DATE DUE

DEMCO 38-296

REFLECTIONS OF A CULTURE BROKER

REFLECTIONS
OF A
CULTURE BROKER

A VIEW FROM THE SMITHSONIAN

RICHARD KURIN

SMITHSONIAN INSTITUTION PRESS
WASHINGTON AND LONDON

GN 36 .U62 D5775 1997   h Thomson

Kurin, Richard, 1950-
                                          1 Data

Reflections of a culture
 broker   from the Smithsonian / Richard Kurin.

       ISBN 1-56098-789-8 (cloth : alk. paper). — ISBN 1-56098-757-X
     (pbk.)
         1. Smithsonian Institution—Management. 2. Smithsonian
     Institution—Public relations. 3. Anthropological museums and collections—District
     of Columbia—Management. 4. Museum exhibits—Political aspects—United States.
         5. Museum techniques—United States. 6. Culture conflict—United States. 7. United
     States—Cultural policy. I. Title.
     GN36.U62D5775   1997
     069'.09753—dc21   97-6974

British Library Cataloguing-in-Publication Data is available

Manufactured in the United States of America
04 03 02 01 00 99 98 97 5 4 3 2 1

⊗ The paper used in this publication meets the minimum requirements of the American
National Standard for Information Sciences—Permanence of Paper for Printed Library
Materials ANSI Z39.48-1984.

For permission to reproduce illustrations appearing in this book, please correspond directly
with the owners of the works, as listed in the individual captions. The Smithsonian Institution Press does not retain reproduction rights for these illustrations individually or maintain a file of addresses for photo sources.

On page iii: In 1982 the occupational folklife of horsemen was featured as part of the Oklahoma state program. Here cowgirl Sheri Lynn Close demonstrates steer cutting. Photo by Dane
Penland, courtesy Smithsonian Institution.

On page v: Thai Buddhist monks from the Wat Thai in Silver Spring, Maryland, honor
Ralph Rinzler at a memorial service at the 1994 Festival of American Folklife. Photo by Richard
Strauss, courtesy Smithsonian Institution.

On page vii: Sakaya Khunpolpitak, a traditional temple painter, drew this interpretation of
the 1994 Thailand program site at the Festival of American Folklife on the National Mall.

For my family, friends, and colleagues,
with respect to my teachers,
and in memory of Ralph Rinzler,
who combined knowledge, artistry, service, and justice
in the most creative and wonderful ways

CONTENTS

FOREWORD

The Smithsonian Institution represents a wonderful idea—the public pursuit and sharing of knowledge. Over its history the Smithsonian has played a key role in representing the knowledge of American and world cultures through its publications, museums, research work, and public programs to millions upon millions of visitors, as well as scholars and policymakers.

These days, there seems to be more at stake than ever before in how peoples and cultures are represented—especially in a highly visible place like the Smithsonian. Our world is getting smaller, with cultures in increasing contact, and even conflict. Therefore, representing someone's culture, even our own, is no easy task. It is not a matter of just nailing a picture on the wall or putting an object in a case. Rather, it requires knowledge and skill, a head and heart for persuasion, negotiation, and deliberation.

Richard Kurin has been at the center of a number of major initiatives, exhibits, programs, and projects, during my tenure, and that of my predecessors Robert McC. Adams and S. Dillon Ripley. His experiences and insights are thought-provoking and illuminate the challenges of the Smithsonian's position and mission. His perspectives are his own, but I think they accurately reflect the richness of intellectual and professional discourse that characterizes work at the Smithsonian. I believe readers—general, scholarly, and professional—will find this book a refreshing look at how peoples and cultures are publicly represented in late twentieth-century America.

I. Michael Heyman
Secretary
Smithsonian Institution

PREFACE

This book is about how various types of major cultural presentations—exhibits, museums, and festivals—are brokered through the Smithsonian Institution. It offers a descriptive and analytic look at this process within a national and international context. My intention is to provide a sorely needed casebook of professional practice. Analyses of how cultural understanding and presentation are developed, enacted, and situated within the public arena illustrate the interplay of scholarship and politics, ethics and advocacy, government institutions and social communities, abstract theories and technical methodologies. I trust that this book will narrow the gap between academic talk and professional action. I am hopeful that it will challenge fellow intellectuals to engage in the formulation of cultural policy, to influence the growing culture industry, and to enliven postdisciplinary studies of culture.

I offer, first, a prologue not of institutional practice but of my own, as an anthropologist in the field. The essay demonstrates quite clearly how my very identity was brokered within another society. Through fieldwork I learned how different conceptual schemes can be brought to bear in a cross-cultural experience, how others could take control of the way I was culturally represented, and how such representations could be negotiated and experienced. Humility is a good but tough teacher. I learned that the culture broker could himself be brokered—and this insight has served me well in my work for the Smithsonian.

The introductory chapter examines the structure of brokering itself and compares the curatorial art of cultural representation to other brokerage roles—in politics, the stock market, and marriage. The first part of the book examines how Smithsonian research and curatorial roles, displays, exhibits, museums, programs, and departments are conceived, internally debated, questioned, and sometimes resolved. One essay explores the brokering of the Smithsonian, how it sought to represent itself, its treasures, and its mission to the American public during its 150th anniversary. Subsequent essays explore how curators broker and negotiate the meaning of objects and collections, how staff failed to understand our role and that of the public and the veterans in the *Enola Gay* exhibition, how some of us debate the purposes of museums, departments, and programs.

The second part of the book examines major public programs produced, in part by the Smithsonian, for the first presidential inaugural of Bill Clinton, the Festival of India, and the bicentennial of the White House, among others. Complex issues arise: How to represent the unity of America after the divisive 1992 presidential election? How to represent another country? How to illustrate the culture of a famous institution? One essay analyzes how Smithsonian staff dealt with Israelis and Palestinians on the proposed representation of Jerusalem to the American public—and how the effort both succeeded and failed. Another essay explains our work with the Olympic Games in Atlanta and how differing ideas of the American South and ways of conveying them to an international audience numbering in the billions were debated and decided for the Olympic Arts Festival. The book concludes with an assessment of scholarly and curatorial roles in today's complex society and offers suggestions for fair, ethical, knowledge-based understandings and presentations of culture in an increasingly commercialized and politicized environment.

ACKNOWLEDGMENTS

T his book is written by an insider, but it is not an "official" accounting of Smithsonian policies, activities, and decisions. Each essay is based on my own firsthand knowledge of the Smithsonian and the particular cultural representations discussed. As the director of the Smithsonian's Center for Folklife Programs and Cultural Studies, I have been a principal in most of the projects. For others, I have been involved in formal ways, as chair of the Smithsonian's 150th Anniversary Program Committee, as an invited discussant for the Smithsonian Council, as chair of the Council of Information and Education Directors, as a planner and summarizer for the joint Smithsonian–University of Michigan symposium on the *Enola Gay* and other controversial exhibitions, as the invited ethnographer/ reporter for the Smithsonian Science and Humanities Dialog, as summarizer of the Smithsonian's "Museums in the New Millennium" conference, as a debater for a Center for Museums Studies minority internship program, as moderator for directors of Latino museums considering the feasibility of a national Latino museum, as a paper-giver at the Material Culture Forum. Yet the interpretations and opinions expressed are my own and do not represent those of the Smithsonian Institution, which I proudly serve. In what I think is the best of an anthropological tradition, I have been a participant-observer, recognizing that in this complex contemporary world ethnographers and folklorists not only study, analyze, and present other people's cultures—but in so doing are often actively involved in brokering their own.

This book could not have been written without my teachers and colleagues. Ralph Rinzler—musician, scholar, producer, and late assistant secretary of the Smithsonian—taught me the "why and what for" of public cultural representation. He creatively and wonderfully combined expert knowledge, aesthetic sensibility, a commitment to public service, and a passion for social justice in the work that was his life. And in exemplary fashion, Ralph infected many others with the same spirit. It has been with Ralph's spiritual children—Jeffrey LaRiche, an honest, respectful diplomat; Diana Parker, a preacher's daughter who has organized many a cultural congregation; Barbara Strickland, a Lumbee Indian woman with a talent for talking through the bureaucracy; James Early, a strategist with an attitude and a conscience; and Peter Seitel, a formidable thinker—and with so many of Ralph's friends that this truck driver's son, born in the south Bronx, found an unlikely home in a Washington establishment headquartered in a castle. I share this home with Betty Belanus, Carla Borden, Olivia Cadaval, John Franklin, Amy Horowitz, Marjorie Hunt, Richard Kennedy, Diana N'Diaye, Pete and Arlene Reiniger, Tony Seeger, Tom Vennum, and my other colleagues at the Smithsonian's Center for Folklife Programs and Cultural Studies who continually illustrate the spirit of public cultural representation and its most professional practice. Roger Abrahams, Ray Almeida, Dick Bauman, Roland Freeman, Henry Glassie, Rayna Green, Jose Griego, Bess Lomax Hawes, Kevin Healy, Ivan Karp, Martin Koenig, Enrique Lamadrid, Alan Lomax, Worth Long, Lynn Martin, Scott Raecker, Ethel Raim, Bernice Johnson Reagon, Rajeev Sethi, Gilbert Sprauve, Jack Tchen, Ric Trimillos, Andy Wiget, and numerous others have over the years reminded me of how important is the task of cultural representation and of the necessity of doing it well.

Other teachers include an extraordinary faculty at the University of Chicago—McKim Marriott, Ralph Nicholas, C. M. Naim, David Schneider, Marshall Sahlins, Clifford Geertz, A. K. Ramanujan, Susanne Rudolph, Stanley Tambiah, Terry Turner, Victor Turner—who some two decades ago taught me the importance of listening to the voices of the people anthropologists usually study.

The selections that make up this book derive from a number of intense projects carried out by teams of dedicated people. Though the opinions and analyses expressed herein are my own, I must recognize the efforts and help of numerous colleagues and collaborators. They may be either buoyed or dismayed—or both—by some of the particulars. Yet in the end I have worked with optimistic, hopeful people dedicated to the belief that human beings can indeed better understand and appreciate each other if given the opportunity to do so. In addition to the aforementioned, I thank Bob Adams, Eduard Alexeyev, Merrick Alpert, Jorge Klor de Alva, Suad Amiry, Arjun Appadurai, Jeffrey Babcock, Robert Baron, Ken Bilby, Claudine Brown, Peggy Bulger, Lonnie Bunch, Alice Burnette, Bob Cantwell, Inta Carpenter, Mike Carrigan, Anna Cohn, Tom Crouch, Quint Davis, Alexander Demchenko, Stuard Detmer, Dave Devorkin, Allah Ditta, Maria Downs, Rex Ellis, Meg Gentes, Henry Glassie, Leslie Gordon, Pam Henson, Mike Heyman, Jim Hobbins, Bob Hoffmann, George Holt, Philippa Jackson, Rebekah Jones, Adrienne Kaeppler, Anatoli Kargin, Mark Kenoyer, Bhai Khan, Nita Kumar, Mike Lanza, Ted Levin, Anna Martin, Mara Mayor, Margarita Mazo, David McFadden, Laura McKie, Bill Merrill, Bernie Meyers, Vijaya Nagararan, Connie Newman, Steve Newsome, Dennis O'Connor, Marc Pachter, Jeff Post, Richard and Sally Price, Kate Rinzler, S. Dillon Ripley, Galit Hasan Rokem, Marc Rothenberg, Pat Sawin, Rex Scouten, Sayyed Shah, Lori Sommers, Nick Spitzer, Linda Stephenson, Alfe Walle, Geoff White, and Ornan Yekutieli.

Thanks too are due the many dependable people who have made the work described in this book possible: Carol Ailes, Linda Benner, Francine Berkowitz, Richard Derbyshire, Bill Holmes, Heather MacBride, Fred Nahwooksy, Judy Petroski, Elard Phillips, Jeff Place, Kenn Shrader, Daphne Shuttleworth, Stephanie Smith, and Joan Wolbier.

I am appreciative of the work of many people on the manuscript. Barbara Kirshenblatt-Gimblett offered wonderful suggestions for improvements; Jack Tchen and Diana Parker gave good, encouraging advice. Emily Botein ably worked on notes and photographs, expertly aided by Smithsonian archivist Pamela Henson and photographic specialist Lorie Aceto. Pete Reiniger drew the maps; Danielle Kurin compiled the index. Daniel Goodwin, director of Smithsonian Press / Smithsonian Productions, acquisitions editor Mark Hirsch, production editors Jenelle Walthour and Ruth Thomson, copy editor Jan McInroy, and designer Linda McKnight contributed the professional expertise to bring the book to fruition.

Finally, I also express my appreciation to members of my family—my wife, Allyn, my daughters, Danielle and Jaclyn, and my parents, Saul and Mary—who have often, in the most literal of senses, shared my work.

CHAPTER 1
PROLOGUE
DOCTOR, LAWYER, INDIAN CHIEF

I first worked for the Smithsonian Institution in 1976, for the three-month-long Festival of American Folklife. This extravaganza of American and worldwide music, dance, cooking, storytelling, and performance helped celebrate the U.S. bicentennial. During that summer, I helped visiting groups of Indian and Pakistani musicians and dancers present their culture to American audiences on the National Mall in Washington and in a variety of venues in cities and towns across the United States.

Later, in the fall, it was my turn to present myself to Pakistanis as part of my anthropological fieldwork for my doctoral dissertation at the University of Chicago. The role of a culture broker generally begins not in an institution but out in the field, with the people who are being represented. A number of anthropologists have reported on the ways in which their own roles are negotiated and transformed within the villages, neighborhoods, and sites where they conduct their work.[1] Fieldworkers symbolically manipulate their relationship to the people they "study." These manipulations occur in an active social universe, cast not only within the meanings of the field-worker and his or her discipline but also within the cultural framework and circumstances of the field community. My own experience illustrates this process. And, humbling as it may have been, it taught me that cross-cultural interchanges are quite complex.

Looking for "My" Village

I was full of confidence when—equipped with a scholarly proposal, blessings from my advisers, and generous research grants—I set out to study village social structure in the Punjab province of Pakistan.[2] But after looking for an appropriate fieldwork site for several weeks without success, I began to think that my research project would never get off the ground.

Daily I would seek out villages aboard my puttering motor scooter, traversing the dusty dirt roads, footpaths, and irrigation ditches that crisscross the Punjab. But I couldn't seem to find a village amenable to study. The major problem was that the villagers I did approach were baffled by my presence. They could not understand why anyone would travel ten thousand miles from home to a foreign country in order to live in a poor village, interview illiterate peasants, and then write a book about it. Life, they were sure, was to be lived, not written about. Besides, they thought, what of any importance could they possibly tell me? Committed as I was to ethnographic research, I readily understood their viewpoint. I was *bābū log*—literally, a noble; figuratively, a clerk; and simply, a person of the city. I rode a motor scooter, wore tight-fitting clothing, and spoke Urdu, a language associated with the urban literary elite. Obviously I did not belong, and the villagers simply did not see me fitting into their society.

The Punjab, a region about the size of Colorado, straddles the northern border of India and Pakistan. Partitioned between the two countries in 1947, the Punjab now consists of a western province, inhabited by Muslims, and an eastern one, populated in the main by Sikhs and Hindus. As its name implies—*punj* meaning "five" and *āb* meaning "rivers"—the region is endowed with plentiful resources to support widespread agriculture and a large rural population. The Punjab has traditionally supplied grains, produce, and dairy products to the peoples of the neighboring (and considerably more arid) states, earning it a reputation as the breadbasket of southern Asia.

Given the predilection for agriculture, Punjabis like to emphasize that they are earthy people, having values they see as consonant with rural life. These values include an appreciation of, and trust in, nature; simplicity and directness of expression; an awareness of the basic drives and desires that motivate men—"*zan, zār, zamīn*" (women, wealth, land); a concern with honor and shame as abiding principles of social organization; and for Muslims, a deep faith in Allah and the teachings of his prophet Mohammad.

Besides being known for its fertile soils, life-giving rivers, and superlative agriculturists, the Punjab is also perceived as a zone of transitional culture, a region that has experienced repeated invasions of peoples from western and central Asia into the Indian subcontinent. Over the last four thousand years, numerous groups, among them Scythians, Parthians, Huns, Greeks, Mughals, Persians, Afghans, and Turks, have entered the subcontinent through the Punjab in search of bountiful land, riches, and power. Although Punjabis—notably Rajputs, Sikhs, and Jats—have a reputation for courage and fortitude on the battlefield, their primary, self-professed strength has been their ability to incorporate new, exogenous elements into their society with a minimum of conflict. Punjabis are proud that theirs is a multiethnic society in which diverse groups have been largely unified by a common language and by common customs and traditions.

Given the background of the area, I had not expected to experience much difficulty in locating a village in which to settle and conduct my research. As an anthropologist, I viewed myself as an "earthy" social scientist who, being concerned with basics, would have a good deal in common with rural Punjabis. True, I might be looked upon as an invader of a sort; but I was benevolent, and the inhabitants of villages, sensing this, surely would incorporate me into their society with even greater ease than they had the would-be conquering armies that had preceded me. Indeed, they would welcome me with open arms.

I was wrong. The villagers whom I approached attributed my desire to live with them either to neurotic delusions or to nefarious ulterior motives. Perhaps, so the arguments went, I was really after women, wealth, or land.

On the day that I had decided would be my last in search of a village, I was driving along a road when I saw a farmer running through a rice field and flagging me down. I stopped and he climbed on the scooter. Figuring I had nothing to lose, I began to explain why I wanted to live in a village. To my surprise and delight, he was very receptive, and after we shared a pomegranate juice drink at a roadside shop, he invited me to his home. His name was Allah Ditta, which means "God given," and I took this as a sign that I had indeed found my village.

"My" village turned out to be Chakpur, a settlement of about 1,500 people, mostly of the Nunari *quam* (variously translated as people, nation, tribe, or brotherhood). The Nunari engage primarily in agriculture, growing wheat, rice, sugarcane, and cotton; most families own small plots of land. Members of the Bhatti brotherhood constitute the largest minority in the village. Although traditionally a warrior group, the Bhattis serve in the main as the village artisans and craftsmen.

Being a Nonperson

On my first day in the village I tried explaining in great detail the purposes of my study to the village elders and clan leaders. Despite my efforts, most of the elders were perplexed about why I wanted to live in their village. As a guest, I was entitled to the hospitality traditionally bestowed by Muslim peoples of Asia, and during the first evening I was assigned a place to stay. But I was an enigma, for guests leave and I wanted to remain. I was also perceived as being strange, for I was both a non-Muslim and a non-Punjabi, a type of person not heretofore encountered by most of the villagers. Although I tried to temper my behavior, there was little I could say or do to dissuade my hosts from the view that I embodied the antithesis of Punjabi values. While I was able to converse in their language—Jatki, a dialect of western Punjabi—I was able to do so only on the level of a four-year-old. This achievement fell far short of speaking the *t'et'*, or genuine form, of the villagers. Their idiom is rich with the terminology of agricultural operations and rural life. It is unpretentious and direct, and villagers hold high opinions of those who are good with words, who can speak to a point and be convincing. Needless to say, my infantile babble demonstrated none of these characteristics and evoked no such respect.

Similarly, even though I wore indigenous dress, I was inept at tying my *lungī*, or pant cloth. The fact that my *lungī* occasionally fell off and revealed what was underneath gave my neighbors reason to believe that I indeed had no shame and could not control the passions of my *nafs,* or libidinous nature.

This image of a doltish, shameless infidel barely capable of caring for himself lasted for the first week of my residence in the village. My inability to distinguish among the five varieties of rice and four varieties of lentils grown there illustrated that I knew or cared little about nature and agricultural enterprise. This display of ignorance only served to confirm the already prevalent consensus that the mysterious morsels that I ate from tin cans labeled "Chef Boy-ar-Dee" were not really food at all. Additionally, I did not oil and henna my hair, shave my armpits, or perform ablutions, thereby convincing some commentators that I was a member of a species of subhuman beings, possessing little in the form of either common or moral sense.

That the villagers did not quite grant me the status of a person was reflected by their not according me a proper name. In the Punjab, a person's name is equated with honor and respect and is symbolized by his turban. A man who does not have a name, or whose name is not recognized by his neighbors, is unworthy of respect. For such a man, his turban is said to be either nonexistent or to lie in the dust at the feet of others. To be given a name is to have one's head crowned by a turban, an acknowledgment that one leads a responsible and respectable life. Although I repeatedly introduced myself as "Rashid Karim," a fairly decent rendering of "Richard Kurin," just about all the villagers insisted on calling me *angrez* (Englishman), thus denying me full personhood and implicitly refusing to grant me the right to wear a turban.

Spy

As I began to pick up the vernacular, to question villagers about their clan and kinship structure and to trace out relationships between different families, my image began to change. My drawings of kinship diagrams and preliminary census mappings were looked upon with not only wonder but also suspicion. My neighbors now began to think there might be a method to my madness. And so there was. Now I had become a spy. Of course, it took a week for people to figure out whom I was supposedly spying for. Located as they were at a crossroads of Asia, at a nexus of conflicting geopolitical interests, they had many possibilities to consider. There was a good deal of disagreement on the issue, with the vast majority maintaining that I was an American, Russian, or Indian spy. A small, but nonetheless vocal, minority held steadfastly to the belief that I was a Chinese spy. I thought it all rather humorous until one day a group confronted me in the main square in front of the nine-by-nine-foot mud hut that I had rented. The leader spoke up and accused me of spying. The remainder of the group grumbled, *"Jahsūs! Jahsūs!"* ("Spy! Spy!"), and I realized that this ad hoc committee of inquiry had the potential to become a mob.

To be sure, the villagers had good reason to be suspicious. For one thing, the times were tense in Pakistan—the country was in the grip of a national political crisis, and the populace had been anxious for months over the uncertainty of elections and effective governmental functions. Second, keenly aware of their history, some of the villagers did not have to go too far to imagine that I was at the vanguard of some invading group that had designs upon their land. Such intrigues, with far greater sophistication, had been played out before by nations seeking to expand their power into the Punjab. That I possessed a gold seal letter (which no one save myself could read) from the University of Chicago to the effect that I was pursuing legitimate studies was not enough to convince the crowd that I was indeed an innocent scholar.

I repeatedly denied the charge, but to no avail. The shouts of *"Jahsūs! Jahsūs!"* prevailed. Confronted with this situation, I had no choice.

"Okay," I said, "I admit it. I am a spy!"

The crowd quieted for my long-awaited confession.

"I am a spy and I am here to study this village, so that when my country attacks you we will be prepared. You see, we will not bomb Lahore or Karachi or Islamabad. Why should we waste our bombs on millions of people, on factories, dams, airports, and harbors? No, it is far more advantageous to bomb this strategic small village replete with its mud huts, livestock, Persian wheels, and one lightbulb. And when we bomb this village, it is imperative that we know how Allah Ditta is related to Abdullah, and who owns the land near the well, and what your marriage customs are."

Silence hung over the crowd, and then one by one the assemblage began to disperse. My sarcasm had worked. The spy charges were defused. But my performance did not really clarify my role, and so I was once again relegated to the status of a nonperson without an identity in the village.

I remained in limbo for the next week, and although I continued my attempts to collect information about village life, I had my doubts as to whether I would ever be accepted by the villagers. And then, through no effort of my own, a breakthrough occurred, this time because of another Allah Ditta, a relative of the village headman and one of my leading accusers during my spying days.

Teacher

I was sitting on my woven string bed on my earthen porch when Allah Ditta approached, leading his son by the neck. "Oh, *angrez*," he yelled, "this worthless son of mine is doing poorly in school. He is supposed to be learning English, but he is failing. He has a good mind, but he's lazy. And his teacher is no help, being more intent upon drinking tea and singing film songs than upon teaching English. Oh, son of an Englishman, do you know English?"

"Yes, I know English," I replied. "After all, I am an *angrez*."

"Teach him," Allah Ditta blurted out, without any sense of making a tactful request.

And so I spent the next hour with the boy, reviewing his lessons and correcting his pronunciation and grammar. As I did so, villagers stopped to watch and listen, and by the end of the hour, nearly one hundred people had gathered around, engrossed by this tutoring session. They were stupefied. I was an effective teacher, and I actually seemed to know English. The boy responded well, and the crowd reached a new consensus. I had a brain. And in recognition of this achievement I was given a name—Ustad Rashid, or Richard the Teacher.

Doctor and Lawyer

Achieving the status of a teacher was only the beginning of my success. The next morning I awoke to find the village sugar vendor at my door. He had a headache and wanted to know if I could cure him.

"Why do you think I can help you?" I asked.

Bhai Khan answered, "Because you are a *ustād*, you have a great deal of knowledge."

The logic was certainly compelling. If I could teach English, I should be able to cure a headache. I gave him two aspirin.

Within an hour, my fame had spread. Bhai Khan had been cured, and he did not hesitate to let others know that it was the *ustād* who had been responsible. By the next day, and in fact for the remainder of my stay, I was to see about twenty-five to thirty patients a day. I was asked to cure everything from coughs and colds to typhoid, elephantiasis, and impotency. Upon establishing a flourishing and free "medical practice," I received another title, *hakīm*, or physician. I was not yet an anthropologist, but I was on my way.

A few days later I took on yet another role. One of my research interests involved tracing out patterns of land ownership and inheritance. While working on the problem of figuring out who owned what, I was approached by the village watchman. He claimed he had been swindled in a land deal and requested my help. Since the accused was not another villager, I agreed to present the watchman's case to the local authorities.

Somehow, my efforts managed to achieve results. The plaintiff's grievance was redressed, and I was given yet another title in the village—*wakīl*, or lawyer. And in the weeks that followed, I was steadily called upon to read, translate, and advise upon various court orders that affected the lives of the villagers.

My roles as teacher, doctor, and lawyer not only provided me with an identity but also facilitated my integration into the economic structure of the community. Since my imputed skills offered my neighbors services not readily available in the village, I was drawn into the exchange relationship known as *seipī*. "*Seipī*" refers to the barter system of goods and services among village farmers, craftsmen, artisans, and other specialists.[3] Every morning Roshan the milkman would deliver fresh milk to my hut. Every other day Hajam Ali the barber would stop by and give me a shave. My next-door neighbor, Nura the cobbler, would repair my sandals when required. Ghulam the horse-cart driver would transport me to town when my motor scooter was in disrepair. The parents of my students would send me sweets and sometimes delicious meals. None of my neighbors asked for direct payment in return for the specific actions performed. Rather, as they told me, they would call upon me when they had need of my services. And they did. Nura needed cough syrup for his children, the milkman's brother needed a job contact in the city, students wanted to continue their lessons, and so on. Through *seipī* relations, various neighbors gave goods and services to me, and I to them.

Even so, I knew that by Punjabi standards I could never be truly accepted into village life because I was not a member of either the Nunari or the Bhatti brotherhood. As the villagers would say, "You never really know who a man is until you know who his grandfather and his ancestors were." And to know a person's grandfather or ancestors properly, you had to be a member of the same or a closely allied brotherhood.

Indian Chief

The Nunari people comprise a number of groups. The nucleus consists of four clans—Naul, Vadel, Saddan, and More—each named for one of four brothers thought to have originally formed the brotherhood. Clan members are said to be related by blood ties, also called *pag dā sak'*, or ties of the turban. In sharing the turban, members of each clan share the same name. Other clans, unrelated by ties of blood to these four, have become attached to this nucleus through a history of marital relations or of continuous political and economic interdependence. Marital relations, called *gag dā sak'*, or ties of the skirt, are conceived of as relations in which alienable turbans (skirts) in the form of women are exchanged with other, non-turban-sharing groups. Similarly, ties of political and economic domination and subordination are thought of as relations in which the turban of the client is given to that of the patron. A major part of my research work was concerned with reconstructing how the four brothers formed the Nunari brotherhood, how additional clans became associated with it, and how clan and brotherhood identities were defined by nomenclature, codes of honor, and the symbols of sharing and exchanging turbans.

To approach these issues I set out to reconstruct the genealogical relationships within the brotherhood and between the various clans. I elicited genealogies from many of the villagers and questioned older informants about the history of the Nunari. Most knew only bits and pieces of this history, and after several months of interviews and research, I was directed to the genealogist bards. These genealogists, usually not Nunari themselves, perform the service of memorizing and then orally relating the history of the brotherhood and the relationships among its members. The genealogist in the village was an aged and arthritic man named Hedayat, who in his later years was engaged in teaching the Nunari genealogy to his son, who would then carry out the traditional duties of his position.

The villagers claimed that Hedayat knew every generation of the Nunari from the present to the founding brothers and even beyond. So I invited Hedayat to my hut and explained my purpose.

"Do you know Allah Ditta son of Rohm?" I asked.

"Yes, of course," he replied.

"Who was Rohm's father?" I continued.

"Shahadat Mohammad," he answered.

"And his father?"

"Hamid."

"And his?"

"Chigatah," he snapped without hesitation.

The author (second from right) during fieldwork with village neighbors in Chakpur, Pakistan. Photo by Douglas Smith, Jr., courtesy Richard Kurin.

I was now quite excited, for no one else in the village had been able to recall an ancestor of this generation. My estimate was that Chigatah had been born sometime between 1850 and 1870. But Hedayat went on.

"Chigatah's father was Kamal. And Kamal's father was Nanak. And Nanak's father was Sikhu. And before him was Dargai, and before him Maiy. And before him was Siddiq. And Siddiq's father was Nur. And Nur's Asmat. And Asmat was of Channa. And Channa of Nau. And Nau of Bhatta. And Bhatta was the son of Koduk."

Hedayat had now recounted sixteen generations of lineal ascendants related through the turban. Koduk was probably born in the sixteenth century. But still Hedayat continued.

"Sigun was the father of Koduk. And Man the father of Sigun. And before Man was his father, Maneswar. And Maneswar's father was the founder of the clan, Naul."

This then was a line of the Naul clan of the Nunari brotherhood, ascending twenty-one generations from the present descendants (Allah Ditta's sons) to the founder, one of the four brothers who lived perhaps in the fifteenth century. I asked Hedayat to recite genealogies of the other Nunari clans, and he did so, with some blanks here and there, ending with Vadel, Saddan, and More, the other three brothers who formed the tribal nucleus. I then asked the obvious question: "Hedayat, who was the father of these four brothers? Who is the founding ancestor of the Nunari people?"

"The father of these brothers was not a Muslim. He was an Indian *rājput* (chief). The Nunari actually begin with the conversion of the four brothers," Hedayat explained.

"Well, then," I replied, "who was this Indian chief?"

"He was a famous and noble chief who fought against the Mughals. His name was Raja Kərən, and he lived in a massive fort in Kərənnagar, about twenty-seven miles from Delhi."[4]

"What!" I asked, both startled and unsure of what I had heard.

"Raja Kərən is the father of the brothers who make up—"

"But his name! It's the same as mine!" I stammered. "Hedayat, my name is Richard Kurin. What a coincidence! Here I am living with 'your' people thousands of miles from my home and it turns out that I have the same name as the founder of the brotherhood! Do you think I might be related to Raja Kərən and the Nunari?"

Hedayat looked at me, but only for an instant. Redoing his turban, he tilted his head skyward, smiled, and asked, "What is the name of your father?"[5]

I had come a long way. I now had a name that could be recognized and respected, and as I answered Hedayat, I knew that I had finally and irrevocably fit into "my" village. Whether by fortuitous circumstances or by careful manipulation, my neighbors had found a way to take an invading city person intent on studying their life and transform him into one of their own, a full person entitled to wear a turban for participating in, and being identified with, that life. As has gone on for centuries in the region, once again the new and exogenous had been brokered and recast into something Punjabi.

CHAPTER 2
INTRODUCTION
BROKERING CULTURE

It was spring 1991. Abdou Diouf, the president of Senegal, had just come from a meeting with George Bush at the White House. Now he and several of his cabinet ministers were sitting across from the secretary of the Smithsonian in a meeting room in the S. Dillon Ripley Center, about 70 feet underground, beneath the Enid Haupt Garden, located behind the Smithsonian Castle. Senegal was to be the featured nation at the Smithsonian's Festival of American Folklife that would take place that summer. The festival would include living demonstrations and performances from Senegal and would attract some one million visitors to the National Mall over a two-week period around the Fourth of July.

I stood to speak. "Mr. President," I said, unfurling a site map of the Mall and the planned Senegal festival presentation, "this is how we will represent Senegal to the American people."

President Diouf, a tall, dignified man, turned his head to look up at me and with a most gentle smile responded, "My dear, that is my job. It is why the people of Senegal elected me president!"

President Diouf was, of course, correct. He did have a right and indeed the responsibility to represent his country, his people, and his culture to the American public. On the other hand, very few museums, television stations, book publishers, or theater producers would likely stand aside and give the president of any nation free rein to do anything he or she wanted to do over the host country's media. That would be an abdication of professional responsibility by curators, program managers, editors, and directors.[1]

Representations of peoples, cultures, and institutions do not just happen. They are mediated, negotiated, and, yes, brokered through often complex processes with myriad challenges and constraints imposed by those involved, all of whom have their own interests and concerns. In the end, a series of decisions is made to represent some one, some place, some thing in a particular way. Making these decisions necessitates due consideration of the meanings held by the participants, the public, and the press, the power of the people involved, and the fiscal resources, expenditures, and impacts. Like other forms of brokerage, cultural dealings rely on an extensive base of knowledge, formal and experiential, but they are, in the end, an art.

Ours is a world that has become increasingly sensitized to the importance of cultural representation. People do not like other people talking about them in ways they think fallacious and demeaning. Most folks realize that communicating understandings about cultural subjects to broad publics is important and has serious political and economic consequences. That is why politicians have cultural issues advisers, why national governments hire lobbyists to buttress the public image of their people and customs, why tourism departments spend millions of dollars on advertising to lure visitors to culturally attractive destinations.

In the past few years, academic scholars, museum curators, educators, makers of documentary films, and others have become increasingly concerned with issues of public cultural representation. They have produced museum exhibitions, films, recordings, television programs, multimedia projects, and World Wide Web sites to disseminate representations of culture broadly. A host of scholarly symposia, articles, journals, and books have reported on and examined how professionals in the cultural fields seek to represent culture to mass audiences.[2] Public megaevents—such as presidential inaugurals, the Columbian quincentenary, the Olympics, the anniversary of Pearl Harbor, the bicentennial of the White House, and even the Smithsonian's own 150th anniversary—have provided opportunities both to participate in and to reflect upon largescale representational activities. They have also provided the fodder for internal and external criticisms and debate over who is saying what about whom. Controversies in the academic literature over popular pseudodocumentaries such as *The Gods Must Be Crazy* and counter-interpretations of precolonial rationality in Hawaii (by Marshall Sahlins and Gananath Obeyesekere) mirror public controversies over museum exhibitions from the work of Robert Mapplethorpe to the Smithsonian's "Science in Everyday Life," "West as America," and that planned for the *Enola Gay*.[3]

Scholars who both engage in and reflect upon these activities find themselves and their work somewhere in between the worlds of academia and popular media. But rather than viewing these realms in polar terms, the scholars involved are gaining a growing recognition of their conflation. We know well enough that public displays often reflect cultural policies and broad public sentiments, but they may also serve as vehicles for generating or foregrounding those sentiments and developing those policies. Affecting public knowledge, discourse, and debate can be done with considerable care, expertise, and ethical responsibility. But anthropologists, folklorists, ethnomusicologists, social historians, area specialists, and others have good cause to worry that their voices will not be heard—that hucksters, theme park marketeers, shopping mall operators, and media moguls, to say nothing of writers, filmmakers, journalists, politicians, Webmeisters, and others—will eclipse them in this project.

Public Cultural Representation

Much cultural exchange occurs in the marketplace and in the media. Much takes place intergenerationally through socialization of the young by the old and vice versa. Generally such forms of communication are relatively piecemeal and particularistic. A new type of frozen egg roll that comes on the market hardly represents all of Chinese culture. While television reports or newspaper stories about prostitution in Thailand, or AIDS in East Africa, or ecological degradation in Mexico City, or rap music in New York may reference and reveal aspects of cultural life, they hardly purport to represent the people and culture of those places. Yet, to some extent, they do.

There is clearly a need for broader and better forms of public cultural representation. However, most attempts to convey anthropological knowledge to the general public have been viewed by professionals as somewhat degrading, or beneath their dignity. Museum anthropology is often regarded by the academy as somewhat antiquated and suspect, as it must gear its presentations to its public visitorship.[4] Writing for popular audiences, as Margaret Mead did a generation ago, and appearing on television and radio might make one famous, but such activities have not been well regarded. The work of Cultural Survival, an advocacy organization for indigenous cultures, still seems to need apology for reaching broad audiences, even though it is based at Harvard and has distinguished staff, contributing authors, and associated scholars.[5] Smithsonian Folkways Recordings, popularizing ethnographic music and verbal art, and the Smithsonian's Festival of American Folklife, offering living cultural performances and demonstrations, are similarly suspected of pandering to broad audiences, polluting pure understandings, making light of serious cultural knowledge.

But anthropologists and scholars in other, related fields now run the risk of having their knowledge ignored, their lessons unheeded, their insights and contributions consigned to the margins of popular understanding. The world is buzzing with discussions of culture. Culture has come to the forefront of political and economic life in the United States and around the world. The question is how scholars and educators help or hinder people in their cultural representations of themselves to each other.

Culture at Issue

"Culture" is a rich but problematic concept. Years ago A. L. Kroeber and Clyde Kluckhohn, two distinguished scholars, came up with more than two hundred definitions of "culture" just in the anthropological literature.[6] Add to this several dozen usages from popular parlance, the society pages, legislation, and even corporate self-help manuals, and you realize that this is a formidable, if confused, term. Yet, given its formal birth just in the last century and its currency, "culture" must capture a crucial and resonant characteristic of the modern human condition.

These days, in popular thought, "culture" resides in three general, though sometimes overlapping, worlds—the worlds of entertainment, scholarship, and politics. As entertainment, culture may be thought of as anything from high art—ballet, opera, symphonic music—to popular culture, as in television soap operas, top-hits music, Hollywood films, and mass commodities from jeans to cheesy crust pizza. As entertainment, culture is largely seen as a material product—a piece of art in a museum, a CD recording, a designer dress in a fashion boutique—created by stylish, innovative individuals. You can find culture in music clubs, at art galleries, on television, and in the shopping mall.

Culture in the world of scholarship is a different matter. There, culture is treated in the main as ideas, socially embedded praxes, philosophies, historically situated complexes of values, ways of life, and orientations. Culture is an abstraction that sheds light on individuals, groups, nations, historical epochs, and even species. You don't buy this kind of culture—you study it, using the methodologies of different disciplines, from anthropology to art history, from philosophy to ethnomusicology.

In yet another world, that of social politics, culture is associated with the identities of people, nations, factions, institutions, professions, and segments of the electorate. Culture is the symbolic means through which people express their views, values, and interests—and impose them upon others. Culture, expressed as language, dress, behavioral code, music, and specific beliefs, defines who "we" are. Global communities, nations, ethnic groups, tribes, corporations, occupations, regions, local neighborhoods, organizations, even families and clubs, each may have its own culture.

Numerous commentators over the last century have pointed out the tension between cultural homogeneity and heterogeneity. On one hand, traditional cultures are disappearing from the globe. Scholars have identified some 4,522 languages ever used by humans. Today only a fraction of those, 708 in all, are still spoken.[7] How many ideas, verses, thoughts, insights, and ways of knowing the world vanished with those languages? Hundreds of societies have disappeared, as previously remote peoples have been invaded by settlers and new migrants. Though the descendants of these societies may survive biologically, they have been culturally assimilated into more dominant and powerful ones, thereby losing their forms of social organization, traditional beliefs, and values.

There have been large-scale, state-sponsored programs to destroy cultures in this century—the Nazi attempt to rid Europe of Jewry, Chinese attempts to destroy Tibetan Lamaism, Indonesian attempts to suppress Chinese culture, and so on. Yet many cultures have disappeared through the spread and penetration of mass commercial culture over the globe. Driven largely by consumer capitalism, mass culture has replaced many local cultural traditions, leading to cultural homogenization and what Alan Lomax has called "cultural grey out."[8]

Cultural homogenization is the process through which people become more similar in the way they see and do things. The rapid telecommunication of ideas and the mass movements of people and goods mean that cultural differences are being reduced. More people are speaking the same languages, eating and drinking the same things, hearing the same music, dressing the same, listening to the same stories (via television), watching the same epics (at the movies), and pursuing the same ideals—accumulation of personal wealth, maintenance of health, and achievement of happiness through increased leisure—than ever before.

Cultural sameness isn't all that bad. People can understand each other's language, interests, and motives. Sameness can provide a sense of shared value and identity, so that ideas of a common humanity, a world community, a global village, a planetary society abound—although the bases of such may vary.

On the other hand, sameness doesn't guarantee a world at peace or even a contented community as utopians and science fiction writers have often speculated. Small differences in position, power, status, and desire can lead to conflict and violence. Indeed, sometimes violent crime and conflict within a society can far exceed that between different nations.

Cultural homogeneity does, however, guarantee boredom and diminished creativity within the species. Cultural heterogeneity entails an extant pool of diverse ways of living, any one of which might have evolutionary advantages in the long run. Cultural heterogeneity provides varied responses to the incredible panoply of environmental conditions and historical circumstances faced by humans. And culturally heterogeneous units, differing in occupational specialization, national loyalty, and ethnicity, can join together in complementary ways to form broader alliances.

In an important sense, cultural homogeneity and heterogeneity are not polar opposites on a single, unilinear scale. Contemporary life has become both more heterogeneous and more homogeneous at the same time. New combinations of local and global cultures, traditional and mass cultures, elite and popular, can join to create both new, larger cultural confederations (e.g., environmentalists, Asian Americans) and more-nuanced microcultures (e.g., new cults, voluntary electronic communities). People have the time and the personal freedom to participate in and define small groups, some of which are exceedingly idiosyncratic. And at the same time those people can participate in larger forms of national and transnational macrocultures. Two people, one in Tel Aviv, the other in Delhi, can pray in Hebrew and Sanskrit, respectively, to very different versions of God and then log on to the Internet to have a conversation in English about advanced nuclear physics and cosmology.

One of the characteristics of our age is that peoples of different cultural backgrounds are increasingly being brought together. With modern telecommunications and transportation abilities broadly distributed, the geographical and communicative distances between peoples are decreasing. More and more people who are different have to communicate and deal with each other. Whereas previously people may have been left alone, content to avoid contact with others or unable to reach far enough to be in touch, that is no longer the case. Today, separations are more easily overcome. Markets, nations, electronic networks—all bring together vast numbers of diverse people. And as people converse, buy and sell, and even fight, their cultures are brought into proximity and juxtaposition. How are these cultures translated? How are differences understood and bridged?

Brokering Culture

Professionals in the cultural fields who engage in the public representation of culture through museum exhibits, performance programs, documentary films and recordings, the creation of Web sites, public lectures, and the writing of ethnographies (for an audience beyond specialized technical experts) are brokering culture. Some scholars and curators may resent the term "brokering," thinking that it suggests something untoward, like taking money or implying scholarship-debasing commerce or trade. But professionals do take money for what they do, professors and curators of anthropology and related disciplines included.

I do not suggest that brokering provides a normative or literal model of scholarly or curatorial practice. But in a world where the ability and the power to manipulate symbolic constructs, develop cultural representations, and present them to mass audiences are assuming greater importance, "brokerage" provides a useful metaphor for examining what we do.

Cultural brokering is a form of what Robert Reich, former Harvard economist and U.S. secretary of labor, calls strategic brokering. Reich identifies this occupational form as a relatively new one, arising from the complex, postmodern, symbolic-analytic economy. In his seminal study, *The Work of Nations,* Reich describes the role of strategic broker as "creating settings in which problem-solvers and problem-identifiers can work together without undue interference. The strategic broker is a facilitator and a coach—finding the people in both camps who can learn most from one another."[9] The role of the strategic broker is to marshal the resources necessary to do the job and to keep everyone's eyes on the general goals while encouraging creativity. Strategic brokers are symbolic analysts—they manipulate symbols, they simplify reality into abstract images, which are rearranged, juggled, experimented with, communicated to others, and then transformed back into reality. The tools of the trade are arguments, gimmicks, scientific principles, psychological insights, disciplinary knowledge, techniques for persuasion and amusement—all of which may allow for communication, problem solving, and emergent innovation.

Culture brokers study, understand, and represent someone's culture (even sometimes their own) to nonspecialized others through various means and media. "Brokering" also captures the idea that these representations are to some degree negotiated, dialogical, and driven by a variety of interests on behalf of the involved parties.

There are alternative models for representing culture that do not imply brokering. There is the extractive model, long associated with expeditions, wherein a scholar or curator collects, takes, or steals elements and evidences of culture from others (in the form of objects, documents, sound or photographic recordings of sorts), brings them "home," studies them, and then writes a book about them or puts them on display. In this mode, the scholar-curator is mindful of self and operating within the bounds and tenets of his or her own interests and orientations—personal, cultural, economic, and intellectual. But there is little, if any, active, sentient involvement of the represented in the representation.

At the opposite extreme is the flea market model of cultural representation. Basically, anyone who in some way qualifies as being from or of the culture gets a table, or stage, or room, or lectern, or gallery, or home page into or onto which he or she can put out the stuff of the culture. Representation is a matter of showing up, and it can run the gamut in style from romantic nonsense to sophisticated propaganda.

If there is to be any type of mediation in representing culture, any agency involved on behalf of the representer, the represented, and the audience to whom they are represented, brokerage is involved.

Culture brokers are not necessarily in bad company, considering that the biggest and the most important things in life are brokered—peace treaties by peace brokers, presidencies by power brokers, corporations by stockbrokers, houses and buildings by real estate brokers, spouses (at least some) by marriage brokers, international shipments of goods by customs brokers, the best books by literary brokers, and the last remnants of personal wealth by pawnbrokers. Culture brokers, like these other types of brokers, enable important transactions, interrelationships, and exchanges.

Technicians of the Liminal

The conventional view of a broker is that of a talented individual who brings two parties together in order to conclude or "barter" a deal through some form of direct give-and-take. Marriage brokers bring together bride and groom in an engagement; a real estate broker brings together buyer and seller to sign a contract on a house or property. The parties need not be either individuals or particularized entities. For example, stockbrokers bring together a specific individual or corporate entity with a general other party—the market. Pawnbrokers help transform objects from individual hockers to cash from general customers. In this view, the two parties must be brought "into sync," their differences agreeably bridged through mutual self-interest. The broker occupies the border between them, facilitating their eventual meeting.

Conventionally brokered deals are usually struck along a unidimensional characteristic—money, power, love. Hence a loan broker brings together a buyer and a seller at the point where the price is right. A power broker arrives at an acceptable form of power sharing. The brokered deal has benefits and costs generally known and familiar to both parties and set within a system of common understandings. Hence, a customs broker works to get an importer's goods through the authorities' checkpoints by following the rules and conventions, charging a fairly predictable fee—calculable in terms of both the importers' willingness and ability to pay and the budgetary demands of the official operation. Deals sour when one party fails to negotiate in good faith, or doesn't compromise enough, or reneges on the agreement and the broker cannot bring the parties together to resolve their differences. Nations or factions go to war or fail to reach agreement on the peaceful resolution of conflict because a political broker cannot bring them to the table. Power brokers succeed when the parties involved get enough of what they want. Brokers, if they are good, are thought to be adept in assessing the mutual interests of the parties, representing positions, negotiating, selling, haggling, and clinching a deal.

Brokers perform a service. They guide their clients through a liminal period, defined as a transition from one status to another—from home buyer to owner, from being single to being engaged, from having a manuscript to securing a deal for its publication. Brokers, if adept, also transform values from one domain to another. These transformations are generally known to the parties and are in keeping with their interests and expectations. For example, a marriage broker turns the private desire for a spouse into a publicly recognized wedding; a stockbroker turns money into shares of a company; a peace broker turns physical war into a paper treaty. Successful brokers are skilled at enabling transitions, manipulating resources, circumstances, and practices, and satisfying the needs of the parties involved so that they feel willing and are able to effect the transition.

Beyond the Art of the Deal

Brokering culture through various forms of representation is a bit more complex than executing a simple linear or bartering model of brokering. When cultural representation is brokered, the self-interests of the parties are less clear, often more diffuse and more open-ended than in bartering circumstances. Genres of cultural exchange are more complex than simple monetary transactions. The actors, agencies, and parties are more numerous, and they may have countervailing notions and ideas of the "deal." Indeed, the cultural deal itself is likely to be multidimensional, engendering diverse systems of values and meanings rather than a shared unit of exchange. Styles and standards of negotiation are typically as varied as the cultures. And the outcomes of cultural brokering are less predictable, emerging through more complex negotiations and screens of interest and value than a single shared continuum of cost and benefit.

Culture brokers usually perform a series of sequential, progressive, goal-oriented tasks, though they may have to reiterate some of the steps as situations change during the course of a particular project. Culture brokers empirically and interpretatively study the culture to be represented, arrive at models of understanding, develop a particular form of representation from a repertoire of genres, and bring audiences and culture bearers together so that cultural meanings can be translated and even negotiated. If the process is effectively executed, the culture broker can facilitate participatory cultural transformation and change—both between and within culture groups.

The role of the culture broker is multifaceted.[10] It is not only to barter down the differences along a unidimensional standard. Nor is it to be the tired old bridge over which cultural performances ride. Indeed, just as marriage brokers worry about their reputations and stockbrokers practice their trade in relationship to laws, regulations, and professional codes, so too do culture brokers act within the parameters of their own professional conventions. For many, these are twofold: the practices of their institutions—which have their own historical and organizationally embedded procedures, missions, and goals—and the practices of their disciplines or fields of knowledge—which have their own bodies of empirical findings, methodologies, theoretical orientations, and standards for constructing knowledge and its argumentation. Culture brokers are bound by and caught up in the symbolic worlds of their institutions and disciplines, often having to broker them as much as the "peoples" and the "audiences" they bring together. They often have to debate and resolve factual and theoretical differences within their field, or between subfields and between disciplines, or even within "one's own people." Because the work of culture brokers is based on concrete representations for all to see, because it is so obviously the result of various decisions all so publicly accessible, culture brokers may upset a lot more of their scholarly and curatorial colleagues than others who do their work more quietly and disseminate it to very small in-group audiences.

Similarly, as culture brokers manipulate their own and collaborating institutions, they necessarily demand compromise in order to effect agreements between divergent parties. These institutions have their own organizational culture and their own interests, which can sometimes appear to be rigid and beyond the bounds of compromise. Culture brokers usually get very good at manipulating bureaucratic culture to secure appropriate and varied resources.

Culture brokers are also intimately involved in brokering other organizations and agencies that mediate their relationship to the people being represented—such as governments, officialdom, commissions, committees, and other forms of organization with lesser or greater ties to those being represented. It may be a national government or a ministry of culture quite removed politically, socially, and culturally from the folks being represented; it may be the local, indigenous leadership of that community. Culture brokers often work with mediating organizations in an attempt to define the people and the cultural forms that are to be represented, because such organizations are likely to have their own ideas and interests at stake in the definition.

Culture brokers, if successful, are often talented at securing the necessary support for their activities so that the people and cultures being presented and the audiences will have a suitable setting for the interchange. This means fund-raising and sponsor support. It also means putting into place the human resources—staffing and support systems—necessary to overcome circumstances and constraints likely to affect the presentation adversely.

Culture brokerage also entails management and the symbolic manipulation of the audience, ranging from issuing press releases and articulately framing program purposes in radio talk show interviews to courting specialized audiences to meeting the needs of average visitors, viewers, or readers.

Most important, however, culture brokerage involves an informal learning relationship with the represented. The culture broker needs to be humble enough to listen to the voice of the people, the exemplars of the cultural traditions to be presented. And it takes good sense to know when people do not want to see themselves, their history, and their culture represented to others. Good culture brokers take the issue of how to represent a culture as problematic. Brokerage involves active, respectful engagement, so that a solution emerges in the form of a particular cultural representation that can be presented to an "audience" in a new setting in an honest way that accurately conveys its meaning. Typically, good cultural brokerage operates in an egalitarian way, recognizing the interests of the parties, the varying types of power—cultural, coercive, fiscal—that might be brought to bear in negotiating their transformation and fulfillment. Culture brokers coordinate horizontally in webs of relationships, rather than vertically and hierarchically through chains of command. For culture brokers, cultural representations do not just happen, nor are they commanded to happen. They are negotiated and emergent, the result of strong knowledge, respect, a bedrock of good practice, and a lot of luck.

Styles of brokering may vary in accord with the social distances between groups and the relative similarity or dissimilarity of their cultures. Where there are strong cultural differences between those represented and the audience, and where great distances in geography or interaction are maintained, there is not much contact, and the need for brokering is somewhat limited. Such brokering is usually the province of explorers and ethnographers, area agents distant from the home office. Brokering, when it does occur, is a sensitive, delicate matter that must overcome large-scale public ignorance. Where cultural differences are great and social proximity present, there is a strong and important need for brokerage. Brokerage is political adjudication, arbitration, and tight, calibrated negotiation. The challenge is generally to overcome stereotype and prejudice or romanticism. Where the cultures of the audience and the represented are more similar and distances great, brokers are diplomats, facilitating the contact of peoples in somewhat routine ways. Brokerage is often a matter of overcoming logistical, resource, and technical challenges and circumstances. And where similar cultures are in close interaction or representation is intracultural, people broker themselves. They hire professional insiders and specialists such as lawyers, public relations people, their own writers, directors, and exhibit fabricators, or they enlist friends, family members, or coworkers to represent them.

A Code of Conduct

If people's cultures are to be publicly represented—and they invariably will be—it is entirely appropriate to formulate a code of ethics for those individuals and agencies involved in cultural brokering. Such a code, by necessity, will be a moral, professional, and voluntary one. Yet it can have the force of expectation and example.

Public cultural representations that purport to be educational or scholarly in nature should, to the extent appropriate, possible, and necessary, have the consent and collaboration of those represented as expressed by the people involved and/or their legitimate and recognized authorities.

Public cultural representations should be based on sound knowledge and research as practiced by the scholarly community. They should be accurate and fair.

Producers of cultural representations should be explicit about the agencies involved in sponsoring, supporting, and implementing those activities. They should be willing to answer questions about their authority and qualifications and about the scope of their involvement.

Producers must honor appropriate legal and moral rights of owner-ship and stewardship of tangible cultural property and intangible cul-tural expressions, and they must compensate individuals, groups, and communities through royalties, fees, honoraria, and other forms of re-ward and recognition of services or materials rendered.

Producers should intellectually engage those represented in the practice and problematics of the cultural representations, offering the best of their knowledge while recognizing the value of the knowledge of their subjects.

Essays in This Book

The chapters that follow illustrate various aspects of cultural brokering. I start with how the Smithsonian brokers itself, its images, its objects, mu-seums, and programs. The first essay describes and analyzes how the Smithsonian represented itself to a culturally familiar American public on the occasion of its 150th anniversary and how the forms of represen-tation that were chosen fit with the symbolic needs of audience, polity, corporate sponsors, and other stakeholders. "Making a Museum Object" explores the ways in which curators broker the meanings of things and transform, or fail to transform, them into objects in the collection. "Ex-hibiting the *Enola Gay*" reviews the difficulties faced in this well-known case, in which at least some of the people represented didn't like what the museum intended to say about their history and culture and didn't feel that they were adequately engaged in the problematic of their own representation. "What's with Anthropology?" looks at the field and mu-seum department, with its long and venerable history of representing people and culture, and asks whether it is adjusting to the contemporary needs of cultural brokerage. Similarly, "Debating Racially and Culturally Specific Museums" poses a conversation about how to adequately repre-sent and engage minority cultures in the museum world. "The Festival on the Mall" offers an account of a genre of representation that seems particularly attuned to the problematics of brokerage within a museum programs context.

Case studies of particular examples of cultural brokerage follow. In each case, the Smithsonian took on the challenge of representing people and culture—from India, Jerusalem, and Russia, but also closer to home in the American South, the country as a whole, and the White House.

The processes of cultural brokerage are described, analyzed, and interpreted. In the case of India, artists upend the usual hierarchy of power and aesthetics to change the National Mall, the Natural History Museum, and their own government. In the case of a binational exchange program with the Soviet Union, now Russia, the consequences of the Cold War are apparent in the juxtaposition of knowledge systems and value orientations in defining cultural forms and genres of presentations. With the attempt to present Jerusalem to American audiences, we see the intrusion of political interests, various constraints and circumstances, and the need to overcome great social distance in arriving at an acceptable idea of cultural representation. With the presentation of the American South at the Atlanta Olympics, the overbearing influences of corporate sponsors and mass commercial culture are undone by acts of humanity—both terrible and uplifting. In the White House we find the ways in which people come to grips with power in brokering their own roles. And the study of the presidential inaugural illustrates how various alternative means of representing the American people fit with ideological articulations of national unity. A concluding chapter, "The New Study and Curation of Culture," makes the case for expanding the knowledge base and ethical practice of cultural brokerage, given the political and economic importance of culture as we enter the twenty-first century.

Opposite: Fireworks highlight the Smithsonian Castle during its 150th Anniversary Birthday Party on the Mall, August 10, 1996. Photo by Beth Laakso, courtesy Smithsonian Institution.

PART ONE
BROKERING THE SMITHSONIAN

CHAPTER 3

BROKERING THE SMITHSONIAN'S 150TH ANNIVERSARY

Brokering is not just something done to others. This chapter offers a case study of how, in part, the Smithsonian decided to represent—and, indeed, broker—itself to the public for its 150th anniversary in 1996. The interests and deliberations evident in internal debates provide insight into the political, economic, and scholarly tensions within a national institution. They reveal how a complex organization rationally considers the type of story to present to its constituencies. The outcomes indicate how those tensions were resolved, at least for the time being.

Anniversary Rites

Anniversaries marking particular events or milestones in the life of a nation and national institutions have become a part of late twentieth-century life in America. Maybe it is just a consequence of civic maturity—institutions having been around for long enough. Possibly, given a longtime American insecurity vis-à-vis Europe, the marking of such anniversaries gives Americans a chance to assert their own history, and thus their own permanence. Or perhaps, as suggested by Malinowski's long-lived theory of ritual, such celebrations of longevity help reassure us during times of uncertainty and change.[1]

Publicly celebrated anniversaries like the bicentennial of the United States, the Statue of Liberty centennial, the Columbian quincentenary, the 50th anniversary of the end of World War II, the 150th anniversary of the Smithsonian, the 100th anniversary of the modern Olympics, and a host of state bicentennials, sesquicentennials, and centennials all provide occasions for recalling, examining, and reinventing the past, positioning people and institutions in the present, and developing a vision of the future. Analyses of public celebrations and cultural representations in Western, industrial nation-states by a number of scholars have concentrated on the relationship between the celebrant and the larger society.[2] Studies have generally revealed how institutions or entities organizing public celebrations, festivities, and displays have mirrored societal tensions and forces and have sought, through the invention or selection of "traditions," to resolve those tensions or to position themselves in alignment with or opposition to those forces. This treatment is consistent with findings from ethnographic studies of ritual celebration in agricultural, tribal, and folk societies where celebrations provide a moment in time, a concentration of focus, energy, and attention to renew the social order or to reconstitute it in alternative form.[3]

While macroscopic analyses of such celebrations and the relationships they posit between celebrant and society are useful, there is a complementary need for microscopic examination of just how such celebrations take on the characteristics that they do. Recent postmodern analyses of public museums tend to view these institutions as part of a hegemonic political order—their exhibits, programs, galleries, and scholarly departments reinforcing the understandings, prejudices, and interests of the dominant classes, social groups, and elites.[4] These museums, it is supposed, inflict their interpretations upon unwitting publics and upon those represented—or misrepresented—in their exhibits and programs. Such views often exaggerate the ability, interest, and authority of governments to control museum directors, curators, and educators. Indeed, governments, at least democratic ones, are often themselves deeply divided. Museums may be honored by one administration, ignored by a second, attacked and revamped by a third. Museums can be vehicles for ideas and values incompatible with official positions. They may also have their own historical missions, broad nonpartisan constituencies, and forms of practice that preclude consistent political positions. In fact, public museums are rarely monolithic; professional disagreements, differences of opinion, and divergent interests are common.

Exploring the way in which an institution construes and represents itself to broader publics on an important occasion reveals processes of deliberation and negotiation, affirmations or alterations in institutional philosophy, self-identification, and worldview. This account is that of a participant-observer, for while I am an anthropologist who analyzes public commemorations, I also served as the chair of the Smithsonian's 150th Anniversary Program Committee and the producer of its Birthday Party on the Mall. In this chapter, however, I write as an individual scholar, rather than as an official representative of the Smithsonian.

The Smithsonian Institution

The Smithsonian was founded in 1846 after a long debate over its purpose. The institution was initially conceived by James Smithson, an English scientist who died in 1829. Smithson's will stipulated that if his heir died childless, his fortune would be given to the United States to found an "institution dedicated to the increase and diffusion of knowledge among men." No rationale was offered for this bequest. For a decade, the U.S. Congress debated what to do with the money—a huge sum at the time. Weighing the possibilities of a national university, a museum, an art gallery, a scientific institute, a library, an observatory, and an agricultural teaching institute, Congress finally decided to establish an independent organization with research, gallery, and library functions, to be run by a board of regents.[5]

Inventor and Princeton University president Joseph Henry, chosen by the regents as the first secretary, envisioned the Smithsonian as a learned institute for scientific research; Spencer Baird, Henry's successor, emphasized collecting and accumulating artifacts and specimens and built up the museum side of the institution. The Smithsonian continued to expand over the next seventy-five years, particularly under Secretary S. Dillon Ripley in the 1960s. Currently, several additional museums and programs are in various stages of development.[6]

The Smithsonian now supports more than 6,500 employees, sixteen museums, the National Zoo, major research institutes in tropical biology and astrophysics, a scholarly press, two record companies, television and radio shows, *Smithsonian* magazine with more than two million subscribers, membership programs, shops, catalog sales, and an extensive Internet presence. The museums in Washington attract about twenty-five million visitors annually, and a traveling exhibit service reaches another eleven million people around the United States.[7] Although the

Headquartered between the U.S. Capitol Building and the Washington Monument, the Smithsonian Institution is unique, variously known as the national museum, the nation's attic, and an international scientific and cultural organization. As a public trust supported in part by federal appropriations, it conducts research, operates museums, and engages in a variety of educational efforts in art, science, and history. Photo courtesy Smithsonian Institution.

Smithsonian receives most of its funds from the federal government, it is not a federal or executive agency. It is a unique public trust that has always diligently defended its nonfederal status, while being keenly aware of its dependence on congressional goodwill.

Most people know the Smithsonian as the keeper of the nation's treasures, both popular icons and objects of significance—first ladies' gowns, the ruby slippers from *The Wizard of Oz*, the original Star-Spangled Banner, the Wright brothers' flyer, the *Spirit of St. Louis*, the Teddy bear, the Hope diamond, the *Apollo* spacecraft, pandas, fossils, and moon rocks. The Smithsonian is widely regarded as the "nation's attic," garage, and curiosity cabinet—the place for collections of stamps, old devices, sensational dinosaur bones—where things that were important to someone are deposited and accumulate.[8]

The Smithsonian is extremely well regarded by the American people. Several national public opinion polls and focus groups conducted in the past few years have revealed that Smithsonian name recognition is at about the 83 percent level for the adult American population.[9] Three out of four American adults who have heard of the Smithsonian think it is important to visit it. Some 45 percent of that public have visited the Smithsonian museums at least once, two-thirds of those who have not would like to do so. Even though most people do not know the full scope of its activities, the Smithsonian is regarded as the entity that most captures the American experience—far surpassing the Statue of Liberty, Mount Rushmore, and a variety of other monuments and institutions. Even in the midst of the *Enola Gay* controversy, some 72 percent of the public thought about the Smithsonian in a positive way—in that respect, it outpaced the president, Congress, and the media.

As a scholarly organization, the Smithsonian has historically been a leader in the development of several disciplines and fields of knowledge— natural history, taxonomic studies, aeronautics, astrophysics, anthropology, and library science. Before World War II and the development of numerous postgraduate research universities and the government apparatus to support them, the Smithsonian played a much larger role in scientific research than it does today. Some Smithsonian fields were closely tied to collections and have been eclipsed, perhaps because of the limitations of those collections. Others, like tropical biology and astrophysics, developed and flourished without a collections base. Still strong and vital in many areas, the Smithsonian's research role is largely unknown to the public and somewhat puzzling to Congress, which thinks of the place principally in terms of museums for the enjoyment of visitors.

Marking the Smithsonian's Anniversary

The question of how to celebrate the 150th anniversary of the Smithsonian began to be discussed seriously in 1993. The initial idea was to celebrate "the Smithsonian and the Nation." We would reaffirm the idea that the Smithsonian is owned by all Americans, that everyone can be proud of an institution that helps preserve and promote understanding of a vast and diverse cultural and natural heritage. The anniversary, it was proposed, would focus on the idea of renewing a sense of public ownership of the Smithsonian and participation in its varied activities, whether one is in Washington or not.

Even in 1993, before the transformative congressional election, this idea found a strong resonance within the Smithsonian. National cultural institutions were being seen as somewhat out of touch with the general population. Western governors and congressional representatives were questioning what Washington-centered organizations were doing for constituents in other regions of the country. The hope at the Smithsonian was that renewed attention and participation would lead to greater taxpayer satisfaction, as well as to more people supporting the Smithsonian by giving gifts, buying its products, and joining its membership organizations. The business and development managers called this the "give, buy, and join" strategy. The greater flow of private dollars into the Smithsonian was, and still is, deemed a desirable goal in an era of tighter federal budgets.

Focusing on the "national," however, was problematic for many scholars and scientists because of the international locus of their activities and the transnational, or even non-national, nature of their disciplines. The Smithsonian has ongoing projects in about 140 countries. Some major facilities and enterprises are located abroad. Ocean biologists, paleobiologists, many anthropologists, and even art historians do not use the idea of "nation" as a major domain or concept in their studies. Smithsonian astrophysicists do not even take the planet Earth as particularly relevant. That is, scholars concerned with environments, cultures, traditions, and galaxies did not see "nation" as the key unit around which to build the anniversary. As a result, our organizing group shifted away from foregrounding "the Smithsonian and the Nation" as its theme. A special *Business Week* supplement published for the Smithsonian in April 1994 reflected this repositioning in its title: "The Smithsonian Institution: Connecting People, Knowledge, and the World."[10]

A steering/coordinating committee and three working committees—marketing, program, and community—were charged with developing the anniversary plans. The community committee organized open houses for staff to exchange knowledge of their work, it gave prizes to honor "unsung heroes," sponsored shows of staff artwork, and the like—all aimed at fostering a sense of community among disparate Smithsonian workers, volunteers, and friends. The program committee developed ideas for exhibits, public programs, television and radio shows, the Internet, symposia, lectures, and publications. Some of these, like the exhibit "1846," the "Working at the Smithsonian" program at the Festival of American Folklife, and the international coral reefs conference at the Smithsonian's Tropical Research Institute, built upon work already under way in various units. Others, like the "Museums in the New Millennium" symposium, the Museums-Schools National Teleconference, and the Young Collectors program, developed from committee discussions. The marketing committee proposed ideas for reaching general audiences more effectively, as well as garnering greater donations from individuals and corporations. This committee encouraged Smithsonian participation in the Rose Bowl parade, invented new products, planned gala events in different cities, and proposed television specials and televised "minutes" that would feature the work of the institution.

A need to return to the "nation" theme became apparent in the fall of 1994. The controversy over plans to exhibit the *Enola Gay*, the airplane that dropped the atomic bomb on Hiroshima, and the strong anti-Washington sentiment expressed in the landmark congressional elections led Michael Heyman, the new secretary of the Smithsonian, toward a major flagship exhibit. This exhibit would tour the United States, attract large crowds in major population centers, and illustrate that the Smithsonian reached beyond Washington and did indeed belong to the nation. Heyman and others hoped that the free exhibit and the attendant media attention would renew the public's faith and trust in the Smithsonian. Congress would be encouraged to support its budget, corporations would be pursued to form rewarding partnerships, and individuals would be attracted to buy from, join with, and give to the Smithsonian.

"Smithsonian's America"

The program committee had considered reproducing an exhibit titled "Smithsonian's America" for such a flagship national touring show, if need be. "Smithsonian's America" had been mounted near Tokyo in 1994 for the American Festival—part of a large international exposition. The exhibit was a 60,000-square-foot, $18 million production of the National Museum of American History and the National Air and Space Museum. The committee had concluded that this exhibition would cost too much money, would require substantial reworking for American audiences, and would not be viewed as a blockbuster by the public. Futhermore, it would place a huge burden on the staff. As an alternative, the committee suggested investing smaller amounts of money in promoting extant exhibits touring the nation through the Smithsonian Institution Traveling Exhibition Service. Yet with the perceived need to make a statement to the American public about the Smithsonian through a major traveling show, attention shifted back to "Smithsonian's America."

Could it be done? Could it make sense? What about the costs, the hundreds of artifacts, and the story?

When "Smithsonian's America" was mounted in Japan, the exhibit's production, promotional, and administrative expenses were paid for by Japanese companies. Some 1.3 million people visited the exhibit over the course of two months at an admission price of $20 per ticket. A museum shop sold books, recordings, and other Smithsonian items. Producing, curating, and transporting the exhibit presented an immense logistical challenge, masterfully handled under the leadership of Lonnie Bunch, the assistant director of the National Museum of American History. "Smithsonian's America" had been designed to exhibit treasures of American history and culture to the Japanese public and to increase Japanese awareness of cultural diversity, race relations, and civic participation in American society. At the time, Japanese officials had made statements to the news media about Blacks in America and the alleged dilution of American society by immigrants from Latin America and Africa, and there had also been internal debates in Japan about Koreans and other minorities. Though questions were raised by the Smithsonian's congressional appropriations subcommittee about the wisdom of sending treasures to Japan—"What if they don't give them back?" asked one congressman—little attention was paid to content.

"Smithsonian's America" opened with representations of American icons—Mount Rushmore, the U.S. Capitol, the Statue of Liberty, a replica of the Star-Spangled Banner, and a videotape of Ray Charles's version of "America the Beautiful." But more than a display of Smithsonian treasures, this was a high-resolution exhibit, speaking to a foreign audience in a relatively linear, monological, and didactic way to represent the ideals and realities of participation in the American dream. The exhibit considered how ideas of American nationhood, land, culture, polity, and identity had developed throughout the country's history. Using hundreds of artifacts such as voting machines, key documents, and even Ku Klux Klan robes, as well as explicit expository signage, the exhibit offered views of slavery, women's rights, voting rights, immigration, civil rights, and cultural diversity. Performances by ethnic and regional groups underscored the cultural richness of the American population. Overall, the exhibit had a positive but not sanitized message: The American dream of equality and pursuit of happiness was, by and large, being pursued in a progressive but challenge-laden way, overcoming prejudice and discrimination but not yet fulfilled.

Brokerage often involves unusual cultural juxtapositions. Here, a crew of Japanese workers construct the American Indian teepee at the "Smithsonian's America" exhibit, held in 1994 outside of Tokyo, Japan. Photo by Rick Vargas, courtesy Smithsonian Institution.

For many both within and outside the Smithsonian, "Smithsonian's America" was a strong, successful, accurate show with a reasonable narrative for public audiences—though some of the Japanese audience and sponsors were not pleased about the representation of conflict in American history and society. For a few others, some of them friends of the Smithsonian, the show was disturbingly "unpatriotic," making too much of what is or has been wrong with America.[11]

The question that the Smithsonian now faced was whether to re-create this exhibition or to design an alternative. I think many of the senior managers and curatorial staff who consulted on this decision believed at the time that "Smithsonian's America" was the proper show to mount. It was my opinion that the Smithsonian had as its basic responsibility the increase and diffusion of knowledge, and that the Japan exhibit legitimately and accurately accomplished that goal. No one doubted that it was the Smithsonian's proper function and responsibility to tell a national story, to craft a representation of its history in some narrative form. It was also recognized that doing so had its risks, that a softer, fuzzier, less storied exhibit would be lot safer.

Toward "America's Smithsonian"

In the end, institutional mission and scholarly/curatorially informed practice had to be weighed against the pragmatics of politics and economics. No one told the Smithsonian not to mount the Japan show (albeit in appropriately modified form) and send it around the United States. But there were reasons for not doing so. First, there was the *Enola Gay* affair. The Smithsonian was in the midst of dealing with an unprecedented onslaught of public attention over the plans at the National Air and Space Museum to display the historic bomber that had ended World War II in the Pacific and ushered in the nuclear age. Complaints by veterans' groups, angry letters from Smithsonian constituents, stories in the press, and threats by members of Congress to scrutinize its operations had the institution reeling. Its rigor, patriotism, and competence were being publicly questioned.[12] The Smithsonian could ill afford to present a national narrative that could be considered controversial and become mired in 1996 election-year politics.

Second, and I believe an even more significant factor, were the economic reasons. The exhibit, as well as televised prime time specials and anniversary minutes, had to be paid for by someone else. No federal funds would be available. The plan was to raise $10 million from each of ten corporations as a pilot effort to develop a corporate giving strategy. The anniversary corporate partnerships would establish a precedent for future patterns of institutional support.

Sponsoring corporations would benefit by being associated with the Smithsonian. Our polling indicated that the public was more likely to think well of a corporation if it was associated with the Smithsonian than if it was associated with the Olympics. Support would come not from the philanthropic foundation arms of corporations but from mainline advertising and promotional budgets. Of the ten $10 million gifts, half of each gift would buy commercial time for the television specials—money that the corporations would spend anyway for television advertising. The Smithsonian minutes, for example, would be only forty-two seconds long—the remaining eighteen seconds would tell viewers about the corporate sponsor. In the nationally touring exhibit, corporate partners would each get 3,000 square feet of exhibit space next to—but separate from—the main exhibit. These corporate exhibits could play off elements in the main exhibit and highlight corporate products or services. Corporate partners would put additional money into advertising the national Smithsonian exhibit and would receive privileges for opening galas, special dinners, and other kinds of activities. We presumed that the success of these partnerships would motivate corporations to continue the relationship beyond the anniversary celebrations.

The proposed partnerships were based on a seminal and deeply held corporate folk belief in "image transfer." Similar to beliefs in contagion and the blessedness attached to saints, relics, and holy sites, corporations believe that essential substances or "impressions" flow between people, organizations, and products. Corporations seek to be associated with people, things, places, or institutions that a sizable segment of the buying public feels positive about. Through advertising and other activities, they place themselves and their products and services in proximity to the liked thing, hoping that the image of it rubs off on them. While this image is an ethereal, nonphysical entity, it nonetheless operates in a material-like way. Corporate marketing directors find this process generally efficacious. Because people like the Smithsonian, image transfer is good. However, if "Smithsonian's America" were to be disliked rather than loved by the American market, or became an object of controversy, corporate partners would be turned off. For the Smithsonian, if there were no corporate partners, there could be no exhibit. Therefore, the Smithsonian had to assure corporate partners of "positive image transfer."

The need for positive image transfer to attract corporations mitigated against adapting "Smithsonian's America" to be the flagship exhibit for the 150th anniversary celebration. Instead, the Smithsonian decided to mount a new exhibit, which would be called, cleverly enough, "America's Smithsonian." The change signaled a projection of public and corporate ownership rather than curatorial guidance. The new exhibit would emphasize the treasures of the Smithsonian—its best and most important holdings (save for three off-limits objects: the Hope diamond, the Star-Spangled Banner, and the *Spirit of St. Louis,* restricted because of their value and their inability to travel).

Curators approached the task of developing an "America's Smithsonian" exhibit with anxiety. There was precious little time to research and curate a major exhibition with hundreds of important objects. The inclusion of the "best" or "most significant" items from every museum and collection precluded—for many among the Smithsonian's scholarly staff—the contemporary idea of what a curator does. To them it represented a throwback to earlier museum practice.

In the early part of this century, when the Smithsonian had acquired the image of the "nation's attic," curation was seen as measuring objects, classifying, recording, and arranging them in various configurations. Curators were keepers of objects, knowledgeable about the physical and biographical attributes of disparate artifacts and specimens. Until S. Dillon Ripley became secretary in 1962, relatively few museum curators had Ph.D. degrees. Collections-based research was largely descriptive and taxonomic. During Ripley's tenure, and that of his successor, Robert McC. Adams, curation began to change. As one of my curator colleagues told me, "I came to the Smithsonian not to measure chairs but to examine the social history of seating." Curators—in the arts, history, and the sciences—have over the last two decades used objects metonymically and contextually, to tell stories. They have used objects, artifacts, and specimens as illustrations in coherent narratives. The difference between this type of approach and the "treasures" or "cabinet of curiosities" approach is readily apparent. When the Smithsonian exhibits these stories, the narratives take on a special status—they become "official" in a way, more than the statement of just the curator or the museum director. Curators and directors delight in this—it makes our work seem that much more important to us—but it also means added responsibility.

The peculiar position of curators and directors at the Smithsonian was made particularly clear in the controversy that surrounded the proposed *Enola Gay* exhibit. This exhibit raised congressional, media, and public debate over the role of curatorship: To what extent should museums preserve and display objects rather than analyze and interpret the larger stories they might tell?[13] Some questioned whether museums have any educational function at all. Some suggested that museums merely display the objects, which could "speak for themselves." Others doubted the effectiveness or appropriateness of exhibits that are like "textbooks on the walls." The impact of the *Enola Gay* controversy, coupled with the perceived problems associated with the "Smithsonian's America" show, pushed the Smithsonian toward a non-narrative exhibit of its treasures. An additional positive factor was that despite the logistical and conservation problems associated with surrendering the exhibit's artifacts, such a show could highlight the collections and works of the various museums—and make a strong statement of their institutional standing in an era of increasing decentralization.

Curatorial and Corporate Brokering

The curatorial team for "America's Smithsonian"—led by Anna Cohn, the director of the Smithsonian's Traveling Exhibition Service, and by project director Michael Carrigan, who had coordinated the "Smithsonian's America" production team—grappled with various ways to conceptually organize some three hundred or so treasured objects. No master narrative was proposed. Rather, categories for placing things were identified, ranging from the rather conventional "history," "art," and "science" to the final "discovering," "remembering," "imagining" ably suggested by David McFadden, at that time chief curator at the Cooper-Hewitt. Objects were alternatively, sometimes appropriately and often ambiguously, sorted into categories and subcategories (e.g., oceans, space, American history, presidents, sports, Civil War) by the curatorial committee and coordinator Jeff Brodie.

The curatorial team, of which I was an active member, did try to weave in some content, but largely to answer the question posed by Marc Pachter, overall head of the Smithsonian's 150th Anniversary Committee: Why is this object important enough to be in the Smithsonian? This question provided a doorway to object biographies and could be used to tell stories about nature, about history, about aesthetics, and so on. But answering the question in any depth, it seemed to me, would reflect on institutional practice, revealing how actual curators disagreed among themselves about acquisitions and how collections were shaped by personality, collector interest, and other factors, that might not be so appealing to the viewing public.

To be sure, some object biographies would allow the exhibit to speak about the evolution of the Earth, the understanding of life, the significance of historical events and personalities, the ways in which expression lends insight to human experience—albeit briefly, in piecemeal fashion, and largely through object labels. While this approach might introduce at least some narrative into the exhibit, it essentially replaced a national story with atomistic biographies, commenting more on the holdings of the Smithsonian than on a vision of a larger society. We fully expected the exhibit to be a wonderfully designed display of the Smithsonian's treasures—from the ruby slippers to Lincoln's hat, from the head of a dinosaur to the *Apollo 14* space capsule. I didn't think visitors could find a voice in the exhibit, nor a grand story worth retelling, nor an authorized version of anything, save perhaps that the Smithsonian possesses great stuff, and so, by extension, do the American people—ergo, "America's Smithsonian." I was half wrong.

Curatorial sensibilities were also juxtaposed with those of corporate partners. Some of us, also believing in image transfer, were concerned that the displays of corporate partners situated outside of the Smithsonian exhibition, but in immediate proximity to it, would "rub off" on the Smithsonian. These exhibits, by MCI, TWA, Discover Card, and Intel, would likely be high-tech, trade show–style displays presenting the "wonderful world" of communications, travel, commerce, and computers. "America's Smithsonian," by contrast, would look awfully historical—as if our natural and cultural heritage were a thing of the past.

Smithsonian staff tried to work with corporate partners on their displays. Dwight Bowers of the American History Museum and Amy Henderson of the National Portrait Gallery worked with a cooperative Discover Card staff to curate a scholarly respectable exhibit. Text panels with photographs, album covers, video footage, and sound recordings formed a Discover Card exhibition of music at the Smithsonian, to be mounted alongside the touring "America's Smithsonian" show. In other cases, Smithsonian curatorial staff found no role in working with companies to develop ideas and exhibits for their spaces. Intel, for example, developed a "future world of computers" type of show—a miniature version of what one might see at a world's fair. Its exhibit featured a small theater, characters such as Mr. Chip, and keyboard stations for abbreviated demonstrations of software. Long on design, short on content, the exhibit provided a perfunctory commercial for the company and for computer use in general. MCI developed a site where visitors could make telephone calls, access MCI's Web site, and sign up as customers—all within a jarring urban playground–themed environment.

These exhibits reflected greater and lesser successes of Smithsonian-corporate dialogue. The bottom line was that the partners were entitled to produce exhibits (at their expense) in return for their $10 million sponsorship. And even though the Smithsonian technically had veto rights over the exhibits, curators had little influence and were generally more disappointed with the arrangement than the marketing and development people were. There were some strong internal discussions contrasting the curatorial "purists" and the marketing "sellouts" within the Smithsonian.

Overall, however, the level of engagement between the Smithsonian—at all levels of staff—and the corporate partners was noteworthy. Meetings were held on a regular basis during the exhibition planning process, before and after each incarnation of the "America's Smithsonian" multi-city tour. There were thousands of telephone conversations, E-mail exchanges, and other communications. Corporate people generally shied away from comment or input on curatorial matters in

"America's Smithsonian"—the selection of objects, their conceptual placement, the content of labels, or the content of publications. The Smithsonian's own marketing and development people also had little to say about such matters to their institutional colleagues.

Much of the cross-talk occurred around issues of exhibit design, crowd flow, the locations of corporate exhibits, the ticketing processes, advertising, special functions like gala dinners, and the like. In most cases, the corporate marketing people knew a great deal more than the Smithsonian did about advertising, marketing, promotion, and event management—and they were neither shy nor hesitant in their criticism. There were strong, disturbing, sometimes accusatory exchanges. Corporate partners found the Smithsonian ambivalent—even downright stodgy—about promotional efforts, naive about the services and deals it had procured (particularly with CBS-TV), and uncoordinated in accomplishing its own goals. In some cases, corporate criticism was well-founded, even if we didn't like it. We were inexperienced in the world of mass public relations. We didn't know much about the commercial world of our partners or about the values of corporate productions, consumers, and audiences. Still, the Smithsonian's liaisons with the partners held their own, often noting that we had a reputation to uphold and broader values than those of increasing sales and attendance or serving their advertising needs. Eventually, a working relationship developed; acrimony was reduced to rationality; both sides learned about the value of the "other." "America's Smithsonian" was produced.

"America's Smithsonian"

The largest touring exhibition ever mounted (at about 100,000 square feet), "America's Smithsonian" required a truly Herculean effort to initiate a planned two-year, twelve-city tour, opening at the Civic Center in Los Angeles in January 1996.[14] The exhibition included some three hundred treasures—Lincoln's hat, Washington's sword, Dorothy's ruby slippers, Jacqueline Kennedy's inaugural gown, an *Apollo* spacecraft, Dizzy Gillespie's trumpet, Edison's lightbulb, paintings by Picasso and Georgia O'Keeffe, a Tucker auto, a dinosaur skeleton, a moon rock, and beautiful butterfly specimens. The sheer amount of conservation, planning, design, contracting, security, and logistical work was staggering. Levels of cooperation and organization within the Smithsonian were unprece-

A billboard outside Los Angeles advertises "America's Smithsonian." Photo courtesy Smithsonian Institution.

dented. The city of Los Angeles was awash in street banners heralding the exhibit; daily press coverage was outstanding; a successful politician-studded gala hosted by Dan Rather preceded the opening; tickets for the free (except for the ticket service charge) exhibit ran out. Over the course of the show's monthlong run, some 300,000 visitors passed through the exhibition. Indeed, they did not pass fast enough. Some initial news stories concentrated on the fact that lines were backing up. Organizers had predicted that 15,000 people a day could go through the exhibition if each visit averaged about two hours. People stayed closer to four hours each, holding down attendance and creating logjams.

The attendance and the publicity fulfilled the Smithsonian's goal of establishing the idea that the institution was on the road, that it cared about bringing its holdings to people outside of Washington. The exhibition was a major event in Los Angeles, attracting celebrities, students, and varied populations. It was supplemented by a popular Smithsonian "Voices of Discovery" speakers program, which booked ten Smithsonian scholars and curators for numerous talks at schools, libraries, colleges, and other cultural centers in the area.

A beautifully illustrated catalog and a variety of specially designed museum-shops products sold well.[15] Much less successful was the effort to get visitors to join one of the Smithsonian's membership organizations. Only a few hundred people paid money to join the Smithsonian. A recent in-house study of the membership effort concluded that the benefits of such membership were not well advertised in the exhibit.[16] The study also suggested that people didn't pay to join because they figured their money wasn't really needed, and besides, in a manner of thinking, they already "belonged." That is, "America's Smithsonian" showed how well the Smithsonian was caring for and presenting the treasures of American history, art, and science—why did it need anyone's help? Furthermore, it had the support of the big corporations that had funded the show and were amply acknowledged and accorded their own exhibit space next to "America's Smithsonian." How could individual memberships in the $28 to $60 range matter in the face of $10 million corporate gifts? Realization of one anniversary goal—funding from corporate partners—seemed to undermine another goal—increasing individual memberships.

The Los Angeles reception of "America's Smithsonian" was repeated in Kansas City. Difficulties with parking and ticket acquisition were minor compared to the overwhelmingly positive reaction by the media and 375,000 visitors. In both locations, attendance still remained below the optimal 15,000 per day originally forecast and expected by the corporate partners. Still, the exhibition entranced visitors, and connected with them.

As an exhibition, "America's Smithsonian" presented almost impossible challenges. Designing an exhibition in a convention center is much tougher than in a museum, which has the infrastructure and design components to support it. Convention centers are cavernous rectangular boxes, great for boat shows. The space between things in a museum is often filled by sublime, or dated, or at least interesting interior design. Not so with the drab, cinder-block walls of convention centers. Creating an ambience for an exhibit that makes the surrounding building go away is a huge and expensive task. Nothing about the building or its internal halls lends value to the objects: Given the mammoth size of convention halls, how can a small object, like an insect in amber, stand out? Despite the battles won by Nigel Briggs's design team, transforming such spaces into adequate exhibit galleries was difficult to achieve.

I am an object-speaks-for-itself skeptic. Yet in Los Angeles, even though I found problems and difficulties—with a carousel, the lighting, the hard-to-read labels, the overbearing nature of the convention center—I was also drawn to the objects on display. And regardless of my hardened scholarly nerve endings, I was taken by Lincoln's hat. Despite its state of disrepair, its unassuming nature, it was, after all, Lincoln's hat—the real thing. Then the space suit, the space capsule, Edison's lightbulb. All the real stuff. But what put me over the top was a William H. Johnson painting. Johnson painted vibrant scenes from African American clubs in the 1930s and 1940s. I have a poster of one of his paintings hanging in my home. I see it each and every day. Yet in the exhibit his real painting astounded me. I had never before realized its texture, the heaps of paint that gave it life and color. The difference between the poster representation and the actual painting was the difference between life and pale imitations of it. What I had looked at and enjoyed every day was made fuller and richer. In retrospect, I suppose it was like Plato's allegory of the shadows in the cave—if one has seen only the shadowy reflections of people, how can the real-life, sensually full, animated version possibly be imagined? The power of "America's Smithsonian" was both in such epiphanies sparked by individual objects and in the repeated and cumulative effect of the whole. Over and over, visitors are hit with the impact of this experience—the Marian Anderson stole for some, the Cesar Chavez altar for others, FDR's fireside chat microphone and Dizzy Gillespie's horn for still others.

I was, of course, not alone. The press was full of reports of people connecting with one or another of the various objects in the exhibition. For example, episodes from a *Washington Post* article about opening day, by Sharon Waxman:

> Sandy Mason is standing dumbstruck before a painting of George Washington. Like most Americans, she has seen this portrait hundreds of times, in school books, documentaries, magazines, encyclopedias. But never in person. She is having something close to a religious experience. "I'm astounded," she finally breathes, staring at the powdered, idealized image painted by Rembrandt Peale in 1853. "This is the most beautiful painting I've ever seen." She takes a step back and falls silent, almost as if in prayer. "He looks so noble. Serene. This is—oh—" She pauses, then says it aloud. "It's, it's holy."
>
> "The longer I stay, the more intense it gets," says an emotional Daniel Cabrera, 43, who took two of his children out of school for the opening day. "To see the things that Abe Lincoln wrote, to be so close to something that is woven into the fabric of our history—it goes beyond words."[17]

And numerous times, staff walking the halls found visitors in front of cases, crying, obviously moved. It is no trifling thing to see people touched by an object (indeed "touching" links the dimensionality and the reality of the object). This was especially evident to those directly involved in the production of the exhibition—they affirmed that "America's Smithsonian," rather than "Smithsonian's America," was the right exhibition to have mounted.

The reaction to the exhibition in New York City, the third site, was somewhat different. For one thing, New York is home to several major museums and has hosted numerous blockbuster shows with treasures comparable to those in this exhibition. The New York Coliseum as a venue had problems with design and attracting crowds. In a city besieged by media promotion, the Smithsonian's budget could not fund a large enough publicity campaign to make a dent in the awareness of New Yorkers. Some speculated that many New Yorkers stayed away because they did not know the exhibition was free. In any case, visitorship—187,000—was much lower than expected. The exhibition did not capture the imagination or attention of the city in the way it had earlier done in Los Angeles and Kansas City, or subsequently did in Providence, St. Paul, and Houston.[18]

"America's Smithsonian" was reviewed by *New York Times* columnists Paul Goldberger and Frank Rich, both of whom lambasted the exhibition.[19] The reviews critically raised important issues in the debate over the future of museums—underlining the role of curatorial narrative, the authority of institutions, and the funding of exhibitions. But they missed the two most fundamental aspects of museum exhibition—the power of the experience that allows visitors to commune with objects and the ability of an object to convey value by virtue of its exhibit location. Goldberger's main point hit home: The exhibition lacked a singular narrative. But the story of "America's Smithsonian" was not the exhibition narrative or the lack thereof. Nor was it the aesthetics of the installation that Rich decried in labeling the show "The Nation's Basement." "Basement" implies junky stuff in drab surroundings. Lost on Rich was the reality that when you try to bring the stuff to the people, you may end up doing it in ill-appointed museums, cultural centers, old schools, neighborhood libraries, and tacky shopping malls—basements all!

"Basement" in our consumer age also implies cheap sales—as in "bargain basement." Both Rich and Goldberger were unsettled by the association of corporate partner displays with exhibition space, occasioning a charge of selling out to commercial interests. They missed the dynamic relationship between the feisty, stodgy, ambivalent Smithsonian and its corporate partners in the venture. They surely knew that as corporate philanthropic pledges have been replaced by corporate marketing and promotional dollars over the past decade, museums and related institutions have had to become more sophisticated in using such sponsorships and partnerships to advance their missions and interests. "America's Smithsonian" raised the ante on how this might be done. But it was still a far cry from the commercialization surrounding the Olympics, corporate control over network television programming, or even sales of advertising in the *New York Times*.

What both Goldberger and Rich also missed was the sociology of the exhibit. "America's Smithsonian," in dramatic, unprecedented fashion, took the Smithsonian out of Washington and to the people—not a bad "realpolitik" for a national cultural institution. For Secretary Heyman, seeking to enter the electronic age and heeding demands for the Smithsonian to extend itself around the nation and the globe, the exhibit marked a new age for the institution. As surveys showed, most of the people attending the exhibition were first-time museumgoers. Many seemed to feel that as citizens of the nation they had a stake in the Smithsonian's treasures. The exhibition spoke over the heads of curators and the usual cadre of museum critics to the people. Consequently, many of the usual criteria for assessing exhibit content did not apply. This was not an exhibit to break new curatorial or thematic ground. This was an exhibit to connect the national collections to a broader populace than ever before—and it worked.

The Birthday Party on the Mall

Some of the same issues about the nature of self-representation of the Smithsonian cropped up again with the celebration of its Birthday Party on the National Mall. This was an event that I reluctantly, though proudly, produced.

The Smithsonian's 150th Anniversary Program Committee recommended against a big party on the National Mall for the actual day of the Smithsonian's birthday anniversary, August 10, 1996. The committee found many reasons for not producing a birthday party. Congress would be in recess—and thus would miss any message we might want to give them. Many Washingtonians would be at the beach—and thus attendance might be low. Furthermore, a party signaling the primacy of the

Washington location would work against the thrust of the traveling show. Practically, the birthday party, if done on a significant scale—so as to accommodate several hundred thousand visitors—would be expensive. Finally, holding a party in mid-August in Washington was risky—we could get 100-degree weather, high humidity, and thunderstorms, weather that would surely dissuade crowds from attending.

The desire to have the party was driven by corporate partners and Smithsonian marketing and development staff. The staff wanted a public relations event with a bang, a signal occasion to point to. They also wanted to throw a party that would serve as bait to attract potential corporate partners—whom they desperately needed. The Smithsonian's lead 150th anniversary consultant, 21st Century Marketing, packaged the birthday party with a fund-raising pitch—join the Smithsonian and get front-row seats on the National Mall for a spectacular celebration, they said. The marketing folks won. There was going to be a birthday party. The only question was, How?

How, in the world of cultural brokerage, is almost invariably a question of who. The Smithsonian marketing committee people suggested bringing in an outside firm to produce the party. Disney and Dick Clark Productions were two of the organizations mentioned. Senior Smithsonian marketing staffers came up with ideas for the party—have Michael Jordan flipping and serving hamburgers, get the Disney characters to the Mall, get celebrities to attend, fete the U.S. Olympic team, have gala concerts of the three tenors sort, and so on.

For me, this was most discouraging. The Smithsonian, so noted for representing others—and sometimes taking flak for it (deserved and undeserved)—would now hand off the representation of itself to someone else? We, who take such care with and devote our professional curatorial lives to publicly displaying the history, culture, and heritage of people, communities, and nations, would give up the representation of our own institution to Disney? Scholars, curators, educators, and programmers on the program committee were appalled. I volunteered my staff at the Center for Folklife Programs and Cultural Studies—which produces the annual Festival of American Folklife and other major events—to take on the task.

We started with the premise that the Smithsonian should show off its own culture. We built upon interviews we'd done with several hundred Smithsonian workers in all categories for a Festival of American Folklife program called "Working at the Smithsonian."[20] We wanted

Smithsonian researchers to demonstrate to the public how they conducted their research—whether in astronomy or zoology. We wanted exhibit designers and fabricators to give the public a view of how exhibitions were created. We wanted bureaucrats and managers, museum
directors and plumbers to show and tell the public how they did their
jobs. Second, we wanted to illustrate the scope and diversity of the
Smithsonian's programs and interests through musical performances
and substantive debates that would engage the public. The Smithsonian,
we believed, needed to be seen as a living, vital institution, not just of
stuff but of people and activities. We also wanted to point to the Smithsonian's new role in electronic exhibits and programs. We knew we had
to do celebratory, birthdaylike things, but we wanted to do them in a
Smithsonianesque way. Finally, we wanted to connect the Smithsonian
to a larger, national iconography, so that the connection between
knowledge and democracy was publicly made and appreciated.

Ably assisted by Festival of American Folklife director Diana Parker,
center deputy Richard Kennedy, center staff, long-term collaborators
Karen Spellman and Jeff Anthony, with whom we'd worked on the Black
Family Reunion, and talented temporary staff Jacqui Schraad, Artemis
Zenatou, Zahir Hussein, and others, we developed and implemented the
Smithsonian's Birthday Party on the Mall. The party was held on Saturday, August 10, and Sunday, August 11, 1996, outdoors on the National
Mall. Some 600,000 people attended. The public response was outstand-
ingly positive. The Smithsonian received hundreds of letters and E-mail
messages to that effect. Senator Alan Simpson, a Smithsonian regent,
called it the best event ever in Washington.

Outdoors, the birthday party was fully one mile long, stretching from
the Washington Monument to the U.S. Capitol building. The site was anchored by stages in front of the Monument, the Capitol, and the Smithsonian Castle. Events occurred in the open air, under tents, and in the
museums along the Mall—as well as at the National Zoo and the Anacostia Museum.[21] Musical performances on the outdoor stages and in
the museum auditoriums included a broad range of American and world
music. Musicians were chosen because of their previous and ongoing
ties to the Smithsonian's programs and collections. Gala concert host
Mickey Hart, drummer for the Grateful Dead, had reengineered Smithsonian Folkways Recordings, supported research by Smithsonian anthropologists and ethnomusicologists Tony Seeger, Tom Vennum, and Ken
Bilby, and aided archival preservation. Aretha Franklin served with the

Rhythm and Blues Foundation—begun at the American History Museum; Buffy Sainte-Marie had recorded on Folkways and worked with American History curator Rayna Green on Native American causes. Salsa diva Celia Cruz had done performances for the Smithsonian Associates, and at the birthday party, besides performing, she joined a discussion with Smithsonian curators about her role in shaping Caribbean musical culture. Another star performer, Trisha Yearwood, who had narrated a video for the "America's Smithsonian" Discover Card exhibit, participated in a similar discussion on the growth and character of country music. The Smithsonian's own chamber orchestra took the Stradivarius instruments out of their cases and played them. The Smithsonian Jazz Masterworks Orchestra performed using Dizzy Gillespie's trumpet—borrowed back for the occasion from "America's Smithsonian." Other groups performing at the birthday party—from the Ho'opi'i Brothers and Ella Jenkins to Johnny Gimble and Buck Ramsey, from the Capitol Steps to the Tap America Project, from the Six Nations' Women Singers and the American Indian Dance Theater to Ruth Brown, Little Anthony and the Imperials, and Sheila E., from Boozoo Chavis and Celtic Thunder to the Cambodian American Heritage Dancers, from tenor Robert White to Raymond Wong's Chinese Lion Dancers, and from a Bahamian Junkanoo Parade and the Young Tuxedo Brass Band to Soh Daiko and Klezmer Plus—had a connection to programs at the American History Museum, the National Museum of the American Indian, the Festival of American Folklife, Smithsonian Folkways, the Smithsonian Associates, the Sackler Gallery, the African Art Museum, or some other Smithsonian unit.

Smithsonian pavilions featured researchers, curators, scientists, and educators showing the public what they do, giving people an idea of how they go about their disciplinary, museum, or service roles. The Air and Space Museum offered an airplane cockpit for children to sit in and an astronomer to take questions from the public. American Art had people making sandstone art, the American Indian Museum demonstrated Native American games, the Conservation Analytical Laboratory had people participate in an archaeological dig, the Cooper-Hewitt had children designing clocks around a "time to celebrate" theme, and at the Hirshhorn pavilion, one could become an exhibit. At the National Zoo pavilion, visitors could listen to and decode animal sounds, measure animal tracks, and learn about DNA analysis. At the Sackler and Freer pavilion, people learned by doing Chinese calligraphy and making a Japanese folding screen. Even the service units of the Smithsonian got involved.

For the birthday party, the Cooper-Hewitt National Design Museum worked with the theme of celebratory times
to engage children in an activity exploring design concepts by making clocks. Photo courtesy Smithsonian Institution.

The horticulturalists showed how to arrange flowers, make tussie
mussies (bouquets), and topiaries. Exhibit fabricators showed how to
make dioramas, the masons taught decorative plaster work, and so on.
No high-resolution story here, save the fact that the Smithsonian had a
lot of highly knowledgeable people on staff, doing good work and willing to share it with the public. To the public, crowding into the pavilions, interacting with the Smithsonian in an intimate way, the demonstrations and activities confirmed that the institution was indeed
engaged in its mission—the increase and diffusion of knowledge.

This point was reinforced in many other ways. A series of debates, termed "It's Public Knowledge," was held throughout the weekend. Actor E. G. Marshall served as host. The program, organized with the Smithsonian Associates, brought together academics, writers, politicians, business and media people to discuss contemporary cultural issues. Paul Duke, Maureen Bunyan, Robert Aubry Davis, among others, moderated packed sessions such as "The Battle of the Sexes," with author/linguist Deborah Tannen debating conservative talk show host Jim Bohannon; "Acting Your Age," with *The Golden Girls* star Rue McClanahan and anthropologist Mary Catherine Bateson; "Whose Culture Is It Anyway?" with Kitty Carlisle Hart; "To Web or Not to Web"; and other topics. The idea of holding free public debates out on the nation's front lawn for the citizenry was appealing and popular, and it helped to highlight the Smithsonian's role as a convener of sorts, a forum for national and international conversations.

Such a forum was connected to the next generation through a Young Collectors pavilion, wherein some sixty youngsters from the Washington Metropolitan area had been invited to display and discuss their collections. This was a genuine hit.[22] While there were some of the more conventional things—coins, stamps, baseball cards, and dolls—audiences were amazed by some collections—bonsai trees, antique rulers, and more than a million punched paper dots—belonging to students from Bailey's Elementary School. Collecting was alive and well, and the vitality of the Smithsonian could be assured in the generation of the future.

Electronic exhibits also made the point about the institution's vitality by showing off the Smithsonian's digital world. A huge air-conditioned tent was set up with computers and twenty large projection screens, and inside it scientists, scholars, curators, and educators from across the Smithsonian accessed databases and Web pages, CD-ROMs and enhanced CDs, showing the public how the Smithsonian was making use of new technologies to conduct its research and educational programs.

An electronic birthday card—seventy computer workstations were plugged into a huge Jumbotron screen—was also available. Some 15,000 visitors to the birthday party typed in their messages to the Smithsonian, and those messages became part of the first electronic collection, publicly generated. Their messages were displayed on the twenty-four-foot-wide Jumbotron screen for thousands to see. And they were joined by thousands of others over the Internet.

Indeed, half a million hits were recorded on the Smithsonian Web site over the weekend—more than double the usual volume. Others participated through more passive media coverage of the birthday party, which included some three hundred television stations nationwide. CBS-TV broadcast live from the site during prime time. CNN carried coverage worldwide, as did MS-NBC. Newspaper articles numbered more than a thousand.[23]

Sponsors were also asked to participate—to develop their own educational pavilions. We suggested that rather than set up pavilions to advertise their products, they create displays that explored the knowledge base of their work. TWA pilots, navigators, and flight controllers could demonstrate their techniques; MCI engineers could show and explain how modern communications works; Intel technicians could replicate a "clean room" and show how computer chips were made. In the end, these companies declined the opportunity to put together such a presentation. Discover Card did participate, however. Conceptualizing an occupationally relevant, yet publicly engaging presentation was not easy. The resulting event had children planting seedling trees in the Discover Card tent, posing for family portraits, and drawing on a mural. But no big logos, no sales campaign here. The signage, site, and presentation were integrated into the overall program and design of the Smithsonian's celebration.

The birthday party was not without the usual ritual accoutrements. We commissioned pastry chefs from around the United States to work with the museums to develop ideas for eighteen different birthday cakes. The New England Culinary Institute made a six-foot-long, three-foot-high scale model chocolate cake of the Smithsonian Castle. Nathalie Dupree, Colette Peters, Stanton Ho, Steven Klc, and others chose other subjects, from models of museum buildings to a Tiffany lamp, a peacock (for the Freer's Whistler Peacock Room), African sculpture, and an animal habitat. Lines stretched all the way across the Mall, from morning to evening, to get into Ripley Center to see these spectacular cakes.

The Smithsonian Castle itself became a cake, lit with fireworks by Grucci. In a culmination of the Saturday evening concert, consumable fireworks were fired from the Castle roof, and conventional fireworks from the Haupt Garden to a video of Ray Charles singing "America the Beautiful." This was followed by fireworks over the Washington Monument to music themed to Smithsonian museums—"2001: A Space Odyssey" for the Air and Space Museum, "Diamonds Are a Girl's Best Friend" for the Natural History Museum with the Hope diamond and the National Gem Collection, Woody Guthrie's "This Land Is Your Land"

A Bahamian Junkanoo parade helped celebrate the 150th Anniversary and reprised a 1994 performance on the Mall for the Festival of American Folklife.
Photo by Jeff Tinsley, courtesy Smithsonian Institution.

for the Folkways collection, and so on. The connection of the Smithsonian with national iconography, a celebration of museum, people, and nation, and heritage with popular culture was made.

Other birthday rituals—speeches and ceremonials—were necessary, especially for Washington. The secretary, the Regents Executive Committee chair Barber Conable, Regent Alan Simpson, and others spoke. The Marine Band played. A Smithsonian employee—Manuel Melendez, sang "America the Beautiful." He had to sing a cappella because the Marine Band does not play with non-Marines and therefore would not accompany him, even though he had been a first tenor in the U.S. Army. We unveiled a newly designed Smithsonian flag and negotiated with the United Armed Services Color Guard so that a Smithsonian security officer could carry it in their formation onto the stage—they agreed. We hoisted the new Smithsonian flag to the top of the Castle, accompanied by a jazz fanfare composed especially for the occasion by David Baker of the Smithsonian Jazz Masterworks Orchestra. We unveiled a Smithsonian coin newly released by the U.S. Mint. And we lifted a new Smithsonian bell into our clock tower.

The bell in a marvelous way told much of the tale of the Smithsonian's 150th anniversary and its effort to broker itself. The idea for making the bell a symbolic centerpiece for the institution came from David Shayt, a specialist in the American History Museum. He had noted how the regents back in the early days of the Smithsonian had voted for a bell and had the Castle designed to accommodate one but had never actually commissioned the making of one. Now, if we wanted the American public to hear us, we should bring the old promise to fruition and get a bell. We did, from the Whitechapel foundry in London, the same foundry that struck the Liberty Bell. We argued about how to pay for it. The bell was to be brokered as a symbol of the Smithsonian. I wanted the employees to pay for it by volunteer donations—an average of $6 from each of the 6,500 employees would do. I wanted this because those who work at the Smithsonian and make its institutional culture deserved to have their names on something. Others thought this was perhaps too idealistic and impractical, and instead looked for outside, corporate support. They won. A. T. Cross, the pen company, was also celebrating its 150th anniversary and was willing to donate the $40,000 for the Smithsonian bell, which now bears its name.

The Birthday Party on the Mall provided a means for the Smithsonian to broker itself to itself and the public. And it encapsulated complex alternative ways of thinking about the institution and how it could be represented. Afterward, Secretary Heyman wrote about one of those ways: "If there is one moment that has come to symbolize for me the Smithsonian's identity as a people's place it was that perfect late-summer weekend when we held our Birthday Party on the Mall. As one of the performers put it, for a moment Washington felt like an ideal small town, where we all came together in shared curiosity and inspiration. We don't always get it right; but when we do, this is a magical place."[24]

CHAPTER 4
MAKING
A MUSEUM
OBJECT

As we have seen, whole institutions, like the Smithsonian, can be brokered. Individual exhibitions can be debated, curatorial roles multiply perceived, sponsoring and partnering relationships strongly negotiated. This might seem quite unsettling to the museum purist. At least, some of my colleagues argue, there is stability and certainty in our collections—the bedrock of the modern museum.

What is the nature of the museum object? Is it not also subject to bickering over its worth, alternative views of its meaning and significance, disagreements over its placement and exchange value? Is the museum object subject to brokering by curators, directors, makers, users, and others?

If "objects speak," as Betsy Broun, the director of the National Museum of National Art, has argued, then there shouldn't be much to any brokering role.[1] The objects should be able to tell us what they are, how much they are worth, where they want to live, and why they are important. Often an abstract painting on canvas does chant "contemporary art, contemporary art, put me in the Hirshhorn," and surely the Star-Spangled Banner communicates great importance at first glance. But for the most part, objects, as one of my other colleagues suggested, "babble." Human interpreters need to be close by to sense the object, examine it, and compare it to others, in order to make judgments about its provenance, meaning, worth, and placement.

Though the material objects placed in a museum may make certain demands based on their size, structure, and composition, they largely sit where we put them, next to a label we write. They depend upon curators to squeeze out their meaning. From material analyses to contextual studies, we spend much time trying to ferret out the meanings, uses, attributes, and circumstances that formed them and that led to their use, veneration, denigration, and significance over time.

As scholars and curators of material culture, we are constantly in search of a narrative for our stuff. Finding the right genre of narrative is no simple task. In modern Western intellectual tradition, how the connections between the human makers, users, and signifiers of objects and those objects themselves are portrayed provides a weather vane for contending social theories. In a utilitarian view, humans invest themselves, through their labor, in objects, in order to survive. In a more symbolic view, objects become vessels of human thought, social exchange, and meaning. But whether seen as invention, alienation, or a kind of cognitive-magical investiture, objects take on the characteristics of people, while people become objectified.[2] As Arjun Appadurai notes, things take on a social life.[3] Hence objects made or used by humans acquire names, ethnicity, gender, religion, nationality—e.g., the *Hope* diamond, *Navajo* blankets, *women's* clothing, *Islamic* calligraphy, the *American* flag—while people are objectified, for example, as *the American Indian* in a new museum building. The museum business has tended to reify, even exaggerate this, personalizing objects and depersonalizing human aspects of museums and exhibits.

There is a good bit of debate over how and why museums do this. And even within the Smithsonian's complex of national museums, different museums are recognized as adopting variegated styles for dealing with humanity. Sometimes we needlessly depersonalize museums to make them safe for objects. Museums are better preserved if not many people come to disturb them. A museum like the Freer turns this into a virtue, providing a sanctuary of sort for the appreciator of Asian art that is removed from the hustle and bustle of the more popular attractions on the heavily touristed National Mall. Most museums separate out human provisioning from our exhibit halls, bracketing display areas or galleries as their significant valued spaces. With pressure to generate more income, museum shops have begun to appear in closer proximity to displays in the Natural History Museum. By and large, we tell our visitors to keep voices low and to "look but don't touch," but we have opened dis-

covery centers and insect zoos and hands-on science labs in our museums. Though we increasingly offer more technological interaction, museums are painfully lacking in human sensibility.[4] We don't do much
with touch, we do little with sound, virtually nothing with taste, and except for the zoo, nothing with smell.[5] The National Museum of African
Art has been roundly criticized by its founder for just such a failing. Warren Robbins finds the museum to have been "malled" as it has drifted
farther and farther away from conveying the rich sensory aspects of
African culture in favor of a more scholarly gallery aesthetic.[6] Children's
museums fare better in this regard but are often viewed as more primitive in their attractions and methods; their status as museums is somewhat suspect in professional circles, given their appeal to younger, supposedly less refined visitors. But what of the more sophisticated—the
people who are to understand and view our objects?

Some think that the more we analyze the materiality of the object,
the better we will understand it. Though scientific, technical analyses
may be useful, and can provide some clues to help interpret objects, the
value placed upon this method is often overstated.[7] Analysis of materiality is objective within a particular framework. Limiting the intrusion of
a human subject does allow for repeated and controlled tests on the
same substance, which can yield the same results subject to stochastic
variation. Thus understandings of the object may be deemed scientific.
And this is especially useful when none of the humans who made, used,
collected, captured, conjured, invented, and displayed the object are
around. But when there are such humans around, a lot more information about the object is available. Dealing with human understandings
of an object—the meanings drawn from and imputed to it—makes our
work much more daunting. While we might approach such a task with a
scientific attitude or sensibility, we really have not developed the tools
necessary to do this job exceedingly well. Rather than calling for less-
than-science, an adequate interpretation and understanding of the
meaning of objects calls for something more. I don't think we have yet
found it. But our failure to develop fully the methods of inquiry to deal
with this complexity—the subjective, and intersubjective or social,
world of meaning—does not mean we should write off the phenomena
of meaning-making or consign it to some epiphenomenal status. And
indeed, the attempt by the new National Museum of the American Indian to build a cultural resource center and a program for object examination, veneration, and interpretation by visiting members of the cul-

tural communities that once used and knew the items is a good, strong step in this direction.

While the Smithsonian and many other museums have made positive strides, we still generally fail to consult the people who make, use, and draw meaning from the objects that we study and show. We give a primacy to the object that we control, but we often forget about the people who have investments in these objects as their originators, users, and audience.

The transformation in the meaning of objects within different social contexts makes a fascinating story. Elsewhere, I have written about the Smithsonian's most famous object, the Hope diamond, and how its meaning has changed over a three-hundred-year period and through its sojourn from India to Washington.[8] That diamond, which started its career as a symbol of divine power and royal authority, was transformed in Europe to a token of wealth and accursed revenge, then finally, in the United States, into an object of romance, magic, and fame. Its biography did not end at the doors of the museum, however, when it became a museum object and icon.

In this chapter I focus on the biography of an object, an Ojibwe birch-bark canoe, and how museum people mediate, negotiate, argue, and determine its status and meaning. This canoe has spent its entire life within the Smithsonian. Examining that life provides an understanding of the sociology of the museum object, and of how objects are brokered within the Smithsonian.

Nyholm's Canoe: From Prop to Museum Acquisition

In 1981, Earl Nyholm, an Ojibwe Indian and assistant professor of Ojibwe language at Bemidji State University in Minnesota, was invited to participate in the Smithsonian's Festival of American Folklife. Nyholm was asked to make a birch-bark canoe in the traditional manner and to do this outdoors on the National Mall of the United States in Washington, D.C., in front of thousands of visitors, every day for ten days.

Nyholm's demonstration of canoe building followed on a fifteen-year history of the festival, during which thousands of traditional craftspeople, musicians, and other cultural exemplars were invited to the Smithsonian to demonstrate their knowledge, artistry, and skill for the public. Every summer, almost a million people would visit the festival and watch the keepers of American and worldwide traditions perform and demonstrate their skills in the midst of museumlike signage, scholarly and curatorial presentations, food sales, heat and dust. The explicit ideology of the festival was to show that culture was living, not just stored away in museums or preserved under glass in locked cases. And the festival equated the living bearers of traditions and the objects they made with the treasures in the national museums.

Nyholm was invited by Thomas Vennum, Jr., an ethnomusicologist and scholar of Great Lakes Indian life, who worked at the Smithsonian for the festival. Nyholm was one of several craftspeople and scholars demonstrating and presenting a variety of Ojibwe traditions at the festival.[9] The aim of Nyholm's demonstration was to show that traditional Indian techniques for boat building still existed. Nyholm's birch-bark canoes—typically some ten to eighteen feet long—are renowned among Great Lakes Indians for their quality. Aside from their beauty and grace, birch-bark canoes were used by the Ojibwe up until a generation or two ago for hunting and harvesting wild rice. They had an advantage over motorboats and over steel-and-fiberglass canoes in accomplishing such work—which Nyholm explained to the festival audiences.

At the festival, held over a twenty-acre area bounded by the Smithsonian museums, the Washington Monument, and the U.S. Capitol, Nyholm daily demonstrated his canoe-building skills, assisted by another Ojibwe from the Wisconsin-Michigan border, George McGeshick. Relatively quiet, dignified men, Nyholm and McGeshick went about the work of constructing the canoe struts, bending and shaping the birch bark, and weaving it to the canoe frame. Vennum would come around to them with a microphone and do a short presentation of ten to fifteen minutes, asking questions about the canoe, the building process, and the canoe's function in Ojibwe culture. A small crowd would gather, listen to a few questions, and move on. While around them music blared from stages, other craftspeople made their baskets, and the public munched on ethnic foods, the men kept to their task, building the canoe. And occasionally Nyholm would appear on a "narrative" stage, where he would discuss the canoe with Vennum and others in front of a seated audience.

The canoe that Nyholm made was not a canoe for use in the Great Lakes. It was a prop for his daily performance—demonstrating Indian traditional boat-building skills and artistry. This canoe was approximately eighteen feet long and three feet wide (at its widest), made of beautiful birch bark, with thwarts of cedar, held together by bindings of spruce root and sealed with pine pitch. The canoe was not finished by the end of the festival, so Nyholm stayed on a few extra days to complete it. Even without the crowds or the presentations, he went about his business of making the canoe. He wanted to finish the canoe on the Mall so that he could then donate it to the National Museum of Natural History.

Such donations had happened before at the festival, when the artifacts made there by culture bearers were donated to the collections of the museums. The Smithsonian had thus acquired the embroidery of Ethel Muhammad, the Southern pottery of Cleaver Meaders, the weavings of Epie Archuleta and Norman Kennedy. There were a variety of options for the canoe. It could have gone into the transportation collection at the National Museum of American History (then the Museum of History and Technology) or possibly into the Renwick Gallery or the National Museum of American Art. But the most appropriate placement seemed to be the National Museum of Natural History. The curators from that museum, holding a collection of Great Lakes Indian artifacts, and indeed some older birch-bark canoes, agreed to the acquisition, and after everything from the festival was taken down and the canoe completed, it was turned over to the museum. Earl Nyholm's performance prop was now a museum object.

Nyholm was proud of the donation and acquisition. Objects take on an additional value when they become part of the national museum collections. This flows from proximity to and association with other national icons—the monuments, national institutions, the museums themselves, and other valuable, famous, treasured objects. Although Nyholm had donated his labor and some materials to make the canoe, he could rest assured that he had made a worthwhile contribution to the national collections. His accomplishment, knowledge, and skill, and that of his community, would now have a place and be recognized as a national treasure permanently—or so he thought.

Borrowing and Deaccessioning the Artifact: When Is a Canoe a Canoe?

In 1987, the Festival of American Folklife included a program on the state of Michigan. Various musicians represented the sounds of Detroit and Motown, and others demonstrated everything from cherry growing and ice fishing to Dutch shoe and furniture making. Earl Nyholm's mother, Julia, demonstrated fingerweaving and bead working. George McGeshick returned to the festival, with his wife, Mary McGeshick, from Iron River, to demonstrate various crafts, including cradle board decorating. Tom Vennum suggested bringing out Earl Nyholm's canoe to enhance the Ojibwe presentation. The canoe would offer a good visual and tactile cue to visitors, interesting them in the demonstrations.

The festival staff arranged for the temporary loan of the canoe from the Natural History Museum collections. The canoe was brought down to the Mall and used during the ten days of the festival, then returned to the museum.

In 1989, Vennum again curated an American Indian program at the Festival of American Folklife. The theme of the program was cultural continuity and access to resources. Tom and our staff worked with members of the Yaqui, Iroquois, Mandan, Hidatsa, Sioux, and Ojibwe tribes, with researchers, and others to define the program by looking at a range of natural and cultural resources vital to the continued health of various Indian cultures but now endangered. Yaqui Indians came to the Mall, building a *ramada,* demonstrating *pascola* and deer dances, and discussing how the U.S.-Mexican border, which cut through their territory, made it difficult for residents on either side to obtain the cocoons used to make anklets for their sacred dance. The Plains Indians discussed how they managed their buffalo herds, demonstrated buffalo dances and rituals and art, and illustrated animal-raising skills on buffalo brought down to the Mall. The Iroquois staged lacrosse games between Onondaga and Tuscarora boys, made lacrosse sticks, and discussed how rules for competition lacrosse made it difficult for them to compete in their own game on an international level. Ojibwe Indians built a small rice camp on the Mall and demonstrated some of the techniques of collecting and processing wild rice in the Great Lakes—now under threat because of industrial pollution and recreational boaters.[10]

Vennum figured that the birch-bark canoe in the Natural History Museum collection would come in handy as part of the Ojibwe presentation. Since Earl Nyholm was coming back and would use the boat for demonstrating techniques of harvesting wild rice, it seemed quite appropriate to ask the museum to lend us the boat. The boat would also be useful for comparative purposes. The festival that year also featured a program on Hawai'i. Wright Bowman, a Hawaiian *koa* wood boat builder, would be demonstrating his skills. The two kinds of boats have similarities and building them relies on the passing down of traditional knowledge. Having the two boat builders together, discussing the construction, features, cultural significance, and traditions connected to their work seemed like a good idea.

Numerous telephone conversations, discussions, and memos later, we seemed to be at a standstill in getting permission to borrow the canoe. Our request to have Nyholm use the canoe was not going to be approved. I called the collections manager at Natural History to ask for the canoe. I paraphrase our conversation:

KURIN: Why can't we use the canoe?

MANAGER: Because it's a museum object.

KURIN: But this is a loan to another part of the Smithsonian. Isn't that okay?

MANAGER: But you don't know how to care for it. You don't have conservators.

KURIN: But Earl Nyholm, the guy who made the canoe, will be here to care for it.

MANAGER: Well, he's not trained in conservation. Besides, the canoe is in disrepair.

KURIN: Well, then, Earl can fix it. In fact, we can video him doing it to add a level of ethnographic information we otherwise would not have. This will be good.

MANAGER: I don't think we can give the canoe to you. The last time you had it you did not care for it well.

KURIN: What happened?

MANAGER: It was supposed to be kept under a tent, and under a tarp at night. It wasn't. It was often out in the open and on the ground.

KURIN: Well, what was the damage?

MANAGER: It was left outside, and when it started raining it got wet.

KURIN: Oh, come on. It got wet. I'm sure staff tried to get it under cover as soon as possible.

MANAGER: Well, that didn't happen. And it got wet.

KURIN: Look—it's a f——in' canoe, it's supposed to get wet!

I persisted. The result was that the National Museum of Natural History agreed to give us—not loan us—the canoe. That is, the canoe would be deaccessioned as a museum object and given (back) to Folklife. After the festival, the canoe would not be accepted back into the museum's collections because it would be, as the collection manager told me, "contaminated." If this was not ironic enough, when we went to physically

Earl Nyholm talks about his birch-bark canoe (left) at
the 1989 Festival of American Folklife in a session with
Hawaiian boat builder Wright Bowman. Photo by Dane
Penland, courtesy Smithsonian Institution.

move the canoe, we were informed that it was in an asbestos-
contaminated museum storage facility. We would have to pay to get it
cleaned.

The ritual contamination that living people would bring the canoe
stood in marked contrast to the physical contamination visited on the
canoe in museum storage. The idea of ownership implicit in the actions
of the collection manager is noteworthy: The rights of the person who
made the canoe—his knowledge, his skill, his labor—were viewed as antithetical to the status of the object as museum object. If his rights, or
ours on his behalf, were to be asserted, the canoe could no longer be a
museum artifact.

From the Museum into the Living Room

The canoe was a living object with an active biography. The museum required that an object be placed in cultural formaldehyde. The canoe needed living room—I just didn't know it would be mine.

I expected that the Natural History Museum would relent after the festival program and take back the canoe. It did not. And so there was the problem of what to do with it. The most appropriate home for it seemed to be the newly emerging National Museum of the American Indian. But no suitable facilities yet existed in Washington, and the New York storage unit was overcrowded and in disrepair. The American History Museum was also a possibility, and indeed, Rayna Green, head of its American Indian Program, was quite empathetic and thought the canoe would make a wonderful one-object exhibition in the future. Unfortunately, nothing could be done right away.

Earl Nyholm still wanted his canoe to rest with the Smithsonian, which had indeed accepted it as an appropriate item for the national collections of the United States. The canoe was a good illustration of the culture and history, the knowledge and artistry of the Ojibwe people. The festival office, which does contain hundreds of donated objects, could not accommodate the large canoe. The festival lacked any climate-controlled space adequate for storing the canoe. What to do?

The canoe—a national treasure, kicked out of Natural History, contaminated by the festival and by its maker, found temporary refuge in my indoor garage for a year. But when I remodeled my garage, the canoe ended up in my not-very-large living room, atop sawhorses, for a second year. Every time anyone in my family wanted to go from one side of the living room to another, he or she would have to duck under the canoe. My children found it amusing; more staid adult visitors did not. It made a wonderful conversation piece but not much else.

I imagine that many donors of objects to the Smithsonian think their thing is going to find a place on a pedestal in a museum, with a nice light shining on it and a label next to it, giving the particulars of the donation and its meaning. This is rarely the case. Only 1 or 2 percent of the Smithsonian's holdings of 140 million items are on display. The vast majority are in storage. The canoe was able to join the ranks of these objects when we finally stored it with other festival materials in a secure and adequate location. But we still await the day that Earl Nyholm's canoe will find a better home. I have a feeling that its story is not yet at an end.

A buffalo calf, Nasca Nacasire, is born on the National Mall during the 1989 Festival of American Folklife. Photo by Richard Hofmeister, courtesy Smithsonian Institution.

And a Buffalo Too

Interestingly enough, the canoe was not the only object that the summer subjected to brokering over its museum acquisition and display. Another was an object that I was more than pleased did not end up in my living room. It was a baby buffalo.

Nasca Nacasire, or Summer Calf, as she was named by Mandan elder William Bell, was born in the early morning of June 24, 1989, in a pen outdoors on the National Mall in front of the Washington Monument and the National Museum of American History. Her birth made national press coverage, as the Associated Press put a wonderful photo of her on the wire.

The birth, as any birth does, marked new life. The buffalo's birth was poignant because it came in the midst of a Smithsonian Folklife Festival program drawing attention to the reintroduction of buffalo herding and herd management techniques among Plains Indians. The birth marked the vitality of an Indian cultural tradition—buffalo were still part of a living culture.

The birth also came at a time when the new National Museum of the American Indian was taking shape. The Smithsonian had just completed a deal to acquire the Heye Collection; legislation authorizing a new museum was pending before Congress and was sure to pass.[11] Not too many people, animals, or institutions are born on the National Mall. But the National Museum of the American Indian would be born there, and its building would rise up from the ground under the guidance of American Indian people just as surely as Summer Calf had been born in that semi-sacred space.

Mandan, Hidatsa, and other Native American participants in the festival wrote a letter to Smithsonian secretary Bob Adams and Senator Daniel Inouye, chair of the Senate Select Committee on Indian Affairs, suggesting that the Smithsonian "acquire" Nasca Nacasire. In the letter, signatories made clear that the Mall was Summer Calf's birthplace and that her presence, in a way, marked the territory—of the Mall—as originally hers, and theirs. Thus, the acquisition would represent, in fact, a rightful return. The treatment of the buffalo would be a metaphor for the treatment of Indian peoples more generally—do they have a right to the land of their birth? The letter is transcribed below:[12]

> Dear Senator Inouye and Secretary Adams:
>
> At 2:06 A.M. on Saturday, June 24, a calf was born to the buffalo cow who was on the Mall as part of the American Indian Program of the Folklife Festival.
>
> Mandan and Hidatsa people from North Dakota also had been singing buffalo songs, performing buffalo dances, tanning buffalo hides and making buffalo head dresses and bull boats as part of this Festival. There is also a great exhibit about our people in the Museum of American History. The Indian presence this year is, we hope, only a sign of what is yet to come. All of the Indian people who have been here—Yaqui, Ojibwe, Northern Paiute, Washoe, Western Shoshone, Mohawk, Onondaga, Tuscarora, Rappahannock, Cherokee, Sioux, Arikara—and the Mandan and Hidatsa people who prayed for this calf, sang for her, and named her Nasca Nacasire (Summer Calf), feel that this calf is a great sign of good for the Indian people and for the Smithsonian. We believe our buffalo dance, which calls forth the buffalo, contributes to the mystique surrounding the birth of Summer Calf on the Mall. Mandan and Hidatsa people will pray for her during her entire life, and songs will be made about what happened here.
>
> In that spirit, we are asking you to acquire [her] for the new Museum which we understand will be built on the Mall. Her presence would be a sign to all people that Indian people have been here and have a place on the National Mall, and that there is great hope for the future of this new

museum and the Indian people. It would be a sign that this place was a place of living people and living cultures. No symbol exists like that of the buffalo—perhaps only an eagle—for its significance among the Indian people of North America. She could remain with her mother until weaned, then perhaps could stay in the National Zoo until a place is made for her on her birthplace, the National Mall.

The buffalo at the Festival were rented by the Smithsonian's Office of Folklife Programs from Bob and Shirley Johnson of the Pet Farm Park [sic]. They helped load and transport the buffalo and were most cooperative. They have said they are willing to make arrangements for the transfer of Summer Calf.

We are asking both of you gentlemen to listen to our petition since both of you have been the leaders of actions to bring the new Museum of the American Indian to Washington. We know that you will understand what an important symbol this buffalo would be for the Indian people and for the American people. In a way, we feel this calf was a gift to all of us, to bind us together in a renewed purpose. We hope you can find some way to let this calf come to stand for all the people in this way.

Aho (Thank You),

Carl Whitman, Jr.	William Bell, Sr.
Heath Harmon	Marty Goodbear
Inez Chase	Naomi Foolish Bear
Dean P. Fox	Keith Bear

The acquisition of Summer Calf would have been an important one for the new museum. Since the impetus for the museum had been the desire to create a living museum for American Indians, and not a museum of dead cultures, the acquisition of the buffalo would have imposed a certain kind of stewardship upon the museum. Caring for a living buffalo would have necessitated an architectural program that allowed for life not only in a metaphorical sense but in a real one. The insertion of a buffalo would have pushed the federal contracting, design, and construction bureaucracy to new limits. The museum would have had to have a place for the buffalo to roam, food for it to eat, a means of dealing with its waste. The museum would have had to account for Summer Calf's growth and maturation. A mate, mating, and the propagation of buffalo on the National Mall would have followed. Accounting for life in the midst of Washington, in the midst of its stately buildings and sterile museums, would have made for a good test of whether the new kind of museum—one that accommodates and makes room not only for people but also for other living things—like animals, and ideas—could become a reality.

The acquisition of Summer Calf by the Smithsonian would have also made an interesting historical story. Buffalo had been born on the Mall before—some one hundred years earlier. In the late nineteenth century the National Zoo was located on the Mall. Buffalo grazed on the Mall's grassland and were kept in pens behind the Smithsonian Castle. The idea of the Smithsonian's collection of buffalo was then, originally, conceived of as serving a preservation purpose. And indeed, the contemporary herds of the Mandan and Hidatsa had been built up from the genetic stock of the buffalo preserved on the Mall. In fact, accession number 1 for the National Zoo was a Hockaday buffalo.

But the buffalo had been moved to the zoo's current Rock Creek Park home, and the time for grazing on the Mall was well past. The acquisition of Nasca Nacasire was not to be. The Indian elders and participants who wrote the letter received no response. Their proposal was never seriously considered. The buffalo would be an uncontrollable object, a thing hard to museumify. And so Summer Calf, now grown to maturity, grazes at the Reston Animal Farm, far removed from the place of her birth. Some things are beyond brokerage; they cannot be transformed into a museum object. Or they present such irreconcilable meanings to those involved that their status cannot be negotiated or mediated through display or presentation. But if brokering a canoe or a buffalo within the Smithsonian was difficult, imagine the challenge of dealing with the *Enola Gay*.

CHAPTER 5

EXHIBITING
THE ENOLA GAY

The exhibition planned for 1995 by the National Air and Space Museum of the *Enola Gay*, the B-52 bomber that dropped the first atomic bomb on Hiroshima, touched off a firestorm of public reaction, media coverage, curatorial and scholarly treatment, and political and professional debate about the role of museums, particularly public museums, in American society.[1] The exhibition sought to examine the context for dropping the atomic bomb, and the consequences of that act, for Hiroshima, for the ending of the war, and for the atomic age that it inaugurated. Veterans' groups complained that the exhibit—as depicted in various versions (five in all) of its script—was unpatriotic and inaccurate, an unfaithful way to mark the fiftieth anniversary of the end of World War II. The Smithsonian was exposed to an unprecedented level of public attention and scrutiny over the way it represented events in American history. Some forty members of Congress signed a letter asking that the director of the museum be dismissed. Museum curators shuddered. Scholars in universities complained about censorship and about political calculation replacing good history. The secretary of the Smithsonian decided to scrap the last version of the exhibition and devise a new, simpler one. Martin Harwit, the director of the museum, resigned.[2] And while some protested at the exhibit's opening in June 1995 about what they saw as the "whitewashing" of the exhibit themes, the crisis settled down. The front section of the *Enola Gay* is now on display at the Air and Space Museum.

In April 1995, the Smithsonian and the University of Michigan planned and held a conference to examine issues of controversy with respect to museum exhibition, particularly the *Enola Gay*.[3] The conference sought to address the ways in which controversial issues and topics could and should be exhibited in public museums within a democratic society. More than any other event in recent Smithsonian history, the *Enola Gay* controversy clearly illustrated how museum exhibits are indeed negotiated, how understandings need to be brokered, and how interests, professional skills, and power relations are brought to bear in representing history and culture. Conferees included, among others, Tom Crouch, one of the curatorial principals from the Air and Space Museum; Herman Wolk, a historian from the Air Force; Admiral Kilcline of the Retired Officers Association; and Edward Linenthal, an academic and a participant in the exhibition advisory group.[4] I was asked to summarize issues at the conference during its concluding session. I focused on the consequences of the *Enola Gay* controversy, the lessons learned for the Smithsonian. What follows is based upon that presentation and subsequent developments, including the issuance of new Smithsonian exhibition guidelines and the publication of Martin Harwit's *An Exhibit Denied: Lobbying the History of the Enola Gay*.[5]

The Smithsonian as an Icon of Public Discourse

What we at the Smithsonian do is important, and it is perceived by Americans as connected to our public life. According to a nationwide survey, the Smithsonian uniquely stands for what Americans would hold up to the world as illustrating who we are as a nation.[6] A question at President Clinton's press conference on the eve of the "Presenting History" conference illustrated the connection between the Smithsonian and public discourse.[7] A reporter asked the president—and I paraphrase—"Given the effort to end the Smithsonian's exhibit on the nuclear bomb, is the issue now a taboo subject in America?" The implication was that if the Smithsonian cannot talk about or deal with something, the subject has no place in our public discourse.

The *Enola Gay* issue is familiar to much of the public, and everyone seems to have an opinion about it. This is quite different from the lack of public attention to the "forgotten bomber," the *Bock's Car*, long on display at the U.S. Air Force Museum in Dayton, Ohio. The *Enola Gay* is controversial and subject to public treatment maybe because it was the first, rather than the second, bomber, but more so because it serves as an icon in a more elaborate, contentious historical narrative created by the Smithsonian in its role as the national museum.

That national history should be a subject of contention should not take anyone by surprise. We are in a period of exacerbated nationalism— new and heightened senses of nationalism resulting in the creation of new nations, as well as widespread challenges to national authority and identity. These challenges, from within through increased localism and regionalism and from without through the global economy, political multilateralism, and transnational cultural flows, apply to a host of countries, including the United States. In the United States we find the idea of the "public" itself shrinking, receding, and even problematic.[8] We wonder about our ability to hold together, given our diversity, disparity, and divisions of wealth, race, culture, language, and interests. We worry that civic discourse is becoming more and more contentious and difficult. And we find civic institutions less able to meet public expectations. The presidency, Congress, government departments and programs, public schools, public libraries, television, and movies—all seem to be failing us.

Is the idea of a nationally unifying, good, pure, responsive public institution attractive but maybe too good to be true and beyond what Americans can believe in anymore? History, when done publicly, can become a field of passionate contention and strong debate—especially when it purports to stand for us as a nation. If people don't like history in a book, they don't buy it. If they don't like a television historical documentary, they change the channel. But history, when done by the Smithsonian as a public institution, when presented as an exhibit, a public display that has a permanence, a solidity, and a powerful location, is not so easy to ignore.

Public Trust and Responsibility

The things the Smithsonian museums hold we do not own. We hold them in trust for the people. This idea of public trust, which goes to the very inception of the Smithsonian, is profound. No curator was elected to represent anybody or anything. Our authority derives from the knowledge we possess and the years of accumulated knowledge, good sense and judgment, esteem and respect, that adhere to the institution, built up over generations by honorable people engaged in the same task.

The American people, and indeed people the world over, expect us to be fair and honest in seeking and presenting knowledge—whether it be historical, cultural, natural, physical, or artistic. When we violate that trust, people, understandably, get upset.

We have a responsibility to the people of the United States, for whom we are an instrumentality. We have responsibilities to the Congress, to scholarship, to sponsors, partners, and employees. Sometimes these responsibilities are difficult to sort through, sometimes they are even in conflict. Reasonable people recognize such conflicts and expect the Smithsonian to navigate through them in good faith, using good, solid knowledge, not preachy moralism or politics or commercialism as our compass.

Lonnie Bunch, head curator of the National Museum of American History, conceives of the Smithsonian as being in the world of public scholarship—poised between scholarly and official domains.[9] Public historians must give the public something of value. Their scholarship is for the larger public benefit. But it must be guided by sound method, intellectual honesty, and high disciplinary standards. At the same time, such public scholarship needs to be presented and is rightfully subject to public scrutiny; it carries a degree of legitimacy beyond that of an individual's academic or scholarly pursuit. After all, it does involve a public investment in the work of the scholar.

The Search for Truth and Narrative

One problem we all seem to have is that knowledge is not such an easy and clear path to the truth. Indeed, the truth is not what it used to be in the days when the Smithsonian was founded. Defining the truth seems a lot harder now than it did in the epistemological realism of the Enlightenment and the early days of the empirical sciences. We have moved from a pre- to a postdisciplinary world in 150 years. In human studies we deal with multiparadigmatic, deconstructed frameworks that make multiple versions of reality a fact of life.

Scholarly searches for the truth are challenged on a number of fronts. According to some historians, there has long been a deep-seated anti-intellectualism at work in our public life. Alternative sources of knowledge and legitimation, often grounded in religious doctrine and belief, have in some cases proved antithetical to scholarly pursuits.[10] The rise of the middle class in the post–World War II era and the GI Bill nurtured a large population often intent on making up its own mind and distrusting others to do it for them. The Civil Rights Movement spawned alternative views of historical and cultural truth that ran counter to conventional knowledge.

Within the academy, a high value is placed on revisionism and on contra-versions of events, theories, and understandings. Doctorates are awarded for new contributions to knowledge—not for the retelling of conventional truths. This is particularly the case in the social sciences and the humanities. Accolades and rewards are oriented toward the rewriting, recasting, and upending of conventional stories. History has gone well beyond the mundane search for the facts and is now solidly concerned with how the facts are interpreted and woven together in some narrative form. Not that historians are alone here. Some of my anthropologist colleagues think that the presentation of ethnographic knowledge is akin to the "writing of culture."[11] While in some respects a useful insight into anthropological practice, such a position may undermine the epistemological status of good research work. In the formulation, disciplinary scholarship may be fallaciously reduced to the status of literary fiction.

Maybe this trend has gone too far and the pendulum will swing back to a stronger empiricism, though I think most have recognized that strong scholarship is thorough and evidentiary, that historical facts have to be substantiated by evidence. We increasingly recognize our own role in combining and weaving those facts into coherent narratives to tell to our audiences. And we need to be increasingly clear about how we fill in gaps with our own interpretations and conjectures.

I suggest three correctives in the presentation of historical and cultural exhibitions—greater rigor in the assessment of the factual data we present, a clearer understanding and choice of the various possible narrative frames that we might construct, and giving the audience a better sense of how our presentation came to be, such as through author-attributed museum signs and articles in catalogs. Exhibit scripts such as that for the *Enola Gay* distinguished too little between fact, narrative frame, and speculation. For example, consider the oft-quoted text of one of the signs in the exhibition's first script: "For most Americans, this war was fundamentally different than the one waged against Germany and

Italy—it was a war of vengeance. For most Japanese, it was a war to defend their unique culture against Western imperialism."[12] Numerous such examples were found throughout the exhibition script.

Anonymous scripts convey a sense of disembodied authority—a "word of God"–like quality that we know to be inappropriate. Finally, we need to give more thought to the pragmatics and context of presentation—the tonality of our signage, the juxtaposition of objects, photographs, labels, and exhibit elements—and the audience (whether the seven-minute cruisers or the subjects of the exhibit) to whom our stories are being presented.

Not only has knowledge become more problematic to certify and present, it is also arguably more distributed than it was in the nineteenth century. Given levels of worldwide literacy, the spread of newspaper, radio, and television, and now the Internet, knowledge is widely distributed around the world and within most classes of society. Rather than emanating from a few, knowledge is now seen in the many. Scholars and curators aren't the only ones to possess knowledge and then to share it through books and exhibits with those who don't possess it.

Indeed, with historical knowledge, the data of which are almost always first oral rather than written, personal and experienced rather than aggregated and structured, people—as actors in history—are vitally and centrally important. Veterans, scientists, officials, and others who played a role in the *Enola Gay*'s mission are possessed of the knowledge of what they did and thought they did. Their voices needed to be considered in the determination of facts, the construction of possible narratives, and the development of exhibitions. Although this was done to some extent, the effort was not adequate. While the Air and Space Museum leadership believed that it listened to the voices of the veterans, the veterans believed that they were not heard, that what they said was not seriously considered.[13]

This becomes abundantly clear in Martin Harwit's own revisionist account of the *Enola Gay* affair. Harwit's view is generally that he was pursuing the truth and that others tried to obscure both the search for it and its presentation.[14] Harwit brings a pre-Kuhnian physicist's sensibility to his interpretation—he naively believes that there is an absolute historical truth and that all it takes is perseverance and sound method to ascertain it. He fails to see or account for his own biases, motives, and goals in telling a historical story—and then chides the veterans, politicians, and Smithsonian officials for having their own interests. Harwit wants the facts but fails to acknowledge his own weavings of them. He saw the brokering of the *Enola Gay*'s history as a purely political act, devoid of useful content, whereas such negotiations were actually attempts to articulate legitimate, countervailing interpretations of the factual.

Many veterans reacted angrily to the suggestion that their history was any less incisive or truthful than that of the academics or of the museum historians. And, as Geoffrey White rightly notes, academic history writing is always embedded in cultural values and commitments.[15] Such an orientation leads to particular ways of defining, documenting, and interpreting facts.

Harwit erroneously assumes that because veterans had contributed to the restoration of the *Enola Gay*, they therefore endorsed his particular approach to its display. He assumes, by a selective reading of comments from historian advisers, that because people say good things about parts of the exhibition script they agree with the whole of it. Consultations with the represented and with expert scholars can always be manipulated.

Museum curators have to listen to the voices of the represented not only because of political expediency and goodwill. They should actually try to hear those voices, because there may be something insightful and valuable in the substance of what they actually have to say. And this is the case whether we are talking about the voices of veterans in the *Enola Gay* exhibit or those of Africans in a Natural History Museum Africa Hall or those of American Indians in the new American Indian Museum. It does not mean that curators and scholars give up their responsibilities. But it does mean that they fully and honestly intellectually engage those whom they seek to represent. The presence of those voices should not lead to bad history any more than bad history should be allowed to silence those voices. As John Shy has put it, history plus memory equals good history.[16]

Techniques for Producing Exhibitions

Clearly, in a museum, particularly a national museum, we have to find room for the meaningful participation of those being represented. Sometimes, in museums such as the National Museum of the American Indian or the Holocaust Museum, this charge is explicit. This ups the ante on what we do, for the people we talk about in the exhibit will let us know how our curatorial stories and theirs square. But it can also serve us well as a museum technique, for most of what we ourselves might want to say as curators has been said by others, or a multitude of others, implicated in the historical events that we seek to display. In many but certainly not all cases, we can let the varied voices of the past speak directly to our audiences to convey the complexity of past events.

But as Barbara Kirshenblatt-Gimblett observes, we generally start not with people but with the objects in the collection, using them as the touchstones to tell those stories. The problem here is the limitations of the objects in telling stories.[17] For one, the Smithsonian, though it possesses millions of objects, still comes up short. There are many histories we cannot tell, many people and many Americans left out because we do not have the objects on hand to tell their stories. Some stories that should be told are not object-driven. In some cases the objects can lead us away from processes and events that are the stuff of history. And the physical characteristics of the objects may not mirror their semiotic character in a story—big objects do not necessarily assume large importance.

On the other hand, there is something about the power of stuff. The objects provide a sense of the real, the authentic, and the power that accompanies it. Cared for by conservators, guarded by Smithsonian security, occupying pedestals and other prime real estate, the objects become distillates of meaning. In parallel fashion, the work of the historian is to cull from the infinite flow of personal experience, events, and occurrences, an understandable extract. Events, dates, periods, eras are defined, placed in close association, and conceptually bound. In writing history, the historian compresses time. An exhibit brings together a disparate assemblage of stuff and compresses it into a limited, defined space. Doing both—producing an exhibition of history—compresses time and space, creating a potent blend—a symbolic world. This symbolic world becomes especially valuable when enshrined in a national museum.

One question is how and to what extent we use this blend. Do we want more or less resolution in our historical exhibits—more of just the raw stuff of history or a more reasoned, clearer choice of alternative stories laid out so the audience can make up its own mind? Is the exhibit a station in a national pilgrimage offering low-resolution ritual catharsis, or is it a court case with visitor as juror?

One can go around the Smithsonian and find enough of each—the ritualistic display and the reasoned argument—in its museums and exhibits. And I don't think they have to be one or the other all the time. But we might have to be more clear to ourselves and our audiences about the types of exhibits we do.

Much of the time the curators are the priests of the temple, and the public, we believe, like it that way. But sometimes the curators and scholars want to be the prophets, not repeating the familiar liturgy but changing the language of the whole service. This is a fine thing to do. But when we do it, we had better do it because we have a strong case, with clear evidence and well-supported interpretations, as well as some savvy about its reception. Curators might get out ahead of their audience or constituents because they have crafted a justifiable, important reinterpretation of history that rightfully should be shared with the public and those represented. And even if some folks are upset that we have discovered something new or previously unknown that challenges dogma, we have a responsibility to let people know—after all, we are not a private institution. There is nothing wrong with new knowledge, a refutation of previous knowledge, and upsetting of history otherwise taken for granted. Contention and controversy may be good for creativity. But again, given where we sit and how we say it, we had better have a strong case. And knowing whether or not we have a strong case takes a considerable amount of judgment, for if we know we are going to ask the public to accept something controversial, we had better be prepared for the answer—which may well be no!

Clarity of Purpose

The purposes of exhibitions have to be clear. President Clinton mirrored Secretary Heyman's analysis of the problem with the *Enola Gay* exhibit—that it conflated two very different ends, the commemoration of the end of World War II and the reexamination of the decision to drop the bomb and the consequences of that decision.[18] I think many veterans and others felt the same way.

My dad was a merchant seaman during World War II. At the time the bomb was dropped on Hiroshima he was stationed on a ship anchored off a small atoll a few hundred miles southeast of Japan. His ship was loaded with munitions, likely to support an invasion if needed. As he tells it, "We had so much ammunition aboard that no other ship would come anywhere close to us. If we had been bombed, we would have left a hole in the ocean." When the bomb was dropped, he and his mates celebrated, relieved that the war was over. Relief. That's what my mom felt too. Her recently wed husband would return to her. When they found out how devastating the bomb's destruction had been, they were both awed. They did not celebrate the destruction, they were merely glad the war was over, albeit at a terrible cost—not only at Hiroshima but throughout the world.

To have a script that was perceived and reported as putting the onus of guilt upon Americans, blaming American servicemen for dropping the bomb on innocent women and children, and putting on their shoulders the start of the cold war, nuclear waste, nuclear terrorism, and other horrors was too much of a stretch. The veterans, and others, rightly felt that the national museum was theirs and that it was doing them a disservice. I do not believe that most felt the Smithsonian should merely, and perhaps mindlessly, celebrate an idealized form of selective history. Herman Wolk's argument is telling: Many felt that the exhibit was history poorly done in terms of the stipulation and weaving of the facts.[19] Further, for some veterans the narrative unfairly placed them in a history that was not of their making. The Air and Space Museum narrative for the *Enola Gay* exhibit—at least the first draft—offered veterans a history that was not of their memory, and also a history that was not how they wanted to be remembered. Had this been done by others, it might not have had much consequence. But as President Clinton implied, when the Smithsonian does it, it *looks like* it is being done officially, speaking of and for the nation as a whole.

National Museums and Curatorial Work

We at the Smithsonian have a way of doing our work that makes it look official—that's the good news and it's also the bad news. So what recourse do people have when they disagree with what the Smithsonian says—start their own new national museum? Again, it's easier to publish a book or write a critical review or even a letter to the editor to respond to something in print. It's much more difficult to respond in kind to a museum and an exhibit—you have to come up with some prime real estate, spend $100 million on a fancy building, a few million for an exhibit, and then get seven or eight million folks to come through the door. It is frankly easier to write the Congress and call a press conference.

The Smithsonian, though certainly responsive to the state, is not an agency of government. Many from other countries are confused by this, thinking we are like a ministry of culture. But, somehow, some way, there was the foresight 150 years ago to cast the Smithsonian as a trust held in the name of the people, with a purpose—the increase and diffusion of knowledge—that transcends the policies and politics of a particular government. This was good. But it means that our scholars and curators are neither beholden to government nor entirely free to pursue their own individual interests. They have a responsibility to the public and must be accountable to it.

This formulation seems to be particularly profound in a democratic society. There is a long record of national museums accountable only to the state. The museums of Nazi Germany, of the Soviet Union, of South Africa under apartheid are monuments to the dangers of the official museum, to the problems that arise when national governments determine the content of museums and view them as instruments of their own purpose. I think we, the people, would be deeply distrustful of museums under the dictates of the state. Distance from the state, and even dissonance, are required so that scholars and curators can fulfill their responsibilities and seek the truth as best it can be known. Curators often succeed and sometimes fail.

If you walk around the Smithsonian museums, you can see a fascinating archaeology of these various ways of pursuing and displaying knowledge. We have exhibits that hark back to ways of looking at things through nineteenth-century eyes, exhibits that disagree with each other and present contrasting points of view. Our research and exhibit work simply does not conform to anyone's singular party line—not even that of Smithsonian secretaries (which sometimes generates considerable angst). And in the context of national nervousness over our sense of self, where the celebratory seems so attractive, we still need curators and exhibits to strive for the analytical, the questioning, the challenging. This is part and parcel of a healthy national civic life.

The sobering, analytic view is needed not as a subversion of the public trust but as part of our responsibility to it. If historical museums are going to generate discussion, public debate, and conversation—so be it. Hard feelings, disrupted careers, public hearings, and media attention may sometimes be the price. But what is the alternative? Look at places around the world where the civic dialogue has stopped and been replaced by violence and destruction.

If we take the broad view here, the controversy was resolved through the larger democratic process. I, and many others, resented the innuendo, the personal attacks, the questions raised about the public service and credentials of Air and Space curators and the former director. Plac-

ing the issue of the *Enola Gay* within the debates over political correctness and attributing the character of its display to leftist curators were
most unfortunate. The politicizing of the affair in terms of liberal versus
conservative partisanship might have been unavoidable, but it obfuscated the more central issue. Linenthal's charges of "cultural McCarthy-
ism" and the American Legion's attempt to "regulate public history"
were as misfounded and as incendiary as presidential candidate Pat
Buchanan's call for Smithsonian "house cleaning."

But in the end, it was citizens talking to their national museum, directly and then indirectly, that led to the crisis and to its resolution. It
was a free press that aired the issue, however imperfectly, for the public.
And indeed, it was the desire for civil discussion, reflection, and responsible action that motivated various panels at scholarly and professional
meetings and in other forums, and that is likely to inspire continued
analysis and interpretation of the case.

As a result of the *Enola Gay* discussion, the Smithsonian secretary
promulgated guidelines for dealing with controversy.[20] The guidelines
rely on museum professionals and public scholars to utilize their art and
skill. They call for museums to air curatorial ideas with broad advisory
groups, for museum directors to be responsible for the exhibitions under
their purview and to consult with Smithsonian leadership in the cases
likely to prompt significant public discord. But they do not seek to steer
the museums away from tackling difficult, controversial topics. They ask
that such topics be addressed competently, rationally, and wisely. The
guidelines are not onerous, but they do require judgment, calibration,
and wisdom in their application. And they do not absolve Smithsonian
scholars and curators from the central task of disseminating knowledge
to the public.

Curators generally believe that theirs is an optimistic enterprise, a
task that fundamentally celebrates the human spirit and its accomplishments—even as it understands the role of doom, misery, destruction,
evil. Curators stand at the crossroads of understanding and celebrations
of self, nation, world, and humanity. The curatorial art is combining and
juxtaposing analysis and memory, celebration and revelation, heritage
and history. Like other brokers, curators are always at the border, engaged
in efforts of cultural translation and symbolic transformation, making
meaning for the disparate audiences and constituencies who have a
stake in what they do.[21]

CHAPTER 6

WHAT'S WITH ANTHROPOLOGY?

A mong other things, the *Enola Gay* controversy illustrated that the National Air and Space Museum was "out of touch" with some of the people that the museum sought to represent. The more out of touch an institution is, the more the categories and understandings of the museum and the people represented are out of kilter, the more language seems irrelevant and inapplicable, the more interests are seen as divergent, and the more brokering and negotiation are necessary if a relationship is to be forged, maintained, and remain vital.

This also happens with disciplines that have been nurtured within the Smithsonian but have a much wider breadth than the museums. Anthropology has a venerable history at the Smithsonian. Ethnology and the study of Native Americans were included in the table of organization, the vision statement produced by the first Smithsonian secretary, Joseph Henry, in 1846. Key figures in the founding of American anthropology worked at the Smithsonian—John Wesley Powell, Otis Mason, Alex Hrdlička, and others. The Smithsonian, through the Bureau of American Ethnology, became a repository for collections of record, documenting the lifeways of American Indians. Through collections from various government-sponsored expeditions, as a repository of skeletal remains, and as a sponsor of field expeditions and a storehouse of information gathering, the Smithsonian came to be a world-renowned center for anthropological study.[1]

Today, anthropology—as a field of study, as a discipline, and as a museum department—faces considerable challenges.

Challenges for the Field

Anthropology, as a coherent field of scholarly inquiry and activity, is subject to serious debate—much of which occurs within the ranks of professional anthropologists and some of which occurs beyond those bounds. Key issues raised about the field have focused on its multiparadigmatic character, the coherence of its traditional, American, four-subfield approach to human study, and the diminished importance it has placed on collections and other empirical data. But perhaps the most serious challenge to the field has had to do with the relationship between anthropologists, particularly cultural anthropologists, and the people they purport to study and represent in their work.

Anthropology formed as a discipline in late nineteenth- and early twentieth-century Great Britain and America as evolutionism was being applied to humankind and cultural phenomena. Evolution, as a concept, does not now drive the field. Indeed, there are numerous competing paradigms still operating—from forms of diffusionism to structural, functional, ecological, symbolic, and various eclectic approaches. Despite a recent attempt by sociobiology to reassert a neo-evolutionary paradigmatic preeminence, the field is characterized by a large variety of theoretical orientations and derived methodologies that result in different types of anthropology being done. This lack of a single dominant paradigm will continue for the foreseeable future and mitigates against a unified discipline, such as has been achieved in the natural sciences and in economics.

The same is true with regard to anthropology's sense of itself as either a scientific or a humanistic enterprise. Most anthropologists would agree that they are scholars, approaching the study and understanding of humans, cultures, and social processes in a rational, disciplined manner. Smithsonian anthropologist Adrienne Kaeppler calls this a "scientific demeanor."[2] But are anthropologists doing science? On this question, the field is divided, as a recent series of articles in the *American Anthropological Association Newsletter* reveals. Many anthropologists use a variety of techniques that rely on scientific principles—particularly in archaeological and physical anthropological studies. They draw freely on chemical, biological, and physical analyses. The methods of ethnological investigations—at least some of them—also use scientific techniques drawn from mathematics, statistical analyses, and the like. Recent congressional debates over the funding of the National Science Foundation and a proposal to phase out one of its directorates, which grants funds for social scientific and anthropological research, have drawn a stiff reaction and perhaps motivated a stronger than justified argument for anthropology as science.

If "science" is used in its broadest sense as a self-questioning, rational, disciplined methodical examination of empirical reality using logically construed theory, then anthropology, in any one of a number of its varieties, is science. But if "science" is meant in a more restrictive sense as experimental and objective, with knowledge discerned through the testing of hypotheses designed to establish universal laws, anthropology is not a science.

One might suppose that anthropology's disciplinary unity is to be found in its subject matter. Most academic anthropology departments are organized into four subfields, like the department of anthropology at the Smithsonian—sociocultural anthropology or ethnology, linguistics, physical anthropology, and archaeology.[3] Most university departments have kept these subfields together, more, I would argue, out of a practical imperative within their institutions than out of theoretical purpose or methodological similarity. Some university departments have split the subfields up, with linguistics as a separate unit or part of cognitive science and physical anthropology as part of human biology. The coherence of the four subfields varies over time, depending upon paradigmatic orientations. Physical anthropology and ethnology were very close in the last century and earlier in this century, when culture was perceived to be innately related to biology—and head shape, for example, was thought to be correlated with social organization—a relationship long studied at the Smithsonian. Archaeology and ethnology were close within functionalist and civilizational approaches of the mid-twentieth century, a relationship still evident in some of the halls of the Natural History Museum. Linguistics and ethnology were seen as closely aligned in structuralist studies of the 1970s and are evident in some of the ethnoscience work conducted at the Smithsonian that now reposes in our collections in the form of flora organized in folk categories.

The questions are, How much sense does it make to group these subfields together and how much do they contribute to each other's discourse? Perusal of the American Anthropological Association's subunits would indicate that the subfields are the major lines of fissure in the overall discipline. Most anthropologists would agree that they probably share more with people outside their discipline than with colleagues in some of the other subfields. The marriage of subfields may at this point be more an artifact of history—and it is convenient in terms of academic bulk vis-à-vis other university departments. But the grouping of subfields hardly seems motivated by current and compelling conceptual design or elegance.

Anthropology, since the 1960s, also seems to have put less emphasis on empirical data collection activities, instead promoting more theoretical, analytical, and synthetic work. Collections of material culture have had a diminished importance since earlier in the twentieth century. The study of artifacts and material culture generally is of little more than marginal importance in ethnology and has long been so. It is of no importance in linguistics. Its main continuing importance is in physical anthropology and archaeology, but even then only as a first step in examining larger issues. Within certain paradigmatic frameworks, artifacts and human remains are of greater and lesser significance. Much of artifactual-based museum anthropology as practiced in the nineteenth and early twentieth centuries is well out of date and quite irrelevant to current concerns.

But more than just collections, data collection of any kind is today generally regarded with lesser, if not minimal interest by cultural anthropologists. Sets of data are used as conveniences for higher-level theorizing or inventing new paradigms. The descriptive, natural historical impulse not only of museum anthropologists but also of structuralists like Claude Lévi-Strauss, in collecting myths and observations of the landscape, or like Clifford Geertz, in earlier deep descriptions of social action, seem quite muted.[4]

More than even these "internal" matters, anthropology is challenged by its relationship to the people it seeks to represent. It has a post–colonial era problem of representing "other." George Stocking, a leading historian of anthropology, views the discipline as a stepchild of colonialism.[5] It clearly grew as a way of "us" understanding and representing "the other," sometimes sympathetically, sometimes not. The post–World War II demise of colonialism saw Third World populations educated on their own terms and speaking for themselves. It also saw immigrants from former colonies going to Great Britain and France. In the United States, the post-1965 immigration brought "other" into "our" society.

Many of the former "others" can speak for themselves about their culture, history, values, accomplishments, social theories, and so on—and do so in English. They can also read what anthropologists have writ-

John Wesley Powell (left), renowned Smithsonian anthropologist, observes the Pauite circle dance on a research expedition to the Kaibab plateau near the Grand Canyon, 1871–75. Photo by John K. Hillers, courtesy National Anthropological Archives.

ten about them. There is, in many societies, a resentment toward anthropology. On the one hand, this concerns the content of what is said about them, but more, it concerns the fact that anthropology is perceived as speaking arrogantly, through organs of power, without engaging them—mainly intellectuals, but also "the common man"—as sentient subjects. Anthropologists, some might say, are, like their subjects, either safe—distant and unresponsive—or dead.

Anthropological subjects, i.e., the people and cultures being represented, do not have to limit themselves to waiting for an anthropologist to study them in order to find meaning in their lives. The "other" and the former "other" write books, engage in artistic commentary through painting, music, literature, and poetry, act and react politically, and so on. They do not depend upon anthropology to represent them. This reveals a contradiction in anthropology and indeed in other human studies fields that claim insight and knowledge into a people, culture, or society. If we know so much, how come the sons and daughters of "others"

An early twentieth-century diorama in the Smithsonian's National Museum offered visitors a voyeuristic view into a "foreign" culture. The Smithsonian has a
long history of making realistic-looking mannequins in a life grouping—first
used for the 1893 Columbian Exposition in Chicago. William Holmes, a leading
Smithsonian anthropologist who was also an artist and the first director of the
National Museum of American Art, was particularly fond of these displays to
represent other cultures. Photo courtesy Office of Smithsonian Institution Archives.

are not flocking to our courses, reading our books, and visiting our museums? Can it be that what anthropologists are finding out is not what
people want to know?

If anthropology is discovering new insights, increasing the store of
knowledge, and providing the research basis with which humans can
live a better life, it is not letting the world in on its accomplishments—
at least not on a major scale. In the early part of the twentieth century,
Franz Boas and his colleagues at Columbia University and New York's
American Museum of Natural History were quite involved in an attempt
to affect public understandings of race in light of the massive immigration of eastern and southern Europeans to the United States.[6] But while
there was some effect within professional policy circles, the effort to affect popular understandings of race largely failed. Despite the solid phys-

ical scientific findings and the comparative cultural data that could have been marshaled and applied, anthropologists were not successful in seeing their view of race predominate in American mainstream discourse. Instead, even today, intelligent laypeople, reporters, politicians, and civic and business leaders continue to operate with nineteenth-century folk notions of race.

Anthropology has a poor track record on major issues of the immediate past. Few anthropologists—among them Ruth Benedict, Ashley Montagu, and Margaret Mead—became public figures, known beyond the field and closely related social sciences, who tried to encourage broader discourse on cultural issues.[7] Mead, the most famous of this group, was derided by many within the field for her public role. With some minor exceptions, individual anthropologists have not followed Mead. And the word "anthropologist," heard by most Americans, is likely to conjure up an image of Indiana Jones (a generation ago it was Carlos Castenada)—someone involved in esoteric studies of little-known, exotic peoples. Perhaps the most well-known current anthropologist is Richard Leakey—whose public stand on environmental and wildlife issues is more a product of his former governmental, political, and activist role than it is of his scientific, disciplinary work. Indeed, the field as a whole seems to discourage public engagement.

Anthropology's inauspicious track record on major concepts of broad public concern—such as race, the environment, human rights—portends poorly for the future. Why should various American minority groups, peoples of the Third World, indigenous peoples, and the like rely on anthropology to make sure that their cultures are properly understood? Indeed, "culture" is no longer seen as the exclusive domain of anthropology. Cultural studies, literary analysis, ethnic studies, and other fields are also claiming "culture" as their subject of study and discourse.

Further, no one is asking anthropologists to inject their knowledge into public discourse, a state of affairs that some anthropologists bemoan.[8] Instead, public talk about culture is taking place on television, radio talk shows, the op-ed pages of newspapers, in political campaigns, and even at PTA meetings. Museums have actually done more than the academic departments in bringing their specialized knowledge to the public, but they have generally seen this as a low-priority service rather than a major responsibility.

The relative inattention of anthropology to current issues of public concern is a loss. A host of current issues can and do engage some anthropologists, but by and large the academic and museum fields have remained aloof from these issues, reacting when they have to, but rarely taking a proactive position. Among such issues are questions of cultural survival among indigenous peoples throughout the world, the relationship between culture and development, cultural rights and environmental sustainability, the culture of the inner cities of this country, youth and violence, cultural property rights, contemporary issues of ethnicity and nationalism, and public cultural representation. These are often regarded pejoratively as "applied," trendy, not serious scholarship, mere advocacy, public service, social work, or lowly popular education.

New Trends: Needs and Opportunities

The internal challenges that beset anthropology are likely to remain for some time. And while the gap between the field and the public, the discipline and the people, the living culture and the museum looks large and perhaps unbridgeable, some bright spots can be identified.

There is always good work being done by anthropologists in university departments and museums. But the experimental moment belongs to those anthropologists working outside of traditional disciplinary structures. Anthropologists increasingly work in a greater variety of settings. In academia this includes medical schools, schools of education, law, development institutes, and many other departments in addition to anthropology. In the government, anthropologists work in a variety of federal agencies, from the Agency for International Development, the National Park Service, and the Bureau of Indian Affairs to the Departments of State, Justice, Energy, and Education. Anthropologists are quite active in the World Bank, UN agencies, and the full array of nongovernmental organizations (NGOs) involved with development. Anthropologists form the core of Cultural Survival and are active in indigenous peoples' networks and organizations around the world. Even at the Smithsonian, anthropologists are found in many different museums, research, and program units, including, among others, the Center for Folklife Programs and Cultural Studies, the Smithsonian Tropical Research Institute, the National Museum of the American Indian, and the National Museum of African Art. This diversity of placement is bound to yield new ways of looking at and doing anthropology.

There is also an increasing desire and need for articulation between sectors of practice. There are more anthropologists working outside than inside academia. The ideology of the discipline has not yet caught up to this fact. And while there is still a suspicion within academia that outside policy work, public and applied anthropology are less than pure or ideal, there is a broadly recognized need to contribute to policy and public education work. Nonacademic practice is an interesting new source for empirical findings, new methods, and theory. Better articulation of theory and practice is likely to revitalize anthropology much as it has other social sciences, particularly economics and the mathematical and natural sciences.

With greater collaboration and an eye toward larger issues of public concern, anthropologists have become more sophisticated about how they work. There is a growing recognition of the desirability of teamwork and long-term projects, rather than reliance solely on individualistic and intermittent fieldwork. Indeed, archaeologists and physical anthropologists have long recognized and practiced this mode of research, well ahead of their ethnological brethren in this respect. Many units, inside and outside the academy, now value the idea of a "project," with a critical mass of faculty, scholars, or researchers looking at a class of phenomena over an extended period of time and/or area with a concerted and focused plan of action. Such efforts should have strong paybacks.

Over the past decade, many humanistic anthropologists have reflected upon their own culture of inquiry rather than dealing with others. But if anthropology is to survive and even flourish, it must engage in greater collaboration with the subjects of its inquiry and understanding. In some cases, anthropologists have successfully worked in increasingly collaborative modes, whether by desire or compulsion, with community members and culture bearers, academically trained professionals, and lay scholars. This has become important in participatory research for development projects, in ethnomedical research, and in research for cultural presentations. At the Smithsonian, the Anacostia Museum's Black Mosaic project, a variety of National Museum of the American Indian projects, Smithsonian Folkways Recordings and Festival of American Folklife projects exemplify this approach. The tribulations of Natural History's Africa Hall—initially shut down, and mired in distrust between the Smithsonian and the community—offered a striking contrast.

Additionally, if anthropology is to remain vital, it must be used as a tool to broker understandings and representation within various communities. Perhaps the most dramatic illustration of this type is Jomo Kenyatta, who, after studying anthropology at the London School of

Economics, returned to Kenya to lead his country to nationhood. Internationally, anthropology has a checkered record. In some cases—as in India, Mexico, and Japan—anthropology has become a useful vehicle for intracultural dialogue.[9] In most other nations, however, anthropology is hardly practiced and is quite marginal to public cultural debates.

In the United States, only about 10 percent of the members of the American Anthropological Association are from "minority" communities. This does not augur well for disciplinary engagement with the cultural life of a growing segment of the American populace. Anthropologists from such communities would have a major role in developing and brokering presentations in museums, cultural programs in schools, people's participation in social and civic organizations, styles of therapeutic practice in the health care system, and so on.

Anthropologists are also becoming increasingly sophisticated in closing the gap between research and public communication, using multiple channels to disseminate knowledge. They continue to write books to communicate their findings, but they also use videos, films, television documentaries, recordings, and on-line Web pages, databases, exhibits, and bulletin boards to make their research known.

This allows for broader public distribution of anthropological knowledge. The growing awareness of the need to reach a greater proportion of the public is tempered by a gnawing ambivalence about doing so. Academic departments have been relatively slow to adapt to larger, general audiences. But NGOs have developed forms of mass communication, cause-related marketing, television special series, radio programs, and large-scale public exhibitions to do so.

The need to reach mass audiences coupled with cutbacks in government and foundation support has led some organizations toward increased exploration of entrepreneurial possibilities. Cultural production—in the form of knowledge, goods, performances, and sites—can become fodder for the culture industry. This industry, including entertainment and tourism, has now become one of the world's largest. The buying and selling of culture, the representation of culture in theme parks and on television, are now facts of contemporary life. Increasing attention is being given to cultural resource management, cultural heritage policies and activities, culture-sensitive development strategies, rights in intellectual and cultural property—all of which engender the economic uses of culture. Anthropologists are lagging behind others in attending to the consequences of these movements. And yet there are roles for anthropologists to play in assuring accurate representations of culture, fair and ethical treatment of culture bearers, policies that assure cultural continuity rather than destruction, and so on.

Some anthropologists in the museum world are making the shift from curating collections of objects to curating the systems, and the people, that produce them. Anthropologists have long recognized a moral responsibility to the people with whom they work. And they have long recognized that their study or curation of some small abstraction of the studied culture is dependent upon a much larger system. Rather than curate the dead or captured specimens of a culture, curators are increasingly concerned with the living larger whole. Bill Fitzhugh's work in developing an Arctic studies center in Alaska, Adrienne Kaeppler's work on Hawaiian *hula,* and Bill Laughlin's work with Mayan Indian playwrights offer strong examples of this development in the Smithsonian's own department of anthropology. In other Smithsonian units, African Art's Phil Ravenhill works to establish community-based cultural documentation projects in West Africa, and Tony Seeger encourages the continued creation and re-creation of local musics by publishing Smithsonian Folkways Recordings and paying out millions of dollars in royalties.

Where this broadening of the field of engagement has not swept through academic anthropology departments, it has resulted in alternative programs. Over the past two decades, and particularly the last one, there has been a proliferation of anthropological-like programs, and they are certain to increase. Whatever they are called—anthropology, cultural studies, folk culture, area studies, ethnic studies, comparative culture, contemporary culture—they appear to place more emphasis on involving and working with the subjects of study as colleagues, paying more attention to contexts, needs, and uses of study and understanding. They generally encourage more population-sensitive approaches and tend to be more broad-ranging in the uses of and types of representation than traditional programs. Their orientation is to more profoundly and pragmatically connect cultural work to political and economic circumstances in a global world, and to communicate much more effectively with constituent audiences and appropriate publics. This reorientation calls for an increased role as adept manipulators of symbolic constructs—culture brokers. It requires not a retreat from research and its specialization to some amorphous generalized anthropology but rather a shift toward new specializations attuned to the complex challenges of cultural life in the twenty-first century.

CHAPTER 7

DEBATING RACIALLY AND CULTURALLY SPECIFIC MUSEUMS

nthropology, as a discipline, claims to cover the broad panoply of human studies. All groups, all cultures, all people are supposed to be included. Similarly, an American history textbook seemingly would cover the historical activities, events, and accomplishments of the American people in all their diversity and variety. A comprehensive art museum, it could be argued, would include examples of all the great art produced by the world's people, past and present. Unfortunately, our museums, disciplines, fields, and texts that have claimed universality have, in fact, rarely achieved it. Too many people feel they are left out of authoritative, comprehensive accounts of historical, cultural, and artistic achievement.

In the 1980s, with increasing attention to issues of cultural diversity among staff, programs, exhibits, and audiences, the Smithsonian began to come to grips with the coverage of peoples, cultures, arts, and histories in its museums. There emerged, among key Smithsonian staff, and with the Smithsonian's congressional oversight committees, the realization that many ethnic, racial, and cultural groups were excluded from coverage by the museums. At a 1989 congressional hearing, John Kinard, then director of the Anacostia Museum, was explicit about the poor treatment of African American history and culture at the Smithsonian.[1] In 1989, legislation for a new National Museum of the American Indian was signed by President Bush. Senator Daniel Inouye, its lead supporter, urged the Smithsonian to finally treat American Indian culture with the respect it deserved. The Latino Task Force was formed in 1992 to study treatment of Hispanic peoples in the Smithsonian. The group's 1994 report, *Willful Neglect,* called for significant increases in Latino staffing, collecting, and programming.[2] The report also called for the possible creation of new museums. During the same period, the Smithsonian pursued legislation, held up by Senator Jesse Helms, to establish an African American National Museum. By 1995, with the legislation tabled, this project became the Center for African American History and Culture, to be located in the Arts and Industries Building on the Mall, adjacent to the Smithsonian Castle. And, by the end of 1995, work had begun to index Asian American collections and resources.

The building of new museums is costly. And at a time of federal deficits and retrenchments, it is unlikely that they will be largely supported by federal dollars. Indeed, the legislation for the National Museum of the American Indian called for the Smithsonian to raise one-third of the cost of the new museum on the Mall—approximately $35 million. A contemplated extension of the Air and Space Museum, destined for the Dulles Airport area of northern Virginia, is to be funded entirely from private sources.

But issues of cost aside, does it make philosophical sense to build new museums for different ethnic, racial, and cultural groups? Should the current roster of museums incorporate the stories and cultural accomplishments of people who have been left out? Or should new museums be built because of a fundamental inability to restructure existing ones to account for a broader, more realistic view of American history and culture?

The question of whether we should build new, racially and culturally specific museums was raised in a debate sponsored by the Smithsonian's Office of Museum Programs (now the Center for Museum Studies) in July 1992 for minority interns resident at the Smithsonian. Amazingly, it is the only time, to my knowledge, that the question has ever been formally debated within the Smithsonian.

Two groups were assigned to debate the issue. I and two interns—Lidia Mendoza Huante, of the Fine Arts Museum of San Francisco, California Palace Legion of Honor, and Pamela Mays McDonald, of the Seattle Art Museum—were asked to argue for the resolution that our society does not need culturally or racially specific museums. Claudine Brown, then Smithsonian deputy assistant secretary for the arts and humanities and director of the African American Museum Project, along with Yolanda Muhammad, of the Sun Cities Art Museum, and Alma Jean

Smith, with the Rhode Island Black Heritage Society, were asked to argue that our society does need such museums.

The Case against Racially and Culturally Specific Museums

We, as well as most other museum professionals, recognize the historical worth of racially and culturally specific museums and the valuable role they have played. Scores of local and regional African American museums, museums of particular Indian tribes, museums for Japanese Americans, Czech Americans, Alaskan Natives, Masons, Jewish Americans, and so on have generally addressed the history, culture, arts, and even sciences of peoples left out of so-called mainstream museums. These museums have redressed the omissions and misinterpretations represented to society by public institutions. They have provided fertile ground for new ideas and reinterpretations, generated important collection activities, enabled communities to see themselves in a significant and familiar way, and proved to be a nurturing ground for professional development often denied elsewhere.

But given the historic role and function of these museums, the question really is, Do *we* need to build more of them, presently and in the future? And since by "we" I presume we mean the public, the question becomes, Should public funds be used to build more of these kinds of museums?

Racially and cultural specific museums arose as separate institutions because their messages could not be found and their audiences could not participate in other, extant museums. These new museums were not only separate, they were unequal, often lacking public money or the support of rich donors, operating with small, often volunteer staffs, few professional positions, and virtually no access to sources of power and money. Most of these museums are still separate and unequal. Building more of them will merely encourage their separateness and inequality. By and large they are not going to reach the audiences of the mainstream museums; they are never going to have the resources. Their ideas, personnel, collections, and activities are likely to suffer and to become increasingly marginalized. This will not well serve their intended, specific audiences, nor will it contribute to a rethinking and reconceptualization of the mainstream.

Simply put, if we are to channel our energies anywhere, it should be toward changing the mainstream. Our first priority should be to use the ideas, people, and lessons drawn from culturally specific museums to re-define and restructure our public institutions. We should use what we have learned from a Black history museum, an Indian art center, and a Latino *casa de cultura* to change the way all museums deal with American history, art, and culture.

There are several reasons why now is the time to do this. First, the mainstream itself is in transformation and is reconceptualizing ideas of American identity and culture. It is an ideal time for redefinition.

Second, with demographic changes in the United States and increasing consciousness of our own long-standing diversity, our multicultural artistic, historic, scientific, and cultural heritage is now broadly recognized. The idea of monocultural American history or monoaesthetic American art is belied not only by intellectual currents but also by popular culture. Whether it is Americans eating more salsa than ketchup, or teenagers using rap in the Whitest of Midwestern elementary school playgrounds, everyone knows that our society is multiculturally complex. There is no way to unravel this complexity and separate it into its monocultural elements.

In which museum do we put the Beatles—the Anglo museum because of their birthplace, the African American museum because of the deep influence of rock 'n' roll and its Black expressive roots on their music, or the Asian Indian museum because of their use of the sitar and the influence of Hindu mysticism in their lyrics?

Third, we realize more and more that we live in a global society. Our art, culture, history, and science have always been inexorably tied to those of many, many others. Take any daily object in American life, any object that could be in a museum. Toilets come from France, cotton from Egypt, paper from China—all via circuitous routes, transformations, contributions, modifications, and adaptations by numerous culture groups along the way. It is very difficult, if not impossible, to create a monocultural museum.

The fourth reason for not creating more such museums now is that we have turned the moral corner on creating separate and unequal institutions. Civil rights legislation here, human rights accords both here and internationally, have made institutional discrimination immoral. Granted, it is still practiced and even advocated—but more so on the extreme fringes of society and to the moral repugnance of publics worldwide. That these museums came into being to redress wrongs is understandable and justifiable. To continue to create them at a time when moral pressure pushes for public institutions to become more inclusive of and responsive to the broadest range of society is irresponsible. Who would now advocate a return to segregated schools? Or separate legislatures (as was practiced under South African apartheid) for Blacks, Whites, Latinos, American Indians, and Asian Americans in the United States? Instead, it is important to reinvest in the idea of civil society that joins people of varied backgrounds into a common nation. In the case of the United States, the framework for citizens' rights and participation transcends race, creed, language, ethnicity, and gender. Enshrined in the Declaration of Independence, the Constitution, and the laws of the land, our definition of a common American citizenship, with equal protection and equal rights for all, is our greatest contribution to world civilization. It is a model for others divided by ethnic, religious, and racial conflict around the world. And it has stood the test of time. The urge to build separate museums runs against the grain of common, national participation.

The rational course of action would be to resist self-marginalization and to participate in the democratic process, to contribute to and, if necessary, attempt to change the mainstream. To create more monocultural museums is to drop out of a larger societal discourse, to flee from a healthy struggle and debate with fellow citizens. Such a course is irresponsible, especially when advocates of inclusion believe their point is both morally and empirically sound.

What is the alternative offered by monoracial or monocultural museums? They will never influence broad recastings of art, science, history, and culture because by definition they will not be comparative, disciplinary, or inclusive. How can one learn about slavery, holocausts, immigration, diasporas, ecological adaptation, ways of seeing the world without some type of comparative perspective, without a view of the interrelationships between cultures and peoples? How can we understand the history of any cultural group—say, the Irish—without reference to others—say, the English? How can African American culture be understood without placing it in some relationship to its diverse African cultural roots, the creolized cultures of the Caribbean, the Native American bases of Maroon and Black Seminole cultures, the religious, economic, and linguistic cultures of the colonial Spanish in Colombia, the French in Haiti, the Dutch in Surinam, the English in the United States?

Not only does our understanding improve from seeing the relationships between cultures, but so too do we gain from comparisons. Minimally, we benefit intellectually and as human beings from recognizing similarities and differences. The African diaspora is unique, as perhaps is the Jewish diaspora, the Cambodian diaspora, the Chinese diaspora, the Tibetan and Palestinian diasporas. We can look at all of these as independent moments in the history of a people, separate events of different peoples occasioning spiritual, artistic, musical, narrative expression. But it may also be useful to look at the processes of diasporas and ask about similarities and differences. It may allow us to see the commonalities and singularities and to understand the conditions of diaspora itself and the dialectic between diaspora and identity. That is, a museum about diasporas, a museum about immigration, a museum about adaptation, a museum about urban arts, all are likely to produce greater insight about the human condition in all its varieties than will a monocultural or monoracial museum.

Monocultural or monoracial museums will have limited disciplinary contributions—they will not, by definition, challenge general views of what constitutes "art" or how "culture" develops. They will lack money and broad audience. They also lack definition.

Just what is meant by the notion of a racially or culturally specific museum? First, consider the notion of race. There is no such thing as race as a biological or natural identity. Race was invented in the post-Columbian European colonial world to categorize, define, and assess the worth of people. It defined peoples as species, fixed, different, advanced, and primitive on the basis of a few alternatively selected gross physical characteristics. Race was born as a concept in a system of racism, and its birth predated twentieth-century genetics and molecular biology. It is still with us as an insidious "folk" concept, even though every biologist and physical anthropologist knows it has no natural basis, no "essence" or "substance."

Every human being shares some 95 percent of her genetic material with chimpanzees and 99 percent of her genetic material with every other human being. We are much more similar than we are different. But are there races? No. Though we still use racial classifications as if they were real, there is no such thing as a race. There are merely distributions of genetic traits. And, after several million years of mixing it up, no one is a pure anything. Indeed, there is as much genetic variation within purported "racial" groups as there is between them—although again, you have to somehow pre-identify the race to measure it.

If we were to have racially specific museums, what would those races possibly be? Does a museum of old-time Caucasians make any sense? What would a museum supposedly based on biological traits look like, anyway? What would an examination of genes and DNA or nose size tell us about art? Of course, we could subdivide the big races, so we'd have a museum of the Irish, the Scots-Irish, the Irish with Catholic blood and those with Protestant blood, and then the Irish American race, and the museum for the race of Scots-Irish Americans who married with Czech—not Slovak—Americans. No, there can be no racial museums; they are only the creation of confused minds that attempt to forcibly place and displace humans in a system they say is legitimated by the natural order. The racial museums in history are those marked by the middle passage, the Trail of Tears, and the seared bodies of Auschwitz.

What about culturally specific museums? They are better than racially specific ones but still problematic. Presumably culturally specific museums would deal with the common, learned experiences and expressions of a self-identified group of people through time. Usually, for museums, culture is taken as ethnic culture and a group or people as an ethnic group. So we'd have a Latino cultural museum, a Filipino cultural museum, and a Native Hawaiian cultural museum, among many others.

One problem is that there are other types of culture besides ethnic group culture. Regional culture, for example, that has Puerto Ricans, Jews, and Pakistanis talking New Yorkese in that city, or that has Old New Mexican settlers, Basques, Czechs, and African Americans cooking with chile peppers in the Southwest, or Hawaiians, Portuguese, and Haoles playing steel guitar in Honolulu. We can't ignore the existence of regional, local, and territorial culture, and so we would need specific museums for those cultures as well.

And of course we'd need religious culture-specific museums. Religious culture may also cut across ethnic cultural lines, dividing Irish into Catholics and Protestants but also unifying under syncretic forms of Catholicism Latinos and Native Americans or, in Islam, Javanese, Berbers, and Tajiks. Other types of cultural groups are based on language, occupation, and family, so we would need a great many museums. And that is without even subdividing. After all, an Italian American museum would not do. Many Italians came to America before there was an Italy. They came as Sicilians and Genoans and Milanese. Those were the culture groups, and thus we'd need a museum for each. Right now, the Smithsonian receives numerous proposals for different culturally specific museums. It could, I suppose, take the "Baskin-Robbins approach" and create a museum for every flavor and variation of human. But if we were to get a great migration of folks from Indonesia, with its more than three thousand ethnic groups, we would need considerably more separate culturally specific museums, so we had better decide how we are going to approach the issue before they come.

The simplicity of the resolution for culturally specific museums belies the complexity of culture and cultural identification. Not only is there a multitude of cultures represented in the world and in our own nation but those cultures are interrelated in tremendously complex ways. A culturally specific museum would fail, by definition, to tackle and understand those interrelationships. A culturally specific museum would also find it hard to account for the multicultural nature of each of us. Multiculturalism is not only "out there," it is inside every individual. Each of us participates in a multiplicity of cultures, and we often, through our lives, through each day, code-switch from a professional museum language to a family language to a neighborhood language to a national language to a computer language to an ethnic and sometimes religious language. We dress up and down, we eat certain ways in different circumstances. We all participate, almost without choice, in a global culture through technology, telecommunications, and the marketplace. We participate in the occupational culture of the workplace and our profession. We participate to varying degrees in American pop culture, in African American culture, in Latino culture, and so on. Often we feel pulled in several different directions and face conflicts of cultural code. And sometimes we of mixed marriages, of lapsed religion, of old and new country are not sure what to tell our children when they ask who they are.

But sometimes the movement about and between cultures is a joy, a celebration of freedom and humanity, signaling our ability to share, trade, argue, bargain, and make sense to each other. Indeed, witness the creative impulses that have led us to new and uniquely American musical styles in jazz, rock 'n' roll, and various forms of fusion. Consider the imagination that created syntheses of cuisine ranging from nouvelle Southern and Southwestern to New York's Chinese Kosher Cuban food.

We can talk about cultural specificity, but there is a lot of it and it is complexly intertwined, even within individuals. To just pretend that there is a pure, accessible, obviously defined culture of a people that if examined will lead to understanding is to oversimplify.

Even if one believes we should build racially and culturally specific museums, why would anyone do so? While such museums have played a historical role in representing those excluded from the mainstream, that need no longer be the case. We need not destroy these museums. But we must raise the question of priority. It is an opportune time to re-define the center and to bring not mere affirmative action but rather fundamental changes in understanding to the center. If we have some-thing to say about who is part of history, who creates art, who is pos-sessed of knowledge and wisdom, and what it is, then we can and should bring it to the center, to the mainstream, and to the broadest public. We can reverse the marginalization, separation, and segregation of the achievements and peoples we seek to represent. And we can do it in big, public institutions in the nation's capital, as well as in smaller, more local institutions that have heretofore promulgated marginaliza-tion and inequity of representation closer to home.

The Case for Racially and Culturally Specific Museums

The argument against building racially and culturally specific museums is strong and forceful, but also flawed and misleading. It assumes that "we" means the public, and so posing the question as one of using pub-lic funds to build racially and culturally specific museums is an attempt to bias the answer. We, as in "we the people" cannot be conflated with the use of public, i.e., governmental funds. Governments are not the same as the people they rule and sometimes represent, as well as misrepresent.

Many citizens and organizations join together in a private, social, nongovernmental way to build and maintain museums devoted to cele-brating, recognizing, commemorating, and chronicling their interests. The impulse to create and maintain a museum is very broad. Some peo-ple like automobiles, and so create an automotive museum. There are museums to Elvis and Dolly Parton, museums for farm tools and bottle caps, holographs and carousel horses.[3] In most cases, there is a commit-ment to mark and preserve forms of culture as important to someone.

Racially and culturally specific museums arise largely because the needs of the people who create and sustain them are not being met through other museums. In fact, calling these museums racially or cultur-ally specific places them in a negative category. It is not that people from such groups are trying to avoid being seen as part of a larger whole. It is rather that in the face of exclusion, they seek something positive to sus-tain them. These museums should more properly be called community-focused museums.[4] People need to see something of themselves in their museums, to feel that it is their history, art, culture, or interest that is somehow important and worth preserving.

I cannot imagine that in the framework of American civil rights— freedom of speech, religion, association, and so on—the government, the Smithsonian, or any group of professional curators would tell a group of people or an organization that they cannot or should not establish a museum that celebrates their community—whatever that community is.

But suppose for a moment that we are talking just about public funds. Should they be used for such museums? The argument against these museums implies that public expenditures are justified for museums that deal with a generalized everyone or with the nation as a whole. The implication is that public funds cannot be used for specific subsets of the population. Aside from the fact that it would be boring to build the same museum everywhere across the land (although this indeed is done in generally totalitarian nations seeking to impose a singular statist view upon their citizenry), this view misrepresents the character of public funding.

Federal, state, and local government funds are expended all the time to support subsets of the population. Local property taxes often pay for schools and the education of children—an age-specific group within our society. But this is thought to be for the public benefit. State funds often pay for highways, which directly serve those traveling those routes. But this too is thought to be for the public benefit. And federal funds are used for entitlement programs like Medicare, which directly serves the infirm—a group defined by a particular health status. Again, this too is thought to be in the public interest. Different programs for the expenditure of public funds support astronomers and cancer victims, soldiers and air travelers. There is no apparent reason for making an exception for museums, or for museums for racially or culturally specific groups. When public funds are used, it does not mean that the benefits have to be evenly distributed to every member of the public. It does, however, mean that the expenditures should be in the general public interest.

The questions then become, Do people have a right and a need to build community-focused museums? And under what circumstances is it in the public interest to do so?

The question of right is easy. Of course they do. There is no law that I can imagine that forbids people from building a museum if they want to. But should they? What needs does museum building serve?

Most public museums have a pretty poor track record in preserving the material culture of minority groups. The artwork, the artifacts, the stories, the significant objects of various peoples are often excluded from such museums. And without the material or documentary evidence, those people may disappear from view in a larger national or regional story. It is in this light that many of the community-focused museums have performed a service to their constituents, preserving the evidences of cultural and historical accomplishment and passing them on to the next generation. These museums have fulfilled their role with limited resources and virtually no public support. They have endured immense challenges, but the truth is that if they had not taken on this role, the history and culture of many peoples would be lost to all of us.

The need for such museums continues. There is no reason to suppose that the so-called mainstream museums have changed their tune and are likely to be responsive to including those who were previously excluded. Most change in the museum world has come about very slowly, if at all. Most mainstream public museums lack adequate minority staff. They do not have the collections from the racial and cultural groups that they would purport to represent. Nor are they necessarily interested in acquiring such collections. Why assume that trustees, directors, senior staff members, patrons, and sponsors want to include more racial and cultural minorities in their museums? And why trust that these museums will take on the collection, study, and exhibition of minority material culture with any urgency at all?

This is particularly true during times of limited funding—which in the museum world is a fact of life. Almost all racially and culturally specific museums—from the Latino Museum of Contemporary Art to the Daughters of the American Revolution Museum—depend upon numerous volunteers, piecemeal budgets, and local community support. They have learned to get by and have endured because they believe in what they are doing and are fulfilling the felt needs of their community—however imperfectly. Public museums at the national and state levels are often also in need of funds, but they generally turn to minority communities as a last resort or when they are under pressure. They can represent the culture of such communities, but only if there are sufficient funds—which there never are. Unless such museums make the representation of minority culture a priority, there will always be the spoken intention, maybe even a line in an annual report about the worthiness of doing so, but it will never get done.

Instead, both now and historically, community-focused museums have proved to be the vehicles for preserving and presenting the heritage of their communities. Though acquisition funds might typically be nonexistent, these museums have nonetheless attracted donors and important collections. Artifacts and artwork have been accessioned, cataloged, exhibited, interpreted, and shared within and beyond the community. Public programs, publications, and educational materials have often resulted. Academic and lay scholars have gained experience and have grown from the ranks of these museums. Curators, educators, and directors have become adept at understanding, representing, translating, and transforming cultural knowledge within and beyond the community. And such museums have provided an important locus of community involvement, a symbol of their legitimate standing in society.

Given the need for representation, and the lack of representation in the more general museums, who then is included in these supposed communities? The argument against community-focused museums would have us believe that Black people don't know who they are. That because the boundaries of Latino-ness are fuzzy, there's no such person, people, or identity. Surely there is a problem with scientific definitions of race. Certainly race is a constructed concept. But, if indeed scientists are ready to unequivocally declare that race does not exist, it seems doubtful that the world will listen. Race has a reality as a concept for thinking about people that goes beyond the scientific community. If race is declared a fiction, will racism disappear? Hardly.

Similarly, it is wrong to argue that just because it is hard to associate culture in any one-to-one type of way with particular people we can't say anything about it at all. Just because it is hard to identify academically doesn't mean that cultural identity, self-styled and imputed, ceases to exist in people's minds and in their social relationships. Given the same argument, one might assume that Catholics, Protestants, Jews, Muslims, and Buddhists could not build houses of worship because some of their members have multiple identities, intermarry, or have beliefs that put them both in and outside their canonical religion.

There is nothing wrong with people forming museums around their culture, any more than there is something wrong in people forming self-help societies, social clubs, lodges, churches, temples, and so on. Museums often reflect on the self-conscious achievement of such groups, the things they see as important within their community. Community-focused museums are a source of pride and education. And they hardly detract from larger unities—indeed, they can give people a sense of self and a security that makes inclusion in larger nations or regions less threatening. And they need not diminish people's loyalty to or understanding of the larger, more encompassing society. Rooting for one team or another does not necessarily lessen one's loyalty to the game of baseball; reading a favorite author does not destroy one's appreciation of reading. Quite the contrary.

The argument against community-focused museums is that in part they are unpatriotic, that they are divisive and threaten the broad sense of being an American. This is fallacious. Having various museums dedicated to art—one to portraiture, another to contemporary art, yet another to photography, and yet another to sculpture—does not detract from an appreciation, treatment, or understanding of, say, American art. There are textbooks on general history, and then specific case studies of particular periods, regions, personages. Does writing a biography of George Washington somehow detract from an understanding of the broader, bigger American history? Does a detailed study of the Civil War mean that it is unnecessary to study and write about other periods? Do a museum about the history of Iowa and another one about the history of New Jersey detract from a sense or appreciation of the United States? It is hard to see how.

Furthermore, community-focused museums can deal with topics, issues, and events that go beyond the bounds of the community itself. There is nothing that stops the Chinatown Historical Museum from doing a comparative exhibit on patterns of Chinese, Irish, Jewish, and Italian settlement in lower Manhattan. In fact, such comparative exhibits, seen from particular and alternating vantage points, could be quite instructive to broader audiences. Given the earlier example, the Beatles could appear in a number of museums—a museum created by ethnic Indians, a museum of Black music, a museum of Anglo-American history. Inclusion of the Beatles in a number of varied community-focused museums could enhance our appreciation of the cultural confluences and flows evidenced in the development of rock 'n' roll.

Given that there is a need and a right to have such museums, should they then receive public support? Is there public interest in building such museums? On what grounds?

The case for public support for community-focused museums can be made in a number of ways. Members of these groups are citizens and taxpayers who have funded museums that, through public institutions, have then left them out. The public museums have a responsibility to be inclusive. There is nothing inherently wrong with public support for a specialized museum, any more than there is something inherently wrong in supporting specialized courses in a public university or community college, or in including specialized books in a public library.

And having separate community-focused museums does not obviate the need for broader, more inclusive, national, regional, or local museums. Instead, such museums can provide the increased detail and nuance that come with specific, focused treatment. And the benefits of that treatment are likely to feed more finely tuned findings, stronger trained professions, more audience-connected programs into the general museums, making them, in turn, better than they otherwise might be. That is, over time, specific museums can help support more general ones.

But the most compelling case for public support is that the public has something to learn from the experience and perspective of the peoples represented in such museums. This is why the U.S. Congress supported the effort to create the U.S. Holocaust Museum and the Museum of the American Indian. The Congress felt that the American people needed to know the story of the Holocaust. A museum, largely though not entirely about this Jewish experience, has lessons for everyone. In this case, education about basic human rights is deemed a public good. The museum benefits those who visit and are exposed to it. Similarly, the relationship between Native Americans and the people and governments of the Western Hemisphere is a poignant and complex one that has had a profound effect upon the shape of society. Having American Indians tell their stories through this museum redresses a historic, recognized wrong. Justice and fairness are public goods. The public can benefit from the museum.

There are no doubt types of community-focused museums that will be built by someone but do not deserve public support. Such museums—an Aryan Nation museum or a museum of eschatological sensualists, for example, may not serve the public interest or provide any public benefits. But others need to be built and need to be publicly supported. For example, Latinos have made a strong case for a national museum to redress their exclusion from the story of America. Here for hundreds of years, settling cities and territory before the Pilgrims or the Jamestown colonists, they have a history that has been erased from public memory. Latinos form a major part of the population and have made manifold contributions to the society; they have a good case for public support. So too do African Americans, whose material culture, social, economic, and scientific contributions have for most of our nation's history been excluded from our museums, textbooks, libraries, and other cultural institutions. Museums that can help African Americans represent their art, history, culture, and knowledge to their fellow citizens provide a means of overcoming deep, painful, and historic divisions within our society.

Community-focused museums can, if done well, contribute to public knowledge and understanding about the human and national experience. They can bridge differences rather than exacerbate them and actually increase the ability of people in a society to work out their differences. Aiding this effort, by building such museums, is a most worthy public goal.

CHAPTER 8
THE FESTIVAL ON THE MALL

The National Mall in Washington, D.C., is a symbolic center of our country. Framed by monuments to Presidents Washington and Lincoln and their singular accomplishments, the Mall begins at the U.S. Capitol, where our participatory democracy is constantly renewed. Bordered by the Smithsonian's national museums, which enshrine our knowledge of history, culture, science, and the arts, the Mall is home to our national civic rites—presidential inaugurations, Independence Day festivities, and victory celebrations. The Mall is also our national town square, where Americans have gathered to speak to each other, to represent themselves and their concerns to their fellow citizens.

Since 1967 . . . the Festival of American Folklife has functioned as a combined outdoor museum and interpretive park, where people from around the country can speak directly to their fellow citizens about their history, their culture, and their lives. . . . The dialogue created at the Festival, in which cultural traditions can be respectfully presented, discussed, and even passed along, is vital to our continued civic health. Sometimes this dialogue is celebratory, sometimes sobering. But to appreciate its importance, one need only look around the globe to places where cultural conversations have stopped and where they have been replaced by intolerance, abuse of human rights, and violence.

The Department of Interior, through the National Park Service, has been a proud partner in the Festival, sharing a commitment to broad-based cultural education. Our work, and our partnership with the Smithsonian and with many others, help Americans understand their cultural heritage and, we genuinely hope, each other.

BRUCE BABBITT, SECRETARY OF THE INTERIOR[1]

One of the ways in which the Smithsonian has, in the last generation, attempted to turn museology outward, to connect with the public and its constituencies, and to include the voices of the represented has been through the Festival of American Folklife. It is a model of cultural representation and brokerage that has been imitated, analyzed, lauded, and criticized. The festival raises historical and ethical issues with regard to the representation of culture and the engagement of people in that endeavor. It is strongly negotiated among its organizers and a myriad of collaborators. It offers insights into the way culture is presented to mass audiences and stands as an alternative type of scholarly curatorial practice that is useful to consider vis-à-vis other forms. Examining the festival as a genre of museum/cultural institutional display provides a benchmark for examining case studies of large-scale public representational events.

Established in 1967, the festival was founded during S. Dillon Ripley's tenure as secretary of the Smithsonian Institution. A 1973 quote from Ripley noted that the festival was developed to "take the instruments out of their glass cases and let them sing."[2] That is, the festival helped enliven the Smithsonian's museum function. By 1986, Ripley offered a reprise—the festival was founded to "take the things out of their glass cages and connect them to real life."[3] This sentiment was echoed by current secretary Mike Heyman, who noted in *Smithsonian* magazine, "It is through the Festival that the Smithsonian shows that history does not stop, that the life of people cannot be reduced to an object in a case or a sign on a wall. It is through the Festival that people speak for themselves, about their lives and accomplishments, and about how they have turned everyday experience into beauty."[4]

Beloved by visitors and the general public, well received by the press and politicians, heartily endorsed by participants, the festival nonetheless has its problems. It is an unfamiliar genre. In combining and crossing various categories such as education and entertainment, scholarship and service, the authentic and the constructed, celebration and contemplation, it may be misconstrued. While more than a thousand cultural scholars have participated in its research and presentation, some find the festival a throwback to earlier, discredited forms of cultural display and voyeurism. And while the festival receives kudos for placing people's culture on the National Mall, others resent its placement, its supposed denigration of traditional museum functions, and its alleged effect on the landscape, trees, and greensward.

Festival Description

The Festival of American Folklife is an annual display of living cultural heritage. It is produced by the Smithsonian Institution every summer for two weeks around the Fourth of July, on the National Mall of the United States in Washington, D.C., in cooperation with the National Park Service. The festival is organized to increase and diffuse knowledge about grassroots cultural heritage. It is an extension of the Smithsonian outdoors, onto the Mall, with the same mission but a somewhat different approach than the museums take.

Since its inception, the festival has featured more than 16,000 musicians, artists, performers, craftspeople, workers, cooks, storytellers, ritual specialists, and other exemplars from numerous ethnic, tribal, regional, and occupational cultures. The festival typically includes daily programs of music, song, dance, celebratory performance, crafts demonstrations, cooking demonstrations, storytelling, illustrations of workers' culture, and narrative sessions for discussing cultural issues. Free to the public, the festival annually attracts about one million visitors.[5] As the largest annual cultural event in the U.S. capital, it receives considerable media attention (about four hundred stories yearly). The festival has often energized the efforts of featured tradition bearers and organizations to continue their own research, education, cultural conservation, and advocacy work. It is fairly well documented and has stimulated the production of other publications and educational products, as well as more static museum and traveling exhibitions.

The festival was initiated by James Morris, director of the Division of Performing Arts, and developed by Ralph Rinzler with support from Secretary S. Dillon Ripley. It was part of a larger effort by Ripley to make the National Mall more accessible to the American public and to make the Smithsonian's programs more exciting and engaging. He believed that citizens should feel a sense of ownership and identification with the national patrimony, represented by the national treasures kept at the Smithsonian but also evident in the buildings, monuments, and sites in the capital that help define American civic culture. He wanted visitors to come to the museums, not be turned away from them. He wanted people to feel welcome on the Mall and to view it as America's front lawn. Ripley also believed that museums had to do more to engage the public, that their artifacts had to be related to the stories and people who made and used them. The festival was a good way to accomplish this.

Ralph Rinzler (right), first director of the Folklife Festival, was known for his flexible role, from fieldworker to performer. Here he plays with (left to right) Charlie and Birch Monroe and Mike Seeger at the 1969 Festival of American Folklife. Photo courtesy Smithsonian Center for Folklife Programs and Cultural Studies.

In its first year, the festival was an instant hit, drawing some 400,000 visitors and the praise of the rather jaded Washington press. Congressional support followed, as many saw their constituents and traditions from back home represented on the Mall, given a national spotlight, and enabled to share their knowledge and traditions with their fellow citizens. The festival's popularity encouraged the development of many programs at the local, state, regional, and national levels. A major part of the U.S. bicentennial celebration, the 1976 festival lasted for three months and involved thousands of participants.

Typically, the festival includes international, regional/state, occupational, and thematic "programs." To date, it has featured exemplary tradition bearers from fifty-three nations, every state and region of the United States, scores of ethnic groups, more than one hundred American Indian groups, and some sixty occupational groups. In any one year there may be three or four major programs—in 1997, "The Mississippi Delta," "African Immigrants to the United States," and "Sacred Sounds"; in 1996, programs included "The American South," "Iowa," and "Working at the Smithsonian." Each program is akin to an exhibition in one of the museums, having its own space (about two football fields for large programs), signage, stages, performances, and boundaries. A good-sized program consists of about a hundred musicians, craftspeople, cooks, storytellers, and about ten lay and academic presenters who help provide background information, introductions, translations, and answers to questions.

International programs have sometimes featured a particular nation (e.g., India, Japan, Indonesia, Mexico, France, Czech Republic, Senegal, Bahamas, Thailand) but also regions (e.g., the Caribbean, the Andes), as well as transnational populations, (Cape Verdeans, Maroons). Indeed, most "country" programs have joined people from the root nation with immigrant populations in the United States. Other programs have featured states and territories of the United States (New Jersey, Alaska, Louisiana, Tennessee, Michigan, Massachusetts, Hawai'i, U.S. Virgin Islands, New Mexico, Iowa) but also regions of the country (the American South, United States–Mexico Borderlands) and a combination of themes and regions ("Family Farming in the Heartland"). The festival has also looked at various forms of ethnic culture, from that of American Indian tribal groups to Lao Americans, from Italian Americans to Russian Americans. Occupational programs have exhibited the worklore of cowboys, taxi drivers, meat cutters, bricklayers, Senators (as in baseball players) and senators (as in members of Congress), doctors, trial lawyers, domestic workers in the White House, and scientists at the Smithsonian. Various thematic programs have cut across cultural groups topically and have included, for example, "Musics of Struggle," "Cultural Conservation," "Culture and Development," "Heartbeat: Music of First Nation's Women."

The strongest feature of the festival is its attempt to foreground the voices of tradition bearers as they demonstrate, discuss, and present their cultures. At the festival tradition bearers, local scholars, and Smithsonian curators speak for themselves, with each other, and to the public. Visitors are encouraged to participate—to learn to sing, dance, eat the foods, and just plain speak to the folks represented in the festival program. While celebrating the diversity of the nation and the world, the festival also celebrates our ability to talk with and join with each other, to appreciate and bridge human differences. The festival has been called

Maroon leaders from Jamaica, Surinam, French Guiana, Colombia, and Texas met each other for the first time at the 1992 festival, joined here by the Reverend Jesse Jackson. The meeting provided an occasion to discuss the cultural history and continuity of these communities, and their common concerns.
Photo by Jeff Tinsley, courtesy Smithsonian Institution.

"a national treasure," and Henry Allen likened festival participation to "attending a service at the First Church of the Great American idea."[6]

Like other Smithsonian exhibits, the festival includes museum-quality signs, photo-text panels, published program book/catalog, learning centers, museum shops, and food concessions. It also attempts to create a physical context for the traditions represented. In the past, it has included, among other things, a race course from Kentucky, an oil rig from Oklahoma, a glacier from Alaska, a New Jersey boardwalk, a Louisiana Mardi Gras parade, a New Mexican adobe plaza, a Japanese rice paddy, a Kalimantan longhouse, a Senegalese home compound, and an Indian festival village. Animals, from cow-cutting horses to llamas, from steers to sheared sheep, have been part of festival presentations. A buffalo calf was born on the Mall one early festival morning and an escaped steer roped to the ground in the Kennedy Center parking lot after a chase down Independence Avenue.

The festival is a research-based, curated production drawing on the efforts of Smithsonian staff, academic and lay scholars from the featured

Logger Gary Winnop of Sitka, Alaska, checks rigging at
the 1984 festival. Occupational presentations have put
barns, threshers, railroad tracks and cars, and computers
on the Mall to help workers demonstrate and explain
what they do for a living. Photo by Jeff Plosonka, courtesy Smithsonian Institution.

states or regions, and plain folks who know a great deal about their communities. Research for the festival and documentation of its presentations has resulted in complex local-level collaborations, training, and an
archival collection held at the Smithsonian and disbursed back to various local institutions. These resources have been used for publications
by fellows, visiting scholars, for the Smithsonian's own Folklife Studies

In 1982 the occupational folklife of horsemen was featured as part of the Oklahoma state program. Here cowgirl Sheri Lynn Close demonstrates steer cutting. Photo by Dane Penland, courtesy Smithsonian Institution.

In 1986 a Japanese rice paddy was re-created on the Mall to provide a context for a rice-planting ritual, performed by the Hanadaue group from Mibu village in Hiroshima Prefecture, Japan. Photo by Jeff Tinsley, courtesy Smithsonian Institution.

series, for Smithsonian Folkways Recordings and for various other educational products that have won Academy, Emmy, and Grammy awards and nominations.

The festival has had a strong impact on policies, scholarship, and folks "back home." Many U.S. states and several nations have remounted festival programs and have used the festival to generate laws, institutions, educational programs, documentary films, television programs, recordings, museum and traveling exhibits, monographs, and cultural activities. In many cases, the festival has energized local and regional tradition bearers and their communities, and thus helped conserve and create cultural resources.

The festival generates a great deal of publicity and has positively affected cultural tourism in many places. In 1994 it was named the "Best Event in the United States" by the American Bus Association as a result of a survey of regional tourist bureaus. It has also been the subject of numerous books, documentary films, and scholarly articles, as well as two recent murder mysteries.[7]

The National Mall

The need and desire for the public American celebration of self goes back to the beginning of the nation. The Fourth of July celebration under President Thomas Jefferson included a festival of sorts, held outdoors—not on the then nearby and swampy Mall but on the grounds of President's Park, adjacent to the White House. Writes White House historian William Seale:

> The Fourth of July was a time to be outside. The President's Park—called the "common"—came alive at daybreak, with the raising of tents and booths soon followed by crowds of people. A regular fair was held, selling food and drink, as well as baskets, rugs, and other cottage products. There were horse races and tests of skill among the men. Cockfights and dogfights took place on the sidelines. In the bare "parade" [ground] kept clear in the middle, the Washington Militia and other military companies drilled between ten o'clock and noon.[8]

Music, too, played, and guests were invited into the White House by the president to celebrate their independence.

Celebrations and performances, particularly musical ones, were held outdoors on the White House grounds through most of the nineteenth century. A bandstand near the south portico served many presidents and public visitors, even during the Civil War. It was not until the 1880s that the bandstand and performances were moved to the Mall and the Smithsonian.

In Jefferson's time the Mall was not an attractive public place. Ending at the Washington Monument grounds and the Potomac River just beyond it, laden with water from the Tiber Creek and Canal, the Mall was said to give off unhealthy vapors. Though designated as a public walk in Pierre Charles L'Enfant's 1791 plan for the Capital City, it failed to take shape as the grand boulevard lined with public buildings and ambassadorial residences that he had envisioned. Though termed the "Mall" on maps by 1804, it remained underused for some sixty years. Crops were grown on it and some private fairs held near Center Market on its northern boundaries in the early 1800s. With the founding of the Smithsonian in 1846, John Quincy Adams and others paced off what was to be known as Smithsonian Park, which then included much of the Mall. The construction of the Smithsonian Castle provided the impetus for improving and landscaping the Mall, resulting in Andrew Jackson

Downing's plan for the Smithsonian Pleasure Grounds or Gardens. Downing's plan, submitted to and approved by the Smithsonian regents, called for a natural style of landscaped garden, a "national park" that would be a public museum of living trees and shrubs in six varied scenarios, replete with labels, so as to educate and edify the public, and that would provide a symbolic, enlightening balance between commercial city life and agrarian country life.[9] Downing's full plan was never achieved, but it did entail the first landscaping on the Mall, the planting of a wide variety of trees and shrubs and the creation of curved paths and carriage drives that persisted well into the 1920s.

As Cynthia Field notes, "By the late nineteenth century, the heart of Washington had neither the clarity of L'Enfant's conception nor the character of Downing's."[10] Railroad tracks crossed the Mall, with a terminus at its eastern end near the Capitol, and the unsightly canal isolated the Mall from the rest of Washington. Various structures abounded. Buffalo and other animals of the National Zoo grazed on it.

This changed in 1901–2, when the Senate Park Commission Plan, informally called the McMillan Plan after its chairman, built upon L'Enfant's vision and developed the current version of the Mall familiar to us today. Central to this plan was the emergence of broad vistas, a straightness, regularity, and uniformity that would impose beauty on a city grown ugly. The principal architects and planners behind the idea were involved in developing the 1893 Columbian Exposition in Chicago, which defined a new period in American architecture and attracted some twenty-one million visitors, who were entertained and informed by exhibits of arts and industries, living ethnological villages, the dancing of Little Egypt, and a Ferris wheel. The exposition provided an idyllic, full environment—a flowering of "City Beautiful" themes, including Beaux Arts architecture, white buildings, great walkways and vistas. As Thomas Hines points out, the strongest feature of the McMillan Commission effort was to develop a park on a grand scale by viewing it as the key feature defining a larger urban environment.[11] The commission developed a uniform building line and architectural program for new public buildings to be constructed along the Mall and foresaw the tearing down of the Smithsonian Castle and the Library of Congress buildings, since they did not fit. The McMillan Plan called for the elimination of hundreds of "intrusive trees" and shrubs and for the plantings of elms in neat rows alongside a central grassy greensward. The plan also called for fountains, kiosks, pavilions, new gardens, a major park at the Washington Monument grounds, and the development of the Lincoln Memorial on recovered Potomac swampland. Most of these recommendations met with strong objections.

Although the recommendations were slow to gain acceptance and many were not implemented, by the 1930s the Mall did emerge in a form similar to that envisioned by the McMillan Plan and recognizable today. The railroad tracks and other buildings—though not the Smithsonian Castle and the Library of Congress—were removed. The Mall's streetscape for new buildings, such as the Freer Gallery of Art, was established by 1913. The Lincoln Memorial took shape in the early 1920s, and three rows of elm trees, rather than the recommended four, were planted in the 1930s. As the Mall developed, so too did its administration. Before the commission, the Mall was divided into several parks and grounds— the Monument Grounds, the Agricultural Grounds, the Smithsonian Grounds, Henry Park, Seaton Park, and the Botanical Gardens, each with its own administration and character. With the establishment of the Commission of Fine Arts in 1910 and the National Capital Park and Planning Commission in 1926, mechanisms for greater overall planning and unity of the Mall were put in place. Further refinements under the National Park Service grew from a Skidmore, Owings, and Merrill plan developed in 1965. The east-west streets running through the Mall were replaced by pedestrian pathways. Denser tree plantings and the development of grand fountains, pavilions, and the Washington Monument park were also recommended but not implemented. In the 1970s, the Metro system station and tunnel were put in underground. New museums and sculpture gardens were planned, designed, redesigned, and developed. Modifications to the Mall continue today, with the building of the new National Museum of the American Indian scheduled for the turn of the century and the installation of walkways to meet the requirements of the Americans with Disabilities Act.

The physical development of the Mall as a national park has always followed from its symbolic relationship to the organization of government, the nation, and the people. The Mall has been viewed as a physical icon of the tie between Congress and the White House, as a symbol of rural-urban utopian union, as a setting for public life. J. Carter Brown, longtime member and chair of the Commission of Fine Arts, noted that "the Mall is a people space."[12]

In ways beyond what planners, architects, and landscapers generally have had in mind, the most dramatic public uses of the Mall have grown out of large-scale mobilizations of people asserting their right and their role in that space. Though this use has some historical precedents in the 1892 Grand Army encampment, the 1932 "bonus army" mobilization, and the 1939 Marian Anderson concert at the Lincoln Memorial, the seminal event was the 1963 March on Washington. This event, immortalized in the public imagery surrounding the Reverend Martin Luther King, Jr.'s "I have a dream" speech for huge crowds, provided a model for staging public marches and demonstrations on the Mall and thus in the nation. Since then, citizens regularly have gathered on the Mall to march for or against one or another cause. Most assert the participation in a single, American civic culture and call for broadening the bounds of inclusion in that culture. Indeed, the unifying notion of the idyllic Mall as mirroring the ideal unity of the people is regularly celebrated through presidential inaugurations and victory celebrations, as well as annual Independence Day concerts and fireworks.

In the 1960s, when he became secretary of the Smithsonian, S. Dillon Ripley called the Mall "Forest Lawn on the Potomac," a rather dreary vision of the nation's center.[13] With the growth of new Smithsonian museums, Ripley installed a carousel on the Mall, initiated the Festival of American Folklife and the Kite Festival, and held a public convocation honoring James Smithson. The Smithsonian, and its "front lawn," the Mall, became a lively, people-filled place, in contrast to other, somber national town squares—Red Square, for example. From family picnics to softball, from inaugurals to flyovers, marches to festivals, the Mall was the "people's place," to be used, enjoyed, and owned by them, much as the national patrimony in the museums and the nation as a political entity.[14]

Living Culture on the Front Lawn

For the Smithsonian, the festival constituted the people's museum, wherein the celebrated national treasures were the people themselves and their traditional wisdom, knowledge, skill, and artistry. In terms of subject matter, the festival was seen as a corrective of sorts, a way of telling the story of the diverse peoples that populated the nation but whose cultural achievements were not represented in the museums or their collections. As method, the festival pioneered the research-based use of living performances and demonstrations. This was consistent with a larger trend in the museum world at the time—the use of "living history" as a presentational or interpretive technique. Having people perform, demonstrate, and expound upon aspects of a tradition provided a lively way to inform an audience. However, whereas living history performances were acted or reenacted by present-day persons, the festival emphasized authenticity—the presence and unscripted participation of the living people who were active and exemplary practitioners of the represented communities and traditions. The festival was powerful because the people were real participants in the represented cultures—not actors. And the festival in turn bestowed additional legitimacy upon the participants by the authority vested in the Smithsonian. The festival occurred in semiotic proximity to the museums (and thus enshrined national treasures) and was located in symbolically potent space—the National Mall—at a symbolically loaded time—the Fourth of July.

This orientation fit very well with National Park Service attempts to present and interpret American cultural history in parks around the nation. In 1973, the National Park Service, with direct responsibility for the Mall, began to work actively with the Smithsonian in support of the festival. A succession of National Park Service directors and secretaries of the interior have reiterated that support in the decades since then.

In 1973 Secretary Rogers Morton noted how the American people had a cherished heritage—"a unique pattern of living woven out of their daily toil." The National Park Service, representing the repository of our natural, historical, and cultural resources, had a role to play in showing Americans that heritage—"living history," he called it.

Indeed, both the National Park Service and the Smithsonian Institution saw themselves, and I think continue to see themselves, as repositories of resources, with a duty to present those resources, for the purposes of public education.

Not only can such living interpretive programs as the festival and those found at many parks be educational and instructive in a technical sense, they can also provide models of civic participation in a democratic society. In the mid-1970s then NPS director Gary Everhardt noted that the festival not only presented a "collage of cultures" but did so in a way that made it a "great national family reunion, that epitomizes the Bicentennial."[15]

Secretary Manuel Lujan, Jr., reiterated the importance of this contribution in 1992:

> Here on the Nation's front lawn, millions of Americans can participate in cultural traditions that reach back centuries and yet still provide meaning

to contemporary communities and individuals. At the Festival you can
meet with, speak to, and be engaged by fellow Americans who forge the
links between our cultural history and our cultural future.[16]

Culture versus Nature?

Producing the festival and meeting its curatorial and logistical needs is
no easy task in itself. It is especially challenging given the need to preserve the Mall's physical resources. Various experiments over the years
with different varieties of grass have yielded turf more resistant to the
millions of human footsteps that pass over the Mall not just during the
festival but during the whole year. Indeed, in 1974, Director Everhardt
pointed to the role of the festival in fostering experimentation, "testing
ways of making mass use compatible with environmental preservation."[17]

Because of the National Mall's special significance, it is difficult to
restrict various uses of it—nor is it necessarily desirable. A 1990 report by
University of Syracuse professor P. J. Craul recommended that all forms
of planned activity be restricted in order to protect and preserve the
Mall as a greensward.[18] Clearly, some forms of regulation are necessary
and are defined by the Code of Federal Regulations and National Park
Service guidelines. But First Amendment activities, national celebration
events such as the festival, inaugurals, and possibly other events are logically and intimately connected with the meaning and history of the
Mall and its public use.

Still the Mall faces resource preservation difficulties. Drainage problems still exist. Traffic moving around downtown Washington may have
a negative effect on the health of the trees. Dutch elm and other diseases
have resulted in tree loss. Compaction of the soil and its possible effects
upon the elm trees remain concerns for both the National Park Service
and the Smithsonian.

An independent empirical scientific study conducted in 1991 by the
U.S. Agricultural Research Service, National Soil Dynamics Laboratory at
Auburn University concluded:

> The elms on the Mall are currently in a state of good health. Given the
> healthy state of the elms and the fact that any damage to the ground cover
> vegetative resource can be repaired, it appears that the NPS has the capabil-
> ity to maintain the Mall in a state of good health and high aesthetic quality
> despite heavy casual and special event traffic that impacts this area. The
> question of whether or not to restrict casual and/or special event uses of

the Mall therefore seems to be not one of biology, but one of management philosophy and economics.[19]

Still, the study recommended that the health of the trees be tracked over time and that various steps could be taken to minimize impact and possible deleterious effects. Over the last few years, the festival has severely limited vehicle use on the treed panels of the Mall, reduced in-ground trenching for cabling by 90 percent, moved more of its high-impact activities out from under the trees to the Mall's non-treed panels, used non-treed plots for storage and staging areas, used more prefabricated structures requiring no ground penetration, rotated panel use, reduced set-up and take-down time, and located trailers and other structures on non-treed walkways. Long-term and regular maintenance is also required and might include stress-avoidance measures, management of watering, fertilizing, and pruning schedules, nondestructive soil aeration, and the possible insertion of mesh elements such as those used in sports fields. Many of these measures apply to other intensely used parks as well. Monitoring of the resources, particularly the elm trees, is also important. A follow-up study in 1993 indicated that the elms were growing vigorously and in a state of good health.[20]

There are other challenges as well. The Mall is currently besieged by vendors selling T-shirts. Setting up shop along the Mall, on the pathways to the national museums, and along the walkways to the monuments, these vendors detract from the serious purposes of these institutions and the aesthetic quality of the park. The right to sell T-shirts and other items is currently the subject of regulatory changes and legal dispute. This, too, has affected the festival, which has long sold publications, documentary recordings, authentic crafts, and other items for the purpose of helping to inform and educate its visitors about the people, cultures, and traditions represented—much like a museum shop or a park visitors center. The legal challenges of distinguishing educational from commercial uses and accounting for quality, consistency, and standards in what is sold, and how, are considerable.

Indeed, the need to meet National Park Service requirements for Mall use affects the way in which culture is represented. For example, in order to reduce stress on the elms, National Capital Region NPS staff have insisted that the festival move the larger-scale events to the middle panels of the Mall, which do not have trees. To festival curators, this is like moving a part of an exhibition out of the main hall, or separating sections of an exhibit from each other because of some arbitrary, non-meaningful characteristic. Hence, performance events may be separated from lower-density crafts demonstrations at the festival, even though they may be closely tied culturally and more understandable in contiguity. Removing food service from food demonstration areas—eating versus looking—makes for sensory disjunctures in the festival. Removing commerce from culture by locating the festival shop off the Mall, on the lawn of the National Museum of American History instead of in proximity to the represented cultures, reduces understanding.

In Search of a Genre

If the Festival of American Folklife is not quite a living history park, neither is it quite a festival. The festival is misnamed, but I don't have a much better word for it. The Festival of American Folklife is not a festival of the same type as a peasant community's celebration of its harvest. Nor does it seem to be a festival of the sort that cities sponsor, a list of events dispersed in space and time called an arts festival. Nor does it seem quite like a folk festival—a concert of pop and revival folk music. Nor does it seem like the international festivals organized by many schools to show off foods, music, games, and costumes only somewhat related to their students' lives.

The Festival of American Folklife has been likened to many things. Existing as part of the Smithsonian's museum complex, the festival has been called a "living museum without walls" and a "living cultural exhibit." Former Smithsonian official Dean Anderson said, "Whereas 'museum' is a noun, the Festival is a verb."[21] This highlights the festival's dynamism and contrasts it with museums, which in the worst case are lifeless, sterile, and silent. The term "museum" originally meant the "place of the muse." A museum without musings, music, and amusement—words of the same derivation—would seem to run counter to the original purpose. The festival can provoke thought, does have music, is amusing at times, has museumlike signs and displays, and so on—but is it a museum? Too temporary, say some. Too outdoors, say others. Too frivolous, says a museum curator. Perhaps if only just the objects appeared and not the people who made, use, and understand them, then it would be serious. "Too messy, but in a good way," says another official in charge of museums.

But if not quite a museum, is the festival more like a zoo, as another colleague once proposed? To be sure, as at a zoo, some living beings come to see other living beings. Zoo organizers provide some information in the form of signs and labels and try to present creatures with a bit of their natural, home setting. By seeing the creatures, visitors learn about them, appreciate their existence, and sometimes even learn about the larger issues that they evoke. Zoo staff provide this context, they say, to help preserve the animals and their habitat as part of our diverse biological heritage. Similarly, festival organizers present people to visitors to display their culture. Signs, labels, banners, reconstructions of bits of home settings, and photographs help visitors understand and interpret what they see, hear, and sense. And hopefully, visitors gain an appreciation of displayed traditions, national and worldwide cultural diversity. But there are big differences between the zoo and the festival. Visitors are just as likely to see themselves on display as "others." And at the festival, people *talk back* and play the major role in shaping their own self-representation.

There are other metaphors for the festival. Festival director Diana Parker calls it a "cultural DMZ [demilitarized zone]." Some people have likened it to a cultural theme park, others to a street fair and block party. To some it is a series of performances and demonstrations; to others, it is an annual lunch break with free entertainment. For famed Cajun fiddler Dewey Balfa it was an illustrated book of cultural practice; for the tour-minded, a quick and easy trip around the world. For Jimmy Driftwood it was an entertaining and substantive graduate course in American culture. For the conspiratorial, it is a form of national theater, in which the state exerts its understandings upon the masses; for the counter-conspiratorial it is a demonstration against the cultural hegemony of the state, a reassertion of the people's ability to make their culture and define themselves. For yet others it is merely a good time.

The Festival of American Folklife is a complex form of institutional public cultural display that accomplishes a number of different purposes and occupies a variety of conceptual spaces. It can be viewed in a number of different ways and its successes and failures tallied accordingly. James Morris, who first had the idea, based it on the American Folk Festival that he had organized in Asheville, North Carolina, in the mid-1960s. Morris's festival was scripted and staged and more like a folk review or a play-pageant.[22] Ralph Rinzler had worked at the Newport Folk Festival, doing field research and developing presentations. His vision was more ethnographically folkloristic than theatrically oriented. The festival got off the ground in 1967 under Morris, with Rinzler hired to develop program and also to plan, with Henry Glassie, a major conference on folklife and its goals at the Smithsonian. This effort was joined by a score of inventive thinkers from a range of fields.

The Festival of American Folklife shared some affinity with folk festivals of the time. In the 1950s Rinzler, with Mike Seeger and Roger Abrahams, had participated in the folk festival circuit. Rinzler was among a group of young musicians gathered around Woody Guthrie in New York and part of the urban folk revival that moved between leftist, union politics, the collections of traditional folk songs, and singer-songwriter entertainment. Rinzler joined the Greenbrier Boys, an urban bluegrass group, helped manage Doc Watson and Bill Monroe and booked them into such venues as the University of Chicago Folk Festival. Rinzler also produced albums for Moses Asch's Folkways Records and was strongly influenced by Alan Lomax, Pete Seeger, Charles Seeger, and Bert Lloyd, who combined politics and scholarship with their aesthetic interest in various folk musics. In the 1960s, Rinzler traveled through the United States, "discovering" and documenting the diversity of community-based roots music for the Newport Folk Festival. And in developing programs at Newport, Rinzler and Lomax drew on the work of other scholars and producers, particularly those working in Pennsylvania. This group—Abrahams, Henry Glassie, Kenny Goldstein, and Don Yoder—eventually formed the core of the folklore and folklife department at the University of Pennsylvania. Don Yoder's work with the Pennsylvania Folklife Festival in particular provided some early models of cultural presentation for the Smithsonian.[23]

Earlier antecedents for cultural presentation existed along the lines of the aforementioned 1893 Columbian Exposition on Chicago's Midway Plaisance. But the 1960s presented a different world. Newport and other folk festivals of the time were not attempts to "display others"— and certainly not in a racial and cultural evolutionary framework. If anything, they were construed more in terms of advocacy—of peoples, causes, and aesthetics. The joining of the folk revival movement with the Civil Rights Movement in such people as Bernice Reagon, Harry Belafonte, Zipporah Horton, Guy Carawan, and in such places as the Highlander Center was mirrored by and crucial to the transformation of the National Mall in the 1960s.[24]

The Smithsonian's Festival of American Folklife followed in the wake of the Reverend Martin Luther King, Jr.'s use of the National Mall as a pulpit to assert civic participation. For Secretary Ripley, the festival was a means of livening up the Smithsonian, of broadening and enlarging its visitorship. Musical performances from band shells and gazebos and "living history" demonstrations would have sufficed for Ripley's purpose.[25] For Morris, the festival could be a device for both signaling and developing the artistic endowment of the American people. Desires to build upon "tradition" through artistic elaboration were expressed in a recommendation after the first festival to establish an American national folk troupe.[26] For Rinzler, the festival could be a massive demonstration of the desire of grassroots people for aesthetic justice. In relation to the museums, the festival would give voice to the people and announce to the public, the media, and Congress that there was "culture" back home and that that culture was worthy of national pride, attention, and respect.[27]

The festival has always navigated between the various axes of art (as entertainment), cultural rights (as advocacy), education (as public service), and knowledge (as scholarship and experience). It has from the beginning sought to broaden knowledge and appreciation of and increase support for art forms and practitioners overlooked in a society whose sense of beauty and value is generally driven by the exercise of power and the commodification of the marketplace. At times during its history, and even within the same year among its programs, presentations and framing have gravitated toward one or another axis. But by and large, the festival's form, contexts, purposes, and place have remained the same.

The Festival as a Festival

In general, festivals provide a time out of time. They separate off the heightened and the accentuated from the mundane, the usual, daily routine. Festivals are liminal moments, temporary pauses or transitions in the flow of events and activities, in which new relationships can be made, old ones reinforced or inverted. Festivals may indeed reinvest the social order with legitimacy—connecting that order to higher powers, cosmic purposes, and sacred history. But festivals may also provide a release valve, so to speak, giving members of society a chance to revolt against the usual order, counter the structure of relationships with either inverted ones or none at all. Festivals typically conjoin and separate people, magnify and compress space and time.

In the Washingtonian scheme of things, the Festival of American

New types of cultural creations and negotiations arise from the juxtapositions at the Smithsonian's Festival. Marie McDonald (left of center), one of Hawai'i's foremost traditional lei makers, had never made one for royalty, since the last Hawaiian king died in 1903. Participating in the 1989 festival, she decided to make such a lei to honor the Ga king of Ghana, who was visiting. When she completed the royal lei, negotiations via walkie-talkie enabled Marie and the Ga king to decide how the lei would be presented. After consultation with his advisers, the king decided to follow Hawaiian custom, receiving the lei over his head with a kiss from Marie. This was followed by a handshake. Photo by Jeff Tinsley, courtesy Smithsonian Institution.

Folklife does operate like a festival. It creates its own space on the Mall, a sometimes jarring presence in the midst of official, neat space. It creates a face-to-face type of community in the shadows of inanimate official buildings and the institutions of state. The festival is messy, it leaks at porous boundaries of participation, time, and event. It does compress time and space, creating an experience and event that are intense but short-lived, in which representations are magnified, pushed together, and then, just as quickly, dispersed. And it brings people together—tradition bearers, the public, scholars, officials, administrators, builders, designers, volunteers, and so on, who would not normally interact. As Margaret Mead wrote, the Festival of American Folklife is "a people-to-people celebration in which all of us are participants—now as organizers, now as celebrators, now as audience, as hosts and as guests, as friends and neighbors or as strangers finding that we can speak the same language of mutual enjoyment."[28]

There is something reassuring in the fact that official Washington can make room for the humanity that it seeks to represent. Washington likes a good show, and though the town feeds on politics and breeds bureaucracy, what it really loves is drama. The Smithsonian's festival provides some of this drama through cultural juxtapositions—a horse-race course from the Capitol to the Washington Monument, a Tennessee moonshine still in sight of the Justice Department, a Hawaiian lei draped over the statue of "the *hoale* guy" (Joseph Henry, the Smithsonian's first secretary), a New Mexican adobe plaza on the national green, a buffalo birth on the Mall, a Junkanoo rush, carnival and Mardi Gras parades blaring at cool stone buildings.

Most festive of all is what happens amongst the people who gather to talk, listen, sing, dance, craft, cook, eat, and watch. Unlike the rules and regulations and authoritative voices that come from the buildings, festival voices are more intimate, more human and inspirited. The lack of direct personal contact so expected in official Washington is contrasted with the folksiness, perceived or real, at the festival. We can hear from and talk with people whom we might not ordinarily meet. Indeed, the social space of the Mall and the festival are endowed with a certain power, what Anacostia Museum director Steve Newsome calls "sanctified." This power, coupled with the sense that the Mall is everyone's and no one's at the same time, enables people to cross boundaries they usually wouldn't cross. And when people speak on the Mall at the festival, they often feel they are doing so with a power they do not ordinarily possess. I think people listen in somewhat the same way.

This makes it hard, if not impossible, for anyone to impose a single, overriding, monological voice upon the festival. And if control over the festival comes from us, the organizers, when it works it is overtaken by the contingents of participants and the contingencies of their participation. We know this, which is why we have to fight both within and outside our own bureaucracies so hard, lest the desire for control be so burdensome as to squeeze out the spirit of the people.

To some extent, and for its limited time every year, the festival subverts the normal order of cultural power along the Mall and is thus also a Smithsonian festival of sorts. A Smithsonian "infomercial" in *Business Week* referred to the festival as the time when "the normally stately institution lets its hair down."[29] A murder mystery by Richard Conroy begins: "This is a tale of an imaginary time [the 1976 festival] when the folklorists tried to take over the Smithsonian Institution, and how they almost succeeded. And how the traditionalists of the museum were driven to the foul crime of murder to prevent this great catastrophe."[30] Museums in their most formal ways can project a sense of the *inside* (spatially and culturally), the serious (almost dour), propertied (laden with valuable objects), and rule-bound (no talking, no touching, restricted access). The festival, by contrast, not only occurs outside physically but also represents the *outside,* associated with the common people, the playful, and the open-ended.[31] Given the great popularity of the festival, the attendance by dignitaries, attention from the press, and the use of the Mall, the normal power relationship shifts—the outsiders are in—if only for the duration of the festival.

The Festival as Cultural Representation

Political and poetic dimensions are linked in cultural displays like the festival. While the festival may, in some literal way, recall nineteenth-century forms of cultural exhibitionism and voyeurism, it has benefited from decades of cultural research and discussions about representation and has become quite different from that.[32] Shifts in authoritative voice, collaboration in self-representation, and treatment of contemporary contexts, as well as the forms of discourse, have changed significantly, thanks in large part to the efforts of people like Ralph Rinzler, Bess Lomax Hawes, Bernice Reagon, Rayna Green, and a generation of cultural workers who have labored at the intersection of scholarship, cultural community advocacy, and public education. Large-scale cultural displays are situated in a public world in which various parties have a stake. Politicians, advocacy groups, rebels, and scholars may use these forms to forward their own agendas, and they have become very sophisticated in doing so, as is apparent in case studies of festival programs.

As a representational genre, living cultural exhibitions like the festival share features with zoo, local fair, town meeting, object-based museum exhibit, ethnographic monograph, talk show, and documentary film. The festival is a low-resolution medium, as Bob Byington, the former deputy director, always said. It differs from a book, film, exhibit, and concert in that it lacks linearity. While it has some highlighted special events, a daily schedule, and structured forms of presentation, so many things happen simultaneously that not everyone experiences the same thing. And levels of mediation in communication vary considerably. Simply, the festival offers the ability—indeed, the desirability—for people (visitors, staff, participants) to chart their own experiential routes through it. The density of the crowd, the significance of the location and time help to make this experience important. Most distinctively, the festival offers the immediacy and sentient presence of people possessed of knowledge, skill, and wisdom, who can and do speak for themselves. At the festival, many different people speak in a variety of voices and styles. For the most part, the authority to speak and the content of that speech are diffuse.

Richard Price, an anthropologist who helped present a program on the Mall a few years ago, turned to me at one session where community leaders from Jamaica, Surinam, French Guiana, Colombia, Texas, and Ecuador were meeting with each other for the first time in the almost five-hundred-year history of *marronage* (Black resistance to slavery and colonial rule)—and said, "What have they got to say to each other?" Well, it turned out, a lot. People who don't usually have the opportunity can use these occasions to talk to a public directly and say their piece. They can cooperate with as well as challenge the ethnographers who claim to—and so often do—represent them. They can engage their exhibitors in dialogue and confrontation. They can speak with, conspire, and learn much from each other, and with all of this gain skill and standing in representing their own concerns in a complex world. At the same time, I think we as practitioners of our own art gain experience and appreciation in both understanding and conveying representational processes.

As a genre, cultural displays like the festival can disrupt the complacent, linear flow of history. The representational act or event can highlight salient issues and challenge public notions of the given state of social life. Almost like a collage, the festival is a display of recontextualized cultural imagery. In offering bits, pieces, and slices of life, the festival allows visitors a way into someone else's life as they are willing to publicly represent it.

Such displays are usually risky. The behavior of participants is somewhat unpredictable. Who knows what the musician from Jerusalem or the Hawaiian nationalist will say when he or she has the microphone and pulpit in front of a few hundred thousand people on the Mall? Yet with risk comes the playful ambiguity of the genre, the way in which cultural styles are brought to the organization and experience of the event itself. The genre shares the interstitial social character that one now finds increasingly in borderland regions and other cultural crossroads. New forms and syntheses of cultural expression may emerge at and be invented through the event itself.

Cultural displays can be used to say new things, foster new understandings, promote old ones, valorize and legitimate stances by governments, peoples, or communities. The very presence of largely working-class folks and people from a variety of backgrounds who are not usually represented on a national or international stage is significant. The institutional investment in their presence and voice helps legitimate their right to speak and adds luster to what they have to say and how they say it. Part of this investment, as Peter Seitel, the Smithsonian's senior folklorist, has suggested, consists of scholar-ethnographers providing a model of listening and respect for public audiences.[33] If scholars and curators can find ways of showing the general population how to listen to and respect the lives and lifeways of "their people," no matter who they may be, we might all be better off. I think this is a good thing that reflects well on the power of educational and cultural institutions in a democratic society.

Others may be more skeptical. Some may doubt whether there is anything to learn from such people. Some entertainers, politicians, and experts who themselves seek the limelight of display (through their performances, appearances, and distinguished lectures) worry about the ethics of the display of "lesser others" who may not have the capacity, talent, or good sense to represent themselves well. Several scholarly critiques of the festival express this concern.

Robert Cantwell, in *Ethnomimesis*, views the festival as too structured, too concerned with its own practice.[34] He believes that participants are overcontrolled, that presentations are far too removed from their original settings, so as to obfuscate and destroy their original meanings. This despite the fact that letters from festival participants, the diaries, articles, and books they write, and the interviews they give indicate precisely the contrary. Indeed, a survey of several hundred participants reveals exceedingly high levels of satisfaction with the festival and their experiences there. Some 90 percent of the participants surveyed from 1989 to 1993 indicated that they would definitely return if asked. They were comfortable with their interactions with staff, and well over 80 percent felt that they had performed, demonstrated, or talked well. Similar numbers were happy with logistics and other arrangements. It is significant that when festival participants were asked about the transmission of knowledge to their audiences, the response was quite overwhelming. More than 80 percent of respondents thought that people actually learned something about their culture at the festival—that it wasn't just mere voyeurism or entertainment. And about 70 percent of respondents thought they did "a real good job" in conveying their cultural traditions to festival visitors—a strikingly high percentage for people who are generally modest about their own accomplishments.[35] That Cantwell finds it "magical"—as in the sense of mysterious—for people from different backgrounds to be talking to each other, singing and sharing with each other, is sad, not so much because it is an inaccurate statement about the festival but because of what it indicates about the attenuated expectations of cultural commentators, the poor faith they seem to have in people, and their cynicism about the possibility for achieving any sense of cultural empathy.

This gap is also revealed in the participant surveys. Among the more problematic concerns to participants were presentations by the scholars—mainly anthropologists and folklorists—who "helped" represent them. Participant ratings of such scholars was about at the level of their ratings of the festival food and payment—at the lower end of satisfaction.[36] This finding can be compared with Richard and Sally Price's report on their experience of the Maroon program at the 1992 festival.[37]

Maroons are descendants of escaped slaves who formed their own societies on the margins of colonial and state control in the Americas. Maroons, comprising people from different African backgrounds but also including some Native Americans, unbeknownst to each other, led the first anti-slavery, independence movements in the New World and formed kingdoms and regional governments, some of which endure today. The 1992 festival brought together Maroon peoples from Accompong and Moore Town in Jamaica, Saramaka and Ndjuka from Surinam, Aluku from French Guiana, Palenqueros from Colombia, Black Seminoles from Texas, and other Maroons from Mexico and Ecuador. It was the first time all these Maroon communities had come in contact with each other. The festival program, focusing on the Columbian quincentenary, conceived this gathering as a way of informing public audiences about the Maroons' important and fascinating, yet little-known, history.[38]

In the Prices' view, the festival is a voyeuristic display of humans as specimens best left consigned to the last century.[39] The Prices offer a litany of complaints about the treatment of participants—some of which they, Richard more than Sally, instigated. Though he is an accomplished scholar, Richard was clearly uncomfortable and inexperienced in his festival role. He yelled at the Maroons to perform, overplayed his authority, and generally refused to consider that other scholars over several decades had come up with presentational strategies that could work. In perhaps the baldest display of the problem, in one area of the festival, Richard placed his books on Maroon culture in front of Maroon participants— between them and the public. He urged people to read his books and apparently resented the fact that Maroons were on display to "speak for themselves." No matter that African American notables like Jesse Jackson, Katherine Dunham, and John Hope Franklin joined the Maroons for discussions, no matter that many of the Maroons were articulate speakers on their own behalf, and no matter that many of the Maroons felt they had represented themselves well and were well served by the festival.[40] This, the Prices suggest, was a sort of false consciousness.[41] One irony here was that the Prices' prize student, Ken Bilby, himself well experienced and well published on Maroon culture, first recommended and then curated the program. I think Bilby has a very different view of the program, the presentations, and the impact of them.[42] And I don't think there is any "false consciousness" in him, any more than there is in many of the Maroon participants and leaders who are and have been quite adroit in matters of self-representation.

Indeed, the far more typical response to the festival and the interface between scholars and community people is along the lines reported by Kathy Neustadt in *Clambake: A History and Celebration of an American Tradition:*

> Having deftly sold the idea of performing a traditional New England clambake on the Mall in Washington, I then had to figure out how to bridge the gap that arose between the needs of the festival programmers and those of the Allen's Neck folks, who were flattered to be invited but not at all sure that they actually wanted to participate.
>
> From a research point of view, I learned more about the nature of the Yankee character through observing the negotiations and interactions at the cultural interface of the festival than I had to date in the more "natural" context. It turned out, happily, after the balking and stalling were over, that the festival experience was deemed a major success by everyone involved,

but particularly by the people of Allen's Neck. . . . Participation in the festival in Washington remains a source of positive memory and pride for most of the people in the Allen's Neck community, and a number of them even refer to it as the high point in their lives.[43]

The readiness of other scholars to accept the horrors of the Maroons' being on display based solely on the Prices' account without themselves having been there or having looked at other information is distressing and bodes ill for the ability of a field to assess its own ethnographic accounts.[44] Worse, it makes me think that if we do to others what we do to ourselves, we are in deep trouble.

It is not that the festival is above criticism or that some of its programs, staff, presentations, and arrangements are not as good as others. The process of conceptualizing, planning, and implementing each festival program teaches us something. In 1987, Kurt Dewhurst, Yvonne Lockwood, Marsha MacDowell, and others used the Michigan program on the Mall to establish an annual Festival of Michigan Folklife, now a decade old. They connected this to a full range of research, education, exhibition, and training projects. We adapted their strategy for other programs, remounting festival programs "back home" and using the festival as a linchpin for producing documentary films and videos, recordings, training programs, traveling exhibits, and publications.[45] Similarly, analytic examinations of festival programs—such as the Indiana University Folklore Institute study of participant experiences of the 1987 Michigan program led by Richard Bauman and Inta Carpenter and the response from Michigan curators, scholars, and organizers—can yield positive results and improve professional performance.[46] Participants in subsequent festivals benefited from our reexamination of procedures, styles of interaction, and information provided to participants.

Yet indictment of the festival genre itself seems to come from a deep-seated insecurity among those who would stand between people, who view themselves as the arbiters, as the elite capable of understanding and translating culture to others. Rather than seeking to broker culture, they seek to control it. When we asked participants about the effects of their festival participation upon their own lives and that of their communities, some 60 percent indicated a significant impact. In many cases, this impact was felt as the ability to represent themselves and their cultures to mass audiences, reporters, scholars, and public officials. This is no mean accomplishment, and it is one that should not be the sole privilege or refuge of the self-selected scholars who position themselves as the intellectual gatekeepers of "their people."

Despite the challenges to and questions about the Festival of American Folklife on the National Mall, it continues to engender a vital public activity, representing an American and human cultural heritage, presenting it to a large audience in an educational way, connecting it to real people and communities in a manner that enhances the national civic culture of our democratic society. And so it is no surprise that other events—from the Black Family Reunion to the L.A. Festival, from the Festival of Michigan Folklife to a national festival in India, from a festival of Hawaiian culture to the indigenous culture and development festival in Ecuador, from the America's Reunion on the Mall festival for the presidential inaugural to Southern Crossroads: A Festival of the American South for Atlanta's Olympic Games—draw inspiration and lessons from it. Indeed, even the venerable old Smithsonian drew mightily upon the festival as genre for the production of its own 150th Anniversary Birthday Party on the Mall. Some of the Smithsonian ancestors might have been quite surprised but, I think, ultimately heartened to learn that the festival genre, historically used to represent others, had become a successful means of representing ourselves.

Opposite: Effigies of demon king Ravana and his cohorts stand on the National Mall for "*Mela!*" at the Festival of American Folklife before being set afire to symbolize the victory of good over evil. Photo by Jeff Tinsley, courtesy Smithsonian Institution.

PART TWO
CASE STUDIES
OF
BROKERING
CULTURE

CHAPTER 9

THE FESTIVAL
OF INDIA

The paradigm of cultural representation implicit in the Festival of American Folklife perhaps reached its apotheosis during the Festival of India in 1985, particularly with a program at the festival called *"Mela! An Indian Fair"* as well as an exhibit in the National Museum of Natural History titled "Aditi: A Celebration of Life."

"Aditi" and *"Mela!"* are exemplary case studies in cultural brokering. They illustrate the complex bridging of individual and institutional interests, varied conceptions of cultural representation and display, and the juxtaposition of diverse purposes and ways of doing. I played an active role in this bridging, coordinating these programs while working with Rajeev Sethi (their creator), Jeffrey LaRiche (the Smithsonian's program manager), and a host of dedicated others. "Aditi" and *"Mela!"* also point to the role that representation can play in enacting and extending a culture, both in a museum and in the daily lives of its practitioners.

Background: "Aditi" and *"Mela!"* as Smithsonian Exhibitions

"Aditi" and *"Mela!"* were organized under the aegis of the Festival of India in the United States. The overall Festival of India was developed as a bilateral official program between the U.S. and Indian governments. Official committees were headed by S. Dillon Ripley, then secretary of the Smithsonian, and Pupul Jayakar, adviser to Prime Ministers Indira and

Rajiv Gandhi. The overall Festival of India, enacted in 1985, with a total budget of some $15 million, included major exhibits on Indian art and civilization at the National Gallery of Art and the Metropolitan Museum of Art, exhibits at the Freer Gallery and the Chicago Museum of Science, a nationwide touring program of Indian musicians, a gala opening at the Kennedy Center, and literally hundreds of other programs.[1]

Both the "Aditi" and the "*Mela!*" exhibitions had been discussed and were in the planning stages before the design of the larger, more encompassing Festival of India. The Smithsonian Institution's Center for Folklife Programs and Cultural Studies (then known as the Office of Folklife Programs) had conducted research, supported collaborative planning, and carried out negotiations with Indian colleagues for "Aditi" since 1977 and for a "*Mela!*"-like program since 1981.

"Aditi: A Celebration of Life" was mounted in the National Museum of Natural History from June 4 to July 28, 1985. The Evans Gallery, a hall for temporary exhibitions, was completely remodeled to suggest a rural Indian environment and house some two to three thousand objects, ranging from museum pieces loaned by the queen's collection in London and more than fifty Indian institutions to contemporary craft items.

The exhibit was arranged thematically, in terms of the life cycle—inspired by but only approximating the Hindu *samsāra* (sacramental life stages). The exhibition began with signals of fertility and continued through marriage, conception, birth, first feeding, childhood, growing up and moving out. Rather than a linear representation of biography, the switch from parents having children to children becoming parents illustrated the truly cyclical nature of life evoked by Aditi, who is in the Vedas both the mother and the daughter of Daksha. The thousands of objects were arranged in appropriate sections of the exhibit associated with their use—fertility objects in the first section, wall paintings in the nuptial chamber, cradles with birth, toys in growing up, and so on. As an alternative to a chronological or spatial ordering, objects—royal and rustic, contemporary and ancient, Hindu and Muslim, southern and northern—were arranged according to the theme in an effort favoring cultural holism over atomistic particularism.[2] Significantly, only a small portion of the objects were in cases. Most were set in mud wall niches, apportioned on platforms, displayed in stalls, and otherwise made directly available to visitors—much to the dismay of our security people.

Complementing and interacting with the objects and their settings were forty folk artists—craftspeople and performers—who worked in designed spaces to illustrate their creative role in the life cycle. A Baul sang of cosmic fertility, a Warli wall painter depicted tribal courtship dances, Rajasthani women applied *mehndī* in preparation for marriage, Muslim Langa musicians sang songs to welcome the newborn, magicians, puppeteers, jugglers, and storytellers initiated children to India's history, myth, and wisdom. Ten of the artists were themselves children. A family with two sons aged nine and four was included in the forty people drawn from thirteen different Indian states.

In addition to objects, people, and settings, the exhibit included considerable descriptive, interpretive, and expressive commentary on signs, as well as translators who interpreted questions, answers, and comments for folk artists and visitors.

"*Mela!* An Indian Fair" was part of the nineteenth annual Festival of American Folklife, held outdoors on the National Mall between the U.S. Capitol and the Washington Monument from June 24 to July 6, 1985. "*Mela!*" served as a much expanded form of the last section of the "Aditi" exhibition, which was devoted to fairs and festivals.

"*Mela!*" was a composite fair, presenting ritual, craft, performance, foodways, and commercial traditions from a variety of Indian regions. More than 100 tons of terra-cotta tile, bamboo, coconut leaves, *shāmī-yāna* (appliqué), and *kanāth* canvas were sent from India to construct the temporary "*Mela!*" site. Some forty-five structures were built, including a masonry facsimile of a temple and stalls for craft sales and demonstrations, and ten tandoor ovens were imported for an outdoor kitchen.

"*Mela!*" was conceptually organized on the basis of indigenous Indian models. Hindu action orientations—*mokshā* (spiritual release), *dhārmā* (moral action), *arthā* (commerce), *kāmā* (pleasure)—informed the selection of activities to be included in "*Mela!*" Traditional Indic notions of the elements (*pānch māhābhūtā*) and their associated sensations (i.e., sound, touch, sight, taste, smell) provided a model for the exhibition's spatial organization.[3]

Animated by thirty-five artisans from India and thirty Indian Americans, ritual activities included daily Ganesha *pūjā* (worship), the mud sculpting of a Durga mother goddess icon, the construction of a cut-paper-and-bamboo *tāzīya* (tomb replica) for the Muslim Muharram festival, and the building and burning of forty-foot-high effigies of the demon king Ravana and his allies.[4] Educational exhibits included an elaborate photo-text panel display on India, its fairs, festivals, pilgrimages, and religious communities.

At the "Aditi" exhibition in 1985, Jacqueline Kennedy Onassis (left) looks on with Rajeev Sethi as Shish Ram, his brother Kailash, and parents Ram Karan and Gotli Devi evoke events from the life of Pabuji, a medieval Rajput chief whose exploits are depicted in the hand-painted *parh* or scroll. Photo by Jeff Plosonka, courtesy Smithsonian Institution.

Sound (associated with ethereal) sections of the exhibition were animated by drummers from different parts of India, performances of Punjabi *giddhā,* Gujarati *garbā,* and Bengali devotional song, and stalls with musical instruments for sale. The touch section (associated with the element air) included cloth, mobile and fan stalls, kitemaker, acrobats, and juggler. The sight section (associated with fire and form) was replete with magicians, a trick photographer, potter, toymaker, impersonators, and shops of varying descriptions. Some forty cooks demonstrated their skills in the taste section—cooking in tandoors, making *jalebī*s (sweets) and serving from *deghchī*s (large cauldrons) 5,000 to 10,000 meals per day. The smell section included incense, essence, and cosmetics stalls as well as a flower garland maker. In sum, the exhibition offered to visitors a sensual event within which, as in *melā*s in India, ritual practice, education, commerce, and pleasure are interwoven and arguably more completely and appropriately understood than when considered in isolation.

The "Aditi" and *"Mela!"* exhibitions were quite successful from the perspectives of the public, the local Indian American community, edu-

cators and staff, sponsoring organizations, and the participants themselves. *"Mela!"* attracted 1.2 million visitors and *"Aditi"* a museum max-
imum (given the capacity) of 130,000 (with two-hour lines on week-
ends). Both exhibitions were hailed by the popular media in both the
United States and India. Hosts of VIPs, including Prime Minister
Gandhi, Nancy Reagan, Jacqueline Kennedy Onassis, and members of
the U.S. and Indian cabinets, visited the exhibitions. Local Indian community groups were mobilized and became involved in the exhibitions,
supplying volunteers and materials and planning auxiliary events. Even
local Indian restaurants and groceries benefited, gaining customers and
attention. To accompany the exhibitions, the Smithsonian developed
several ancillary products: a book catalog, *Aditi: The Living Arts of India,*
with essays by leading Indianists, which sold more than 40,000 copies
and which subsequently won both scholarly and popular acclaim; an
award-winning documentary film on the *"Aditi"* exhibition; an elaborate educational kit on Indian culture distributed to South Asia outreach
centers and museums for primary and secondary schools; an ethnographic film series; a scholarly symposium resulting in the publication of
the volume *Contemporary Indian Tradition;* a *Smithsonian* magazine article
on the participating folk artists and their community; workshops for
teachers and workshops for visiting children in which the Indian folk
artists initiated and instructed hundreds in their artistic practice.[5]

The Politics: Why the Exhibits

It is important to understand that for the Indian folk artists *"Aditi"* and
"Mela!" were not merely exhibitions. The core group of participants were
members of a cooperative, Bhule Bisre Kalakar (Forgotten and Neglected
Artists) living as squatters in a makeshift tent and shanty village in
Shadipur, on the outskirts of Delhi.

These poverty-stricken, low-caste musicians, puppeteers, jugglers, acrobats, and street performers and their families came from all over India.
Originally, and for some even until just a generation ago, these families
were patronized by local rulers and regional courts. Some were attached
to patrons continuously, others combined patronage with seasonal cycles
of itinerancy, visiting fairs and pilgrimage sites, undertaking traditional
rounds or tours of villages. The political demise of local-level patrons,
coming with a particular finality after independence (especially in

Rajasthan) enforced harsher regimens of itinerancy. At the same time that such artists sought new patrons and audiences, popular forms of entertainment—the Indian cinema, radio, and more recently television and videos—mitigated against the public demand for traditional performance.

Many itinerant performers sought the cities for their promise of large audiences, new performance venues, and new forms of patronage. Some succeeded in playing for tourists, for business or celebratory functions at hotels, or even for government agencies seeking to advertise the benefits of family planning through puppet shows. But most, like those in the Delhi slums in the 1970s, had to perform on the streets or continue to travel to local and regional fairs.

Under the law, street-performing artists were regarded as beggars, subject to at least harassment if not arrest. Their art was regarded as a sham, a mere means to solicit donations. In the mid-1970s they were viewed as part of the illiterate, vulgar, urban slum-dwelling population engaged in nonproductive activity. The irony is clear to many of the artists, who perceive themselves as keeping alive valued traditions. The *bahrūpīya* impersonators invoke the power of the gods to play their roles, the puppeteers inspire the young with tales of history, valor, and still-held Indian ideals, and the acrobats preserve in their movements and feats the ancient yogic *āsānā*s (poses).

In a drama recounted so well in Salman Rushdie's partially fictionalized *Midnight's Children,* these artists, along with other slum dwellers, were bulldozed from their homes in old Delhi as part of Sanjay Gandhi's slum clearance and social renewal program.[6] Some fled the region, some were sterilized, and most settled under a bridge on the outskirts of Delhi in a place called Shadipur. In Shadipur they built a squatters' camp on unused public land and began to rebuild their lives.

They formed a cooperative, the purpose of which was to secure a legitimate place in Indian society. The cooperative would lobby for the right to practice their art and build homes upon the land. Bolstered by the talent of designer Rajeev Sethi, the support of folklorist/government adviser Pupul Jayakar, folklorists Komal and Keshev Kothari, ethnomusicologist Nazir Jairazbhoy, architect Hasan Fathy, and many others, this community has sought, through political action, cottage industry and artistic exhibitions recognition of its role and rights to its land and livelihood.[7] The guiding philosophy of these artists has been that recognition of the value of their artistic and cultural achievements will bestow benefits on them as practitioners.

The exhibitions in Washington, as well as two previous incarnations of "Aditi" in Delhi (1979) and London (1982), were conceived by Rajeev Sethi and considered by him, by artists from Shadipur, and by the Smithsonian's Ralph Rinzler and Jeffrey LaRiche (then folklife director and deputy director, respectively) to be a means to this end.[8] The exhibitions were not diversions from reality but tools for its reconstruction. That reconstruction, as it emerged in the cooperative and continues to evolve, envisions an economically and aesthetically viable role for the exemplary practice of particular traditional arts.

At the Smithsonian, the massive media attention—network television coverage by ABC, NBC, and CBS, *Time,* the *New York Times,* the *Washington Post,* National Public Radio—the huge crowds, critical acclaim, and visits by VIPs from Secretary of State George Schultz to designer Mary McFadden to musician Ravi Shankar forced recognition of artistic and cultural achievement. Despite the artists' tenuous survival, their verbal, musical, and material artistry was exemplary and still grounded in community life. When Prime Minister Rajiv Gandhi visited the "Aditi" exhibition, he acknowledged the participating folk artists as India's "foremost cultural ambassadors." This transformation of status was not lost on the people from Shadipur, who a decade earlier had been regarded with contempt by Indian leaders.

In India, the success of the exhibitions led the prime minister to promise to work for revocation of the beggary law affecting folk artists.[9] He also promised to help the people of Shadipur obtain title to their land. The government of India held a national cultural festival in Delhi and established various regional centers for the study and presentation of the folk arts. High-volume sales of Indian handicrafts through the Smithsonian convinced Indian government corporations that such items would be viable on the international market. Millions of dollars in sales were realized, and a Golden Eye Foundation, with the purpose of promoting Indian crafts, was established. The Handicrafts and Handlooms Export Corporation, which cosponsored "Aditi" and *"Mela!,"* sought to revitalize its founding (Mohandas) Ghandian philosophy by supporting and strengthening folk artistic activity at the local level.

The expectations of the individuals who participated in "Aditi" and *"Mela!"* were raised. Some directly benefited economically and artistically from their celebrity status upon returning to India. Others fared less well, finding their efforts exploited by unscrupulous associates. Overall, the publicity, attention, and acclaim received by the "Aditi" and *"Mela!"*

participants did extend to their brethren in legitimating their role in Indian society and ensuring their rights to practice their art and, in some cases, to own the land that they have been promised. The establishment of regional centers, the national festival, and further international manifestations of the Festival of India, as well as new programs by government agencies, demonstrated a heightened awareness of the worth of traditional arts in India's future.

In Shadipur itself, two Dutch sisters, Sterre Sharma-Zegers and Mei Zegers—the first married to an influential Indian politician and former cabinet officer, the other an expert in development, and both relatives of an "Aditi" exhibit volunteer—became involved in the community. With Sethi and the Shadipur cooperatives, they stimulated the founding of a local health clinic, the teaching of adult literacy courses, and other training programs in the community. Regular meetings, reports, and planning ensued within Shadipur.[10]

The dream of Sethi and the Shadipur artists was to have a residential and cultural center in Delhi, a place where they could live in dignity, continue their craft and performing traditions, and at the same time educate both Indian children and tourists about the wealth of knowledge and joy in their cultural heritage. The pride of accomplishment, the memories, and the organization required for "Aditi" and *"Mela!"* sustained the community for more than a decade. During one visit to India, I opined to one government official involved that the tragedy of "Aditi" and *"Mela!,"* and of India, was that it was more likely to establish some kind of Disney-like theme park before it made good on its promise to its own people.

In 1995, after numerous setbacks, the Delhi Development Authority agreed to grant the people of Shadipur the use of well-located land for the development of their residential and artistic complex. Initial architectural plans were drawn up for homesteads, and for the facilities to support performances, crafts displays and workshops, cooking areas, library and archival functions, and the needs of visitors.[11] Plans were developed to establish the necessary operational structures so that artists could make a living on their own labors, educate visitors, and inspire their countrypeople in the process. It took constant attention and pressure to try to bring the artists' goal to fruition. Indeed, I urged Hillary Rodham Clinton to pursue the matter with officials during her visit to India that year.

Unfortunately, a scandal erupted in 1996 that cast the artists' dream into limbo. According to newspaper accounts, Sterre Sharma-Zegers had created her own private trust and gained title to the land that had been designated for the arts complex. Artists from Shadipur protested loudly, seeking official investigation. When Sharma-Zegers's husband, an influential cabinet minister, was formally charged for the corrupt handling of government petroleum contracts, the scandal assumed larger proportions. By early 1997, the project was, at best, on hold.

Events in India illustrate how what we do in the museum and with our programs can have both short- and long-term effects. Some of these effects grow organically out of the experiences of those involved and need but little encouragement. Others require deliberate, focused, and strategic attention over years—and still may not achieve the desired result.

The consequences of the exhibits were felt not only in India. Some issues were mirrored in the Washington, D.C., area among members of the Indian American community. Of the more than three hundred volunteers who participated in the *"Mela!"* and "Aditi" exhibitions, well over 90 percent were Indian or of Indian descent. With only a few exceptions, these volunteers were middle-class people, from relatively high-status groups and from families of white-collar professionals. Most volunteers were older, retired or semiretired professionals, housewives born in India, or bright, motivated teenagers and college students either born in the United States or well acculturated to contemporary American life.

Before the opening of the exhibitions we held training sessions for volunteers to inform them about the particular exhibits, performing groups, and craft demonstrators, about their role as translators and helpers, and other logistical matters. Mark Kenoyer, my assistant for "Aditi," an anthropologist who grew up in India and is now at the University of Wisconsin–Madison, explained in somewhat embarrassing terms the social status of the folk artists who would animate the exhibition. "These people"—I paraphrase Kenoyer—"are like those who come up to you on the streets of New Delhi. If you saw them there, you would walk away from them, or if driving, roll up your window and tell them to 'go away.'"

Thus depicted were the poor, low-caste, "vulgar" street people whom these volunteers were supposed to serve and help. There was a lot of squirming in the room, but little doubt of the honesty either in Kenoyer's remarks or in the way they were received.

While we may have lost a few volunteers, and while some volunteers may have been squeamish about the project, most did participate. Because the exhibit was such a big success, and because it drew such incredible media and VIP attention, the artists became celebrities of a sort, certainly in the eyes of the volunteers. The volunteers felt they were helping the Smithsonian with the exhibit and were proud of their daily interactions with the artists from India who were so famous and well received by the American public.

Some of the older volunteers, who in India might have refused to eat or drink with most of the "Aditi" artists, were now serving food to them, eating next to them, and even taking water and tea to them in the exhibition. Many of the teenagers who were initially ambivalent about Indian culture generally (vis-à-vis American popular culture) and who were familiar with the high value placed on Indian classical dance and music, discovered artistic traditions and lifeways heretofore unknown to them. This discovery led some of the volunteers to take instruction from the artists on how to play instruments, how to dance, and how to perform magic tricks. It led others to intimate, sometimes romantic, personal involvements. The effort to identify with the Indian artists perhaps reached a peak with our good-bye party, during which many of the volunteers dressed up in the clothing of the artists and imitated their personal and performative mannerisms in humorous but revealing skits— amid much hilarious laughter and the enjoyment of all.

The status inversion and leveling apparent in the relationship between volunteers and folk artists had several consequences. Local Indian families and organizations invited artists as distinguished guests to their homes or community functions. Folk artists were continually receiving awards, gifts, and invitations. Second, vitalized older volunteers became more active in presenting their traditions, through lectures, demonstrations, and community events, to the broader American public. Third, younger volunteers became more interested in Indian culture, a culture they knew little about and in which they had not invested much energy. They began talking more to their parents about India, taking courses, and reading books. Several volunteers traveled to India after the exhibitions to meet participants and conduct amateur fieldwork. At least one volunteer, brought in because her mother, an Indian immigrant, was a participant in *"Mela!,"* pursued and has now completed a graduate degree in Indian studies from the University of California at Berkeley.

The volunteer program also helped bring into the consciousness and programs of the Smithsonian a relatively recent immigrant group that had not previously identified the National Museum as being concerned with their culture or history. The Festival of India exhibitions helped the institution reach a new and broader audience. Members of the Indian American community used the opportunity to carry over their participation beyond just the exhibitions or the Festival of India. In 1986, for the Festival of American Folklife, our chief volunteer and perhaps 25 percent of our volunteers for the Japan program were Indian Americans who were first exposed to the festival through *"Mela!"* Some of our volunteers became docents in the Natural History Museum; others took staff positions in other museums and offices in the Smithsonian. And still others began research projects in collaboration with Smithsonian scholars.

The Poetics of an Ethnographically Real Exhibition

As both museum visitor and cultural anthropologist I am often exposed to the generic American museum exhibit. In the generic exhibit, objects find their way into cases, purportedly for insurance and security reasons, to be removed from makers, users, and viewers. If it is considered an art object, it gets a pedestal or a nice place on the wall and a spotlight. If a craft object, it is often displayed in some artistic but arbitrary grouping of like items. Usually the people who make or use the object are not included in exhibits; if they are, it is generally vicariously, through photographs, or through mannequins—frozen representations of people as objects. When authentic practitioners are included in a living exhibition, they usually sit at standard tables or perform on proscenium stages according to a schedule, occupying a space and a time neither designed for them nor suggestive of the usual context of artistic practice. An alternative mode of representation, living history museums, such as Colonial Williamsburg, may replicate such physical settings, but this mode, in substituting actors or revivalists for authentic practitioners, generally disarticulates demonstrated traditions from their biographical, historical, and social contexts.

Museums and museum exhibitions may be considered as forms of presentation with their own cultural roots and richness of meanings. In a museum we expect to see exhibitions; exhibition halls or spaces tend to be separated from people-function spaces. Rest rooms, cafeterias, information desks, and stores are kept distinct from exhibition areas—

enforcing divisions between education on one hand and commerce, provisioning, and maintenance on the other. Whether offering a presentation or a reconstruction, we understand an exhibition to be just that, removed from the reality of those represented, as well as our own. Exhibitions are bounded spatially by entrances, exits, and walls and temporally by daily and grand openings and closings. Exhibitions have their own routinized organization and processes of formation, involving institutional structures, curatorial and support staffs, funding arrangements and sponsors, building management, loan agreements, and so on.

If exhibitions are a nineteenth- and twentieth-century mode for the presentation of culture, one may ask whether the aesthetics of that form are appropriate to that which is represented. If, for example, folk art is distinguished from elite and commercial art in its unification of object and context, pleasure and utility, meaning and audience in familiar contexts, does it then make sense to have exhibitions that generically present the objects of folk art as if they were paintings in the National Gallery or concert performances in the Kennedy Center? If the very conception of "the object" in a particular culture is as a vessel of life, should the object then be displayed as if it were inanimate in a generic museum exhibit? It makes sense for our presentational formats to be consistent with the features of those arts and cultural activities we seek to represent.

Curatorial responsibility for the "Aditi" and "Mela!" exhibitions was vested in the Smithsonian's Folklife unit. With two decades of experience in the presentation of living cultural traditions through the annual Festival of American Folklife, it was able to achieve such an alternative presentational format. This was accomplished partially through design—as a result of Indo-U.S. scholarly, bureaucratic, and technical collaboration—and largely by providing an appropriate context for Indian craftspeople and performing artists to socially act and structure their own environment.

For the Indian folk artists the exhibitions were real in a way different from the way they were perceived by Smithsonian staff and the general public. For the Indians the exhibitions represented a political act; their existence rather than their texts constituted their most compelling feature. For the Smithsonian, exhibition semantics rather than pragmatics were foregrounded, with attention focused on installation, exhibit texts, their interpretations, exhibition artistry, and their relationship to the overall thematic message. For the public, it was a show—a good, engaging, and entertaining one that taught them something about India.

The Indian artists also did not share with the Smithsonian the culture of "museuming." The Smithsonian's notion of an exhibition as a rationally planned, statically ordered, and—above all—predictable set of activities was only vaguely understood and not very realistic or comforting. Despite initial and in some cases continuing efforts from a variety of quarters, Indian artists obfuscated the boundaries that define exhibitions as such. For these participants, the exhibitions were part of life, an organic event calling for creativity and improvisation as a means of dealing with life's contingencies. "What do you mean, an exhibition?" asked magician Nasib Shah, one of the participants, on the opening day of *"Mela!"* in response to my context-setting speech. "I perform at fairs in Rajasthan, in Gujarat, in Haryana. This is just another *melā,* only it's in Washington." And Nasib Shah came prepared to perform his magic and to sell his rings and gemstones.

Despite such differences, both the Smithsonian and the Indian participants had to deal, jointly, with the selection of folk artists who would come to Washington. The Smithsonian's approach, developed over the years of mounting the Festival of American Folklife, is to choose exemplary practitioners of the tradition as recognized within the community. Root forms of the tradition are those with a historical continuity to the past that have been socially integrated into the community of practice. The Smithsonian generally prefers to represent such root traditions rather than derived or evolved forms—though the latter are often presented to illustrate cultural transformations. Performances and crafts intended for in-group audiences/users are preferred over those intended for outsiders or tourists. Traditions represented have been incredibly wide-ranging and are chosen on the basis of program content—theme, curatorial message, the need to accurately survey a geographic/political unit.

In this case, the development of the exhibition themes came about through the efforts of Rajeev Sethi. A brilliant designer, adept at community development, grassroots social organization, and cultural representation, Sethi developed exhibition themes over the years with Shadipur artists and others. The themes were broad enough to serve as a mechanism for including a wide range of artistic activity, and they resonated with Smithsonian notions about the types of activities amenable to public presentation on the National Mall. The ideas of celebrating the life cycle and staging a rural fair were consistent with the folklorists' comfort in presenting display events—expressive forms that artists use to represent themselves publicly. Hence the folk artists would enact in the Smithsonian exhibition context the types of performances and demonstrations usually enacted publicly in India.

Similarly, Smithsonian interest in exemplary practitioners was mirrored by the concerns of Sethi, Indian folklorists, and the artists themselves. Discord over the choices of who was selected was quite limited, involving only the case of the puppeteers. It was within this community, the most populous of Shadipur, that issues of participant selection were absorbed by larger factional and economic conflicts.

In almost all cases artists had to make choices about repertoire. The Smithsonian's concerns for authenticity, root forms, and community-oriented performance were variously debated, rejected, heeded, or ignored. Sethi and other Indian colleagues understood rootedness perhaps more spiritually than literally. In most of the cases root forms and community-oriented performances made sense—they were practiced as meaningful parts of the repertoire. Folk artists themselves made distinctions between traditional songs and film songs, old forms and modern ones. The encouragement of selecting the older root forms generally meant valuing the types of artistic production over which the folk artists had a comparatively larger degree of control. Hence *kāthputlī* puppeteers were encouraged to sing the Mewari songs and enact the traditional tale of Rajput hero Amar Singh Rathor rather than to sing Hindi film songs and enact skits about family planning. The latter had been created by a commercial film industry and government agencies for audiences attuned to aesthetic and social standards quite different from *kāthputlī*-nurturing audiences.

Smithsonian staff, Sethi, other scholars, and artists themselves remained in a continuous dialogue about the nature of tradition, innovation, and adaptation. Encouragement of traditional practice was seen by organizers as a necessary counterbalance to the tremendous weight of commercial forms, exogenous influences, and other factors that generally devalue and delegitimate the skills, knowledge, and artistry of traditional artists. I think artists understood this full well. We were much more concerned with the expressions of the artists than with appeasing an American audience that had limited familiarity with Indian culture. Indeed, artists and organizers operationally conspired to define the nature of tradition, since they were well positioned to do so and since strong commercial competition was lacking. At the same time, we all recognized, sometimes tacitly, that several artistic forms had developed beyond traditional venues, audiences, and means of transmission. Yet they still illustrated continuities with tradition and provided contemporary means of aesthetic and economic self-empowerment. We did not want to rule out these expressions for the sake of enforcing a set of perpetually problematic academic categories. Hence, we were able to avoid potential impasses because Chandrakala Devi from Mithila demonstrated traditional skills on nontraditional life-size papier-mâché wedding figures or because the lost art of glass painting was demonstrated by a Tanjore *brāhman* trained by nontraditional means.

Smithsonian and Indian organizers thus defined the larger exhibition themes, selected participants, and encouraged certain items of repertoire. This was done with considerable scholarly expertise and a clear commitment to cultural conservation goals. It was also done through an active, generally goodwilled but sometimes acrimonious process of dialogue, debate, and conversation among artists, scholars, organizers, and sponsors, both Indian and American.

Within this context, Indian participants in "Aditi" and *"Mela!"* crafted the exhibitions as products, albeit not usual ones, within which traditional attitudes, skills, and creative expressions came to the fore, making the exhibitions quite different from those typically found at the Smithsonian or other similar museums. Here I offer several brief ethnographic vignettes that illustrate the ways in which folk artists defined and modified the exhibition context in terms of their own aesthetic and organizational notions, while at the same time forcing Smithsonian staff assumptions into relief.

Aditi *Pūjā*   The "Aditi" exhibition filled the Evans Gallery in the Museum of Natural History much as any exhibit would have a designated hall. *Aditi* in Sanskrit literally means "unbound," a most appropriate name for the exhibition.

On arrival in Washington, "Aditi" participants expressed the desire for a place to perform *pūjā* (worship) prior to the exhibit's grand opening and daily openings. The appropriate site for this was, of course, at the beginning—the entryway of the exhibition. This, much to the chagrin of museum security and staff, meant the building's Constitution Avenue foyer. To build the necessary shrine, the older women in the group searched for stones and boulders, eventually finding in the museum's collection several meteorites that in their pattern of cleavages and gouges bore a construed likeness to the mother goddess. The shrine was elaborated by several women, who then decorated the marble floor of the museum's foyer with rice flour–drawn *ālpanā, kolam,* and *rangolī* designs, thus making the space receptive to divine presence.

Visitors to the museum and its staff were daily confronted with the group's *pūjā,* singing of *bhajan*s (devotional songs) and distribution of *prasād* (blessed foodstuffs) in the reconstituted foyer. The *pūjā*s were done solely for the group and not intended as part of the exhibition or for demonstration purposes. It was a real *pūjā* for a real event, which transformed the nature of the museum's public space—appropriating it as Indian sacred space in control of the participants rather than museum personnel. Indeed, Dick Fisk, the director of the Natural History Museum came down to look at "Aditi" and remarked, "What happened to my museum?"

Mela! Temple   Since *melā* sites in India usually host a shrine or temple, marking its association with divine figures or saints, it was appropriate to build such a structure on the Mall. After consultation with architects, *brāhman* priests, and scholars, a small masonry temple structure was constructed by Smithsonian workers. In keeping with our attempt to produce an exhibit and avoid overt sectarian displays, we cordoned off the structure and placed signs around it saying that it was a facsimile of a temple, illustrating the architectural form and its association with *melā* sites.

The notion of a facsimile temple did not make much sense to the "*Mela!*" participants. On the first day of the festival, the signs came down. In ensuing days, the "Aditi" potter made a clay *yonī* (divine womb) to match and serve as a receptacle for an exhibited polished-stone *lingam* (divine phallus). The priest painted symbols on the structure indicating a Shiva temple. This precipitated rather heated debate among the Indians about the use of certain symbols and the correctness of their drawing. Once the *lingam* and *yonī* were installed, the flower garland maker created appropriate decorations. A sculpted bull—Nandi, consort to Shiva and mother goddess—also appeared. By the end of the first week, daily *pūjā* was performed in the now no longer facsimile temple. Gujarati dancers performed in its previously undefined courtyard, and *bhajan*s were sung there. Space and a structure intended for one use by Smithsonian staff were appropriated for other uses by participants. This appropriation was achieved in an organic and creative way, as participants contributed their various talents to bring to life not only the temple but also their own status as a community.

Building the *Mela!* Smithsonian staff, including construction personnel, were inexperienced in working with bamboo, terra-cotta tile, coconut leaves, *shāmīyānā, kanāth* (canvas appliqué canopies and walls),
and other building materials sent from India. Production plans called for
an Indian crew of carpenters and craftspeople who could work with the
Smithsonian crew to build the *"Mela!"* structures.

The tool kits, techniques, flexibility, and improvisation of the Indian
carpenters confounded the Smithsonian labor crew, engineers, and carpenters, who valued mechanization, precision of measurement, stan-
dardization, and square-angle construction. After some days of mutual
denial of each other's abilities, the American and Indian crews developed an appreciation of each other's craft—Indian carpenters experimented with power drills and augurs and Americans discovered the need
for flexibility when dealing with bamboo and came to understand the
rationale of interlocking terra-cotta tiles. Indian carpenters, communicating through their work, demonstrated the contingent nature of construction at an Indian *melā*—building around trees and roots and making use of materials at hand. Smithsonian personnel and contractors
who idealized construction as a closed system of actualizing measured
plans gained from these carpenters a new perspective on their own
work. In the end, while Smithsonian engineers reworked stress equations
on their calculators and puzzled as to why the structures stood at all,
scores of American volunteers, including builders and roofers, came
down to the Mall to help and to learn from the Indians.

In one instance, the difference between Indian and American standards could not be bridged. Our plan was to have coconut leaf roofs for
some *"Mela!"* stalls. Woven mats of coconut leaf fronds make for excel-
lent roofing in India. It is a lightweight material and when it rains the
soaked leaves mesh together, making the surface relatively impermeable.
Since we often get summer thunderstorms during the festival on the National Mall, this type of roofing seemed ideal for conveying both the aesthetic and the utility of a traditional architectural form.

In order to bring the ton of dried coconut leaf fronds into the United
States, we were required to have them fumigated in India, to prevent
unintended importation of potentially harmful insects and parasites. Unfortunately, the fumigant made the coconut leaf more flammable than
usual—as fire marshals from the District of Columbia discovered when
they tested the in-place roofs two days before the festival's opening. The
roofs constituted a fire hazard that had to be corrected. The Smithsonian

spent $10,000 in fire retardant, and staff and volunteers worked through the night to dip and spray all the coconut leaf and reinstall the roofs. And then it rained. The roofs leaked. The fire retardant had coated each leaf with a plastic laminate that prevented the leaves from meshing together. We spent the next night installing plastic wrap under the coconut leaf.

In this case, the chain of actions and consequences—Indian and American—did not work out very well. Traditional architectural materials and ideas about their use were confounded by American practices and notions of safety. The interpenetration of functional perquisites from the two cultures was dysfunctional in building terms, although the ironies were well appreciated by the Indian and Smithsonian construction crews.

Cultural Presentation

While the Smithsonian planned the exhibitions to be living ones, the Indian folk artists really meant it. The registrar for the "Aditi" exhibition did not expect to see new objects come into the exhibit every day. Participants would hang new items on the walls or place them on stands or platforms. The Warli wall painter ran out of room to paint in his designated area—so he continued down the hallway. A Mithila painter was inspired to embellish a blank wall in the fertility section. So too did performing artists throughout the exhibitions expand beyond their boundaries. The "Aditi" *bahrūpīya*s would often leave the exhibit hall to wander through the museum and inflict their impersonations on the unknowing, much as they do in India. Acrobats would accost the Internal Revenue Service across the street from the museum with their loud drumming in order to stir up a larger crowd. The monkey men of the *"Mela!" langūr bahrūpīya*s, would hide in trees, throw branches onto the crowds, scamper and yell as befit their role. My daily exhortations to them—"Get down from there. The trees on the Mall are national monuments. You will be arrested by the National Park Service Police"—were taken not as official warnings or as stage directions but as straight lines to be incorporated into the performance routine for the enjoyment of the audience. Similarly, such standard festival operations as tightly scheduled presentations on stages were routinely disregarded—as were at times the stages themselves. For the Indian folk artists, the exhibitions

Despite my repeated admonitions to protect the trees on the Mall, monkey impersonator (*bahrūpīya*) Krishna paid me no mind, much to the delight of festival visitors and staff. The *bahrūpīya* draw inspiration and power to impersonate from the monkey god Hanuman. Krishna later made his way onto the Washington Metro, to the Capitol, and at some point, to television reporter Sam Donaldson. Photo by Jeff Plosonka, courtesy Smithsonian Institution.

were living events that had their own dynamic rhythm and flow, and that was different from any preset, prescribed order.

Bazaar Culture

Of the forty stalls in *"Mela!,"* ten were devoted to the demonstration of various crafts—toy making, kite making, bangle making, and the like. The remainder were intended to invoke the bazaar setting so integral to real Indian *melā*s. Sethi and I both believed that the creation of a functioning bazaar or market at *"Mela!"* was necessary to give visitors a sense of its economic dimension. By inspecting items, asking questions, bargaining, and buying merchandise, visitors would gain a better appreciation of the overall event. We also thought it was a financially viable way to help fund the exhibition, since it would cost a great deal of money to put items "on display only" in all the stalls. Sales would assure that the stalls were well stocked and would pay for the acquisition of merchandise in India, shipping, and the staffing of the stalls.

Other Smithsonian officials and staff were divided in their opinions of this arrangement. Although a concern was raised that sales of merchandise would detract from the crafts demonstrations and performances, it was agreed that the idea had enough countervailing programmatic merit. Stronger objections came from the Smithsonian's business people, who saw sales as their institutional function. Embedding sales in an exhibition was anathema to their museum shop operations. They had the expertise and the infrastructure to sell merchandise, and they did not want to lose possible profits.

Our counterargument was that sales were part of the ethnographic event that we were representing. They were not culture-neutral but rather embedded in a particular event and sociology of exchange. Smithsonian officials in the end gave their approval for bazaar sales. After "Mela!" and in light of the volume of sales (more than $120,000 in ten days), the business people vowed "never again" and traded acrimonious memos with the Office of Folklife Programs in an effort to reassert control over sales.

Still, concessions had to be made. Bargaining, so intricate a part of the social exchange in Indian bazaars, could not take place because of accounting procedures and the need to conform to legal sales tax collection codes. Sales were handled by local Indian American hired help and volunteers, not by real shopkeepers. And, because of our limited "upfront" finances, we could not afford to purchase enough inventory to stock and restock all of the stalls—particularly those whose merchandise might not be in much demand by American visitors. Thus, five of the market stalls (e.g., essences, religious icons, oil lamps) had merchandise for display only—to give people an idea of what such shops look like in India. But in the end, twenty-five stalls did have sales, far more points of sale at the festival than at any time before "Mela!" or since then.[12]

Aesthetic and Social Order

The "Aditi" and "Mela!" participants lived in accommodations with Indianists who spoke their languages. They had Indian cuisine for meals, redesigned toilets, and various other appropriate amenities. Over the years, the Festival of American Folklife has evolved a means for dealing with participant culture shock. One standard procedure is to have various cultural liaisons live with and serve as counselors to participants, thus aiding their adaptation to a different environment. The model is generally one of individual counseling.

For the Indian artists, particularly those of "Aditi," who spent two months in Washington, this model was of limited value. The housing, working, and general living situation more closely simulated a small community or village than it did a collection of individuals. The Indians themselves recognized this quite quickly and constituted a group *panchāyāt* (council) to discuss and regulate their internal behavior toward each other. The group would meet when needed, squeezing into one of the apartments to talk about someone's drinking, another person's verbal abuse, and so on. Problems were openly discussed. Some of the older and wiser artists would be asked to give their opinion. Yelling matches might erupt. Distractions were continuous. The group often proposed restitutive actions and levied fines, and entertainments often followed. Operating much as it might have in India, the group exerted a measure of social control over community activities.

One of the major points of group discussion and conflict concerned the sales of items made by "Aditi" and *"Mela!"* craftspeople at the exhibitions. During *"Mela!"* the staff operated a special stall in the bazaar. Most of the craft items made by craftspeople or brought to Washington by participants were sold there. In other, exceptional cases items were sold by staff or volunteers from the stalls of the makers.

Many of the craftspeople felt they should get the full profit from their items. But most of the musicians and performers objected. They argued that it was their music and performance that attracted so many people to *"Mela!"* Since they helped to draw customers, they deserved a share of the profits. The issue was hotly debated for two days and nights as a group. Finally a consensus agreement emerged. Craftspeople would set a price they wanted for an item. Smithsonian staff would attempt to sell the item at double that price. The income, minus the cost of sales, would be divided into shares. The craftsperson or owner would receive half the profit. The remaining half would be divided evenly among all participants, including musicians, craftspeople, cooks, and others. Smithsonian staff would keep the records and handle disbursements. If artists were found to be cheating by selling directly to the public without reporting sales, they would sacrifice their share of the profits for that day.

In this manner, the group exerted control over a fairly complex and sensitive matter. While some individuals complained about the arrangement, it was generally quite popular and successful. Two people were fined, one day each. Otherwise the agreement held and perhaps mirrored the kind of consensus building, group cooperation, and conflicts that characterize the larger Bhule Bisre Kalakar cooperative to which many of the folk artists belong.

Individuals also exerted aesthetic control over their own experience. The teenaged Krishnagar toy maker, having visited the National Gallery of Art, reduced its sculpture to his own scale by making clay models. The Indian street performers, not satisfied at being mere curiosities, learned enough English to banter effectively and engage American audiences much as they do Indian ones. And after visiting King's Dominion theme park for a roller-coaster ride, Ganga Devi turned her vision of scaffolding into an intricate Mithila-style painting now hanging in the Crafts Museum in Delhi.

Banku Patua, the Bengali *chitrakar,* approached his American visit as an artist and storyteller. He painted a story scroll depicting his experience and composed lyrics in the traditional style. His painting of the airplane that brought him to Washington, D.C., conveys the imagined impossibility of flight. He paints visitors to the exhibit, coming in wheelchairs; people of different castes and religions eating together; evil cleansed on the Mall through the burning of Ravana at *"Mela!"* He paints a Jesus seen at the National Cathedral, and the retreat of the American gods and goddesses from daily public life, and the absence of sociality on the streets of the nation's capital. He even paints the rolling hills of the D.C. area—surprising to the eye of Washingtonians but exquisitely revealing of the comparison with Banku's Bengali flatlands. And now, in the villages of West Bengal, Banku Patua with both pride and humility displays his scroll and sings his song:

> Come and listen all my friends gathered here, all people present.
> I will tell you about America
> When we arrived at Washington airport, Rajeev Sethi and other friends greeted us with sweets and garlands.
>
> And after all of us craftspeople were seated on the bus, the bus started going not on the left but on the right side of the road. This is a delightful country and there are many wonderful things to think about and they are worth knowing.

After coming to Washington, Banku Patua, a Bengali
chitrakar, drew a scroll that narrated his experiences
with the "Aditi" exhibition, including a visit to the U.S.
Capitol. Photo by Tracy Eller, courtesy Smithsonian Institution.

With joy in our hearts we went to Georgetown University and with
     motherly affection we were fed and given beds and all the things
     we needed.
And they came and cleaned for us.
The next day when we came to the exhibition grounds I saw that all kinds
     of people, including those in wheelchairs, came to the exhibition.
And it touched me.
I have made a picture of that, which finds a place in this scroll.

When we went off to have our lunch, Hindus, Muslims, Jains, and Christians all sat down in one place to eat together.
And after a few days, we went out sightseeing.
And I decided to put a picture of the Potomac River in my scroll.

The wonderful things in this wondrous place!
Reflect on them.
There's a lot to learn from this America.

On our way back to Georgetown University we saw the Washington Monument.
And I have portrayed that in my scroll.
It's a beautiful place, and people from this country and abroad come to look at it.

Reflect on this.

And then what did I do?
We went to the church and saw a statue of Jesus Christ.
And that I have captured here in my scroll.
And then what did I do?
On the last day of *Mela!* the effigies of Ravana were burned. And inside that fire, when the effigies were burned, all the bad things which were inside of us were thrown into that fire.

These wonderful things of this wondrous place.
And then we went out for a tour.
I saw this beautiful thing, the parliament of this place, and that I have put at the end of my scroll.

People, I have a lot of shortcomings.
And if in this ballad I have made any mistakes,
I ask forgiveness from all those present.[13]

Brokering Life

Barbara Kirshenblatt-Gimblett, writing about "Aditi" and *"Mela!,"* raised the issue of how so-called living museum exhibitions can contain human beings.[14] According to Kirshenblatt-Gimblett, such containment takes several forms. Most tangibly, humans can be set into museums like objects, occupying wall space, framed by niches, and identified by labels. More subtly, people and their cultural expressions may be contained as a type of symbolic biopsy. Music, narrative, ritual, craft making, and other actions are abstracted from their usual cultural context and injected into another. This other context, that of a festival or museum, or even a concert hall, reduces the semiotic richness of the social enactment. People become signs of themselves, a dance becomes a sign of a larger performance and context, in itself a sign of the larger community, culture, or country. In this view, extended chains of such signification amount to reductions of self and meaning, so that as these chains become elongated the freedom of action open to "participants" is lost. Organizers, familiar with the context of presentation, are in charge of signification, and thus they both orchestrate participants and tell them what they are supposed to do and mean.

Whether this assessment is accurate is to me an empirical question, depending in large part on the kinds of performances and demonstrations, the museum settings, and the actions of participating artists and museum staff. I do not believe it impossible to adequately present living culture in a museum setting. Indeed, if we are surprised or shocked to see people as subjects in museums, it is not because they do not belong there. It is because museums have, sadly, become places where we do not expect to encounter other people. This is often evident in the way in which museums impose controlled settings, cases, pedestals, and spaces for objects, an unwritten protocol that prompts visitors to avoid each other in exhibition halls and to speak in the hushed tones deemed proper for museum conversations. While in one, or possibly two, cases, "Aditi" artists were placed in an "objectlike" position, this amounted to a relatively small failing in the overall presentation. I believe that the overwhelming response by the artists and visitors was exactly the opposite. People were heartened by the ability of artists to take over the museum and inject humanity into its otherwise impersonal halls and galleries.

In their fundamental design, "Aditi" and *"Mela!"* provided space and facilities for living people to demonstrate their art. As indicated above, the performers, craftspeople, and musicians extended their art far beyond those spaces. There was no attempt to insulate participation. To the contrary, in every case volunteers and staff were provided to help translate and interpret so that artists could answer questions and speak for themselves. Unlike objects, artists went to lunch, took *bīdī* (cigarette) and tea breaks, moved around, changed their presentations, and went to the lavatory. I seriously doubt that people were mistaken for objects in this context.

If in the structuring of the experience the Indian folk artists became signs of themselves and other entities, such as Indian folk culture or India itself, there was certainly an advantage in doing so. By being placed, and placing themselves, in a position of representing other members of the cooperative, folk artists, and Indian culture more generally, they strengthened individual voices. Street acrobatics, juggling, puppetry were legitimated as artistic practice by the National Museum of the United States and presented as such back in the Indian community. The ability of the people of Shadipur to advocate their rights was advanced. Many of those involved in the exhibitions understood that they were representing larger traditions, larger communities, larger cultural and national bodies. This they generally interpreted as an honor, as a responsibility, and sometimes as something that could be turned to personal advantage and profit.

There is another side to the semiotic question. What are the psychological characteristics, if any, of becoming a sign of oneself, or of other signs? If the folk artists participating in "Aditi" and *"Mela!"* really felt themselves becoming more and more removed from their home setting, more reduced in meaning, signifying less and less about more and more, then, I suggest, they might have approached an Indian ideal of *nirvana* or *moksha*—the loss of self in a larger universe. But I don't think that was the case. As Milton Singer argues in *When a Great Tradition Modernizes,* in his masterful answer to Max Weber, the character of a group ethos in a psychological sense cannot be formulated or inferred from philosophical principles in the ideological repertoire of the group.[15] A philosophical concept, like *kārmā,* for example, does not stop Indians from pursuing goals in their daily behavior—like eating meals or seeking medical treatment. A semiotic analysis suggesting that people are becoming signs of themselves tells us about the categories of semiotics; it does not tell us anything about the thoughts, feelings, or actions of those people.

I think the "Aditi" and *"Mela!"* participants brought with them the contexts of their own performance and behavior. Aside from the elaborate physical construction of the exhibitions, they brought with them strong notions of why and how they do what they do, and for whom. Exemplary artists have the power to create or re-create these contexts just about wherever they go. And given the chance, they can convey the strength and the beauty of what they do. I would suggest that the participants, rather than living a self- and meaning-negating experience derived from or surgically removed from everyday reality, actually brought with them their own repertoire of self- and culture-defining ways, and this particular experience allowed for a great deal of cultural creativity, of heightened or magnified sense of culture and self.

The Smithsonian staff, Indian American volunteers, Rajeev Sethi, Indian scholars, and Smithsonian officials encouraged participating artists to demonstrate their art, skill, and knowledge, to speak for themselves and for others of their community. This they did, extending their talent far beyond the domain of exhibit and museum. The encouragement was competent and conscientious, perhaps because of the right mixture of staff, experience, and resources. In other cases of poor staffing, lack of knowledge and sensitivity, lack of expertise, resources, or time, I can imagine circumstances that would lead to discouragement, deprecation, and disgruntlement.

If the people who came (and those they stood for) were adequately represented, was it then worth doing? After all, there are real issues of power and control that absorb and affect the people we represent. The modern museum, founded on the democratic ideals of the Enlightenment, sometimes seems to set for itself minor and relatively ineffectual goals with regard to those democratic ideals. Indeed, it is ironic that museums seem to provoke those ideals when they misrepresent people, events, or cultures, as with the *Enola Gay* and historic treatments of American minority groups and Third World societies.

Museums, I argue—and I think the case of "Aditi" and *"Mela!"* well demonstrates—can play a role in effecting cultural democracy. Museums do not equip people from endangered cultures with guns, votes, or plumbing. But they can provide communities and people with a useful service. As social institutions with standing, museums can help legitimate beliefs, practices, people, accomplishments, and interpretations. Second, through exhibits and programs, museums can help in generating and articulating the symbols and symbolic statements through which a community might represent itself. The production and reproduction of meaning is something that museum professionals and academic scholars are trained to do and that can be of great importance to those they seek to study and represent.

The people of Shadipur and folk artists in India have not yet achieved all their goals. But their participation in the Festival of India Smithsonian folklife exhibitions was worthwhile in bringing attention to their cause, generating useful ideas, eliciting promises of help, and even stimulating concrete programs.

If culture is to be conserved, it must live. It cannot be frozen in time and preserved by museums or anthropologists or folklorists or historians. For a culture to live, its bearers must practice that culture, revise, transform, and adapt it to new and changing circumstances, to find new meanings for old practices and old meanings for new practices.

The "Aditi" and *"Mela!"* exhibitions were as good as they were not because the Smithsonian just went ahead and put them together. Nor were they good because the Indian participants did whatever they wanted to do. The exhibitions themselves became an arena for the practice of cultural representation. In this arena, museum culture, the culture of folklorists, of Indian officials, of designers, and, most important, of the folk artists themselves was negotiated in a multilogical environment. The reality of the exhibitions was continually brokered, not on paper but through actions and events that brought into relief conflicting interpretations and wonderful cultural juxtapositions.

CHAPTER 10

BROKERING POST- COLD WAR FOLKLORE

S cholars and presenters of cultural programs often broker meanings with each other. Sometimes these debates are academic and have significance for a small group of scholars specializing in a particular field. Sometimes meanings of culture, art, and tradition are negotiated by those who arrange tours or bookings for programs and exhibitions. And sometimes the debate over culture, whose culture, and what kind of culture can involve authorities of public and official institutions who play a role in articulating the relationship between culture and the national state.

This chapter examines how folklore and related concepts were defined and enacted in a cultural exchange program between the Smithsonian Institution and the former USSR Ministry of Culture and its successors. The program was initiated in 1986, a time of *perestroika,* and continued through 1995, having endured the dissolution of the Soviet Union. The program involved a variety of projects, including the production of festival programs, the publication of sound recordings and scholarly articles, and the conduct of field research. The overall program has been marked by institutional collaboration and frustration, conceptual dissonance and resonance, adaptations and transformations in the understanding and practice of public folklore. The exchange is revealing not only of differences in perspective between Smithsonian and Soviet, Russian, and Ukrainian cultural specialists but also of broader internal debates within two very different societies.

"Folklore" is a problematic enough concept in our own intellectual history. At the popular level, "folklore" generally refers to something that is made up, a spurious belief, an untruth. To many, folklore is that soft, fuzzy stuff of childhood, the fairy tales told to toddlers, the folktales read to first graders. For others in our society, folklore is entertainment—from the rough-hewn songs and ballads of marginal rural and working people to the poignant, if sometimes irritating, lyrics wailed by the urbane, guitar-strumming singer-songwriter. To still others in the arts, folklore is the *ballet folklorico,* the wonderfully costumed and choreographed theatrical performance. For some scholars, folklore represents the grassroots, traditional oral expression that arises informally through social interaction. And for many reporters, folk heroes are those whose grassroots appeal and unsanctioned behavior stand in opposition to official, accepted, hierarchical society. With such a range of meanings to accommodate, folklorists in the United States have a hard enough time conveying their subject matter and practice to each other, other scholars, the media, and the general public. How much harder is it, then, to define and negotiate a folklore exchange with those of another society—that of Russia and the former Soviet Union—particularly at a time when their social categories—of people's culture, state culture, entertainment, art, truth, and fiction are rapidly being transformed?

This chapter offers an anatomy of a binational exchange. It details the ways in which folklorists try to shape their own practice as well as the presentations of others whose cultures they seek to represent. In this creative practice, ideas of folklore and folklife, authenticity, tradition, community, art, and performance have to be constructed, again and again, in variegated forms, for audiences of scholars, the lay public, bureaucrats, government officials, and even the "folks" themselves. Instead of examining how such understandings are debated in scholarly books, journals, and articles, I examine here the ways in which folklore is constructed in public practice. For it is in public practice that the consequences of our ideas about folklore and culture—some commonly held, others vigorously debated—are likely to become apparent.[1]

Presenting and Contextualizing the Exchange

The Smithsonian Institution–Soviet Ministry of Culture exchange program consisted of a series of interrelated projects, including Soviet participation in a "Musics of the Peoples of the Soviet Union" program at

the Smithsonian's 1988 Festival of American Folklife; American participation in the 1988 International Folklore Festival held in Moscow; documentary recordings of *Musics of the Soviet Union* and *Tuva: Voices from
the Center of Asia* on Smithsonian Folkways Recordings; a collaborative
field research project, Soviet and Soviet American Folklife Research and
Presentation; American participation in the 1990 International Folklore
Festival in Kiev; and Soviet participation in the 1990 National Folk Festival in Johnstown, Pennsylvania. These projects were supported by protocols between the two institutions, official visits, and numerous meetings and communications. As a whole, the program represented an
ongoing dialogue about folklife and folklore, their definition, importance, and place in the cultural life of the United States and the USSR.

The program continued even when the Soviet state dissolved. Protocols were developed and signed with the Russian and Ukrainian Ministries of Culture. Field research continued in the United States and in
Russia and Ukraine. Two Smithsonian Folkways Recordings were produced, *Bukhara: Musical Crossroads of Asia* and *Shashmaqam: Music of the
Bukharan Jewish Ensemble,* illustrating the transformation and continuity
of central Asian traditions in the United States. The program "Russian
Roots/American Branches: Music in Two Worlds" at the 1995 Festival of
American Folklife also resulted from the exchange and generated another Smithsonian Folkways Recording, *Old Believers: Songs of the Nekrasov Cossacks.*[2]

The initial impetus for the exchange program came from Smithsonian secretary Robert McC. Adams, who, in 1985, invited key staff to
propose possible collaborative activities with the USSR, then in its early
stage of *glasnost* and *perestroika.* Peter Seitel, then the director of the
Smithsonian's Office of Folklife Programs, wrote to Secretary Adams suggesting that several Soviet scholars be invited to the 1986 Festival of
American Folklife to observe the festival and also meet with American
scholars on the Smithsonian's Folklife Advisory Council. A delegation of
Soviet folklorists, ethnologists, and semioticians was proposed, signaling
a desire to put collaboration with the Soviets on a scholarly footing. This
approach also reinforced to a secretary who was relatively new to the
Smithsonian the view that the Office of Folklife Programs was at heart a
scholarly organization, implicitly countering an alternative view of us as
merely a producer of large-scale public performances.

Many Smithsonian museums and offices were interested in collaborative activities with the Soviet Union. Anthropologist Bill Fitzhugh in

the National Museum of Natural History had long been working with the Soviet Academy of Sciences on the Crossroads of Continents project to research and exhibit cultural materials from both sides of the Bering Strait. As a result of Secretary Adams's initiative, however, collaborative activities were to develop between several Smithsonian units and the Soviet Ministry of Culture. Formal relationships with the Academy of Sciences, the Folklore Commission, and several other organizations also emerged in the course of our work with the ministry. At a meeting in October 1986 in Washington, Deputy Minister of Culture Yevgeniy Zaitsev and his delegation heard presentations from several Smithsonian museums and offices. Folklife described its mission and suggested that a Soviet scholarly delegation visit Washington for the 1987 Festival of American Folklife. Zaitsev invited Smithsonian folklore scholars to visit Moscow in 1988 for the first in a planned series of biennial folklore conferences and festivals. I wrote a lengthy internal memorandum in November, presenting the possibility of long-term joint research on folklife in the United States and the USSR that might result in the production of side-by-side "living exhibition programs" in the two nations in some future year.[3]

The Office of Folklife Programs wanted to position scholars of folklore, ethnology, ethnomusicology, and related fields at the forefront of any collaborative project with the Soviet Union. This would ensure that proposals would be developed from ethnographically based understandings of folk culture. We did not want to consider proposals that conceived of folklore as theatrical performance—as is often the case in the USSR. In April 1987, Secretary Adams carried this point to the Soviet Embassy in Washington and then to USSR Minister of Culture Vasily Zakharov in Moscow, stating that the Smithsonian's Office of Folklife Programs had its mission to study and present unmediated forms of living folk cultural traditions.

Minister Zakharov indicated to Secretary Adams that the Soviet Union intended to undertake a substantial, permanent expansion of its folklore programs and was heartened by possibilities of collaborating with the Smithsonian in this area. Following this meeting, Seitel issued an official invitation "to two of our Soviet colleagues in folklore studies to attend the 1987 Festival of American Folklife." He stated: "I hope the specialists you select will be interested in the analysis of folk culture and of its scholarly, research-based presentation to general audiences for both educational and entertainment purposes."[4]

Ralph Rinzler, then the Smithsonian's assistant secretary for public service, followed up with a letter and a visit to Aleksander Potemkin, the cultural counselor at the Soviet Embassy. In an effort to make sure that the Soviets knew what we were talking about when we said "folklife and its research-based presentation," Rinzler discussed the visit of Igor Moiseyev to the Smithsonian's 1976 Festival of American Folklife. Moiseyev had developed and popularized the genre of Soviet and Eastern European "folkloric ballet," or theatrical folklore. It is a genre characterized by large professional dance troupes, purposefully colorful costumes, highly choreographed movement, orchestral music, theatrical sets, and complex staging. It is usually performed on stages in auditoriums or stadiums for seated, ticketed audiences. Music, dance, sets, and costumes may be loosely based upon or inspired by ethnographic reality, but highly valued innovation and artistic control are vested in a professional staff. Rinzler wrote to Potemkin: "Moiseyev spoke with enthusiasm of our unmediated or uninterpreted presentation which in fact differs from his own theatrical interpretation of folk traditions."[5]

In June we received word that two Soviets, Alexander Demchenko, the director of cultural education programs at the Ministry of Culture and M. N. Nalepin, a folklorist at the Academy of Sciences, would be sent to Washington. Demchenko was in charge of amateur groups in communities across the Soviet Union who dress in costume and perform the folk dances and songs of their region. Nalepin studied American folktales in their written form. Over a two-week period in Washington, Demchenko and Nalepin spent ample time observing the Festival of American Folklife, which at the time included programs on the folklife of Michigan, the cultural conservation of language, and musics of the Washington metropolitan area. They watched many performances and demonstrations, observed visitors' experiences, examined logistics and infrastructure. They had numerous meetings with Seitel, festival director Diana Parker, and Smithsonian Folklife staff to discuss festival philosophy and its means of production. Demchenko and Nalepin stayed at the hotel with festival participants. They also visited Sisterfire, a feminist performing arts festival in nearby Maryland.

During their visit, Demchenko and Nalepin met with Bess Hawes, director of the National Endowment for the Arts folk arts program, and Alan Jabbour, director of the American Folklife Center at the Library of Congress, among others. They toured Baltimore neighborhoods with Maryland folklorist Charles Camp, the Adams Morgan neighborhood of

Washington with Seitel and Smithsonian folklorist Alicia Gonzalez, and rural Virginia with folklorist Charles Perdue.

Demchenko and Nalepin talked about three levels of folklore—theatrical, amateur, and ethnographic. The last was what real peasants and tribespeople traditionally did or do. These forms of folktale, folk music, craft, ritual, and performance were generally considered to be dying out. Folklorists, ethnologists, and ethnomusicologists conducted historical and analytic studies of these traditions. Theatrical folklore was staged entertainment, supervised by choreographers and artistic directors. It was not authentic folklore but rather performance inspired by peasant and tribal life. Amateur folklore was community-based and even research-based, as enthusiasts from a particular area would join together with a common interest in understanding, preserving, and identifying with the traditional culture of their nationality or region. Their activities typically consisted of singing and dancing, making costumes, and perhaps even demonstrating the crafts and occupational skills of a previous era. Demchenko oversaw and, with his ministry department, supported the activities of these groups through budgetary allocations, publications, and sponsorship of festivals.

Demchenko, and perhaps Nalepin as well, were not all that concerned with reinforcing the divisions between these types of folklore. Ethnographic, amateur, and theatrical folklore all had their place, and they were all legitimate forms of human expression. Further, they were interrelated. Theatrical folklore looked to ethnographic folklore for its inspiration. This was done out of respect for traditional cultural forms, and it mirrored creative practices in Russian literature and classical music. Theatrical folklore troupes also recruited members from local amateur groups that were interested in their region's folklore. Amateurs were motivated by strong feelings for their cultural heritage. These groups grew out of community interest, and their expressions sought to re-create in a literal way traditional ethnographic forms of music, song, dance, and dress. These re-creations took place in a society different from that which had originally given rise to those expressions. Amateur groups were preserving those parts of their culture that could be enacted and that could also give them a sense of identity. Preserving all of one's culture for its own sake did not make much sense to Demchenko or Nalepin. No one seriously expected contemporary people to enact daily routines of a bygone era by using ancient methods of getting food and making things when modern means were more efficient. Those who did were indeed traditional.

From our discussions, from visits to different Washington-area communities, and from observations of the Festival of American Folklife, Demchenko understood our idea of folklife as, as he put it, "a slice of life." For him, we were concerned with ethnographic folklore as contemporary people lived it in daily life. More problematic were our ideas of tradition, authenticity, community-based culture, and cultural conservation, particularly in their application. As Demchenko observed in the festival's Michigan and metropolitan Washington programs, many of the musicians and craftspeople did not appear to be very authentic or traditional. A Washington-area gospel choir had a musical director and regularly scheduled performances in town. The blues musicians played professionally in bars and clubs and produced records for sale. Craftspeople made objects like Ukrainian-style Easter eggs not only for their homes but for sale. For Demchenko, tradition referred to a very particular past. A traditional practice was authentic to the degree that it replicated its original, or socially solidified, articulated, or reified version. The problem for the Smithsonian's festival—or for any other celebration— was that if we were to seek the authenticity of tradition in a literal identity between contemporary and historical practice, we would have a difficult time in finding anything that was truly authentic. And even if we did, the social system within which the practice was embedded would be different now than it was in the past. We would be left with quaint survivals, stripped of their original meaning and social functions. For Demchenko, cultural conservation, as advocated by American folklorists, meant preserving these survivals. As a strategy, it would seem to run against the grain of cultural evolution and operate to the detriment of the very people we cared about.

The Smithsonian Folklife program has operated with a more dynamic idea of tradition. It has used the ideas of "root" and "evolved" traditions to speak about and illustrate continuities and changes in aesthetic forms, occupational practices, and ways of knowing. While tradition may be viewed as a natural, received object by culture bearers (and some scholars), Smithsonian Folklife's focus is on living exemplars and practitioners and has long recognized the process of traditionalization—the culturally negotiated way in which the present is connected to the past. While in this sense all traditions are invented and continually reinvented, questions of authenticity still remain. Who is making or re-making the tradition, and for whom? And to what extent do enactments of the tradition exhibit a historical connection with the aesthetics, knowledge, and skills of the subject community? Smithsonian Folklife has stressed the importance of a community of practice and value in as-sessing questions of authenticity. Festival research guidelines and pre-sentations tend to stress the practices of culture bearers who are recog-nized as traditional and exemplary within their own community.[6] Festival participants are encouraged to illustrate in-group performances, skills, and knowledge rather than those directed toward out-groups. Pre-sentational contexts and selection of repertoire are construed to empha-size local or communal aesthetic and cognitive control over cultural practice, rather than the reception and imitation of the aesthetics and knowledge of others.[7] For Smithsonian Folklife, authenticity is a matter of both cultural continuity and community control. Conserving culture is a matter of a community's having the power to bring forth and alter its own aesthetic, cognitive, normative, manual understandings in con-temporary life—to gain some measure of control over technological, economic, social, and cultural change.

The value that we, in our discussions with Demchenko, placed on the importance of considering community-based cultural practice in re-searching and presenting folklife was juxtaposed with our perceptions of state-run and state-controlled folklore in the Soviet Union. Demchenko argued that many of the amateur folkloric groups under his purview were indeed based in communities, controlled by members, and moti-vated by their own interests, values, and sense of ethnic, regional, or na-tional identity. For Demchenko, much of the diversity of Soviet cultures was preserved through the performances, club activities, festivals, and amateur studies conducted by these groups. For me, Demchenko's argu-ment revealed that the state had effectively penetrated and become the community.

What happens when the culture of the state becomes the culture of the community? Rather than encouraging diverse cultural streams, state control of folklore resulted in the cultural homogenization characterized by particular Russian and Communist Party standards. American folk-lorists, I suggested to Demchenko, have a parallel problem—the penetra-tion of commercial and popular culture into local, regional, and ethnic communities. In the United States, commerce and the marketability of cultural production often become the arbiters of local taste, knowledge, and value. Folklorists, even those employed by agencies of central power that to some extent support the cultural edifice of the larger social order, nonetheless encourage cultural diversity, pluralism, and equity rather than cultural homogenization, and community rather than state control over cultural production.

The discussions and conversations with Demchenko were important for understanding a letter of invitation that he carried from Minister Zakharov to Secretary Adams. The letter announced the "commencement of the program of cooperation in the area of folklore and the preservation and development of folk traditions" and formally invited an "American amateur folklore troupe of up to thirty persons to participate" in the International Folklore Festival in Moscow in August 1988. Minister Zakharov specified that "the troupe should have a performance program lasting no more than one hour, and should present upon request a special program 'Man-Labor-Peace' no more than thirty minutes in length and reflecting labor traditions and rituals." Minister Zakharov also asked for a "description of the creative accomplishments of the recommended troupe, their performance program and promotional materials." He also invited the attendance of two Smithsonian staff who could acquaint themselves with the festival and the development of folklore work in the USSR.[8]

Demchenko also proposed that the Smithsonian feature the Soviet Union at the 1988 Festival of American Folklife. Plans for Swedish participation in the festival had been abandoned just weeks before Demchenko's visit. A decision to mount a program on Soviet cultures would bring parity to the exchange and intensify our developing dialogue. We discussed a modest program that would concentrate mainly on traditional musics of the Soviet Union. So overstated was our concern for the "authentic" and "traditional" and the need to avoid both theatrical performers and amateur hobbyists, that Demchenko responded (and I paraphrase), "If you want, I will bring the kind of people who will hunt squirrels, cook over their fires, and eat on the Mall." We accepted Demchenko's proposal and Minister Zakharov's invitation, subject to funding.

Smithsonian Folklife staff also immediately recognized potential problems in our mutual expectations. We informed Demchenko that the notions of a singular American cultural representation, an amateur troupe, and a contrived program—"Man-Labor-Peace"—to be presented in thirty-minute and hour versions implied a type of performance and group in which the Smithsonian's Office of Folklife Programs had neither interest nor experience. This kind of spurious, contrived, and packaged program, familiar to students of fakelore and folklorismus, is popular at many international folklore festivals and world's fairs or expositions.[9] Such events, organized by such agencies as the Conseil International des Organisations de Festivals de Folklore et d'Art Traditionnels (CIOFF), tend to reify the identification of nation with a national folklore that is almost always a romanticized, theatrical version of a mythologized past. If the ministry wanted a crisply choreographed presentation of American national folklore, replete with national costume, square dance, and hillbillies, then it would be better for it to seek a professional or semiprofessional troupe, such as those that might perform a staged potpourri of "folk dance Americana" at Disneyland. If we were to participate in the Moscow festival, we would send people such as those who would appear in the Smithsonian's Festival of American Folklife. We would send not a singular "American" group but rather a group illustrating the diversity of American society. We would need to know more about the range and coherence of the festival theme, but we could certainly select participants whose repertoire included topical songs or performance items concerning peace, humankind, and occupational culture. Demchenko accepted our participation knowing our concerns. Secretary Adams wrote to Minister Zakharov formally accepting the invitation and promising to send "authentic folk performers to the International Folk Festival."

We also recognized the possible difficulties for the Smithsonian's festival. With Demchenko we agreed to host between thirty and forty "authentic folk singers, musicians and dancers demonstrating traditional, non-stylized performances."[10] We also agreed to work in tandem with Soviet folklorists and ethnomusicologists to decide on the genres to be represented, to generate field documentation of musicians, and to make final program selections. We at the Smithsonian wanted to avoid receiving "an amateur troupe" with characteristics parallel to those suggested in Minister Zakharov's invitation of an American group. Unknown to us were Demchenko's thoughts on the matter, for we were essentially asking him to step outside of his own program at the ministry, and indeed perhaps outside the bounds of the ministry itself, to conceive and sponsor a group such as we had in mind.

In the fall of 1987, Smithsonian Folklife staff began to formulate ideas about the genres and themes to be represented by the Soviet group coming to the Smithsonian festival and the American group going to Moscow. For the Soviet musicians, we decided that an illustration of the richness and diversity of Soviet musical culture was quite appropriate for a modest initial program. Most Americans identified the Soviet Union as Russia. A program spanning several republics and suggesting regional, ethnic, and religious diversity paralleling and even exceeding that of the United States was deemed to be a strong one. Consulting with Soviet specialist Nick Schidlovsky and Margarita Mazo, a Soviet émigré with a doctorate from Leningrad and a former Harvard ethnomusicologist then in residence at the Woodrow Wilson Center for Scholars, we developed a detailed list of traditional musical genres from throughout the Soviet Union.

The genres were major ones in the cultural life of the regions and were, we thought, presentable on the Mall. In a letter to Demchenko, we specified that "all groups or individuals should be community-based artists who have learned in a traditional way and who perform in an authentic non-stylized manner. It is understood that we will depend on our Soviet scholarly colleagues to identify and document groups and individuals."[11] Included in the documentation we asked for were sound recordings with accompanying logs, still photos, slides or videos of the musicians in performance contexts, and a written report describing the genres and styles, the social context of contemporary performance, the historical background of the tradition, the biographies of the performers, the repertoires of musicians, and translations of selected songs. We also suggested that Rinzler and Mazo visit Moscow in November to confer with Demchenko, Nalepin, and other scholars, such as one of Mazo's former teachers, ethnomusicologist Eduard Alexeev, who was vice chairman of the Folklore Commission at the Soviet Composers Union.

Our offer on how to proceed was accepted, as was Rinzler and Mazo's visit. Rinzler and Mazo had a hectic weeklong trip in Moscow, meeting with officials and scholars and learning about the work of various institutions, including the Folklore Commission, the Moscow Conservatory of Music, the Gnesin Institute, the All Union Art Research Institute, Melodiya Records, and the Moscow Ensemble of Folk Music. Rinzler was impressed by the serious scholarship at many of these organizations. Scholars carried out field expeditions, generally produced descriptive, analytic, and theoretical works, attended conferences, and occasionally recorded performances of folk performers when they were in town. He noted strong collections of field material and the penchant for those interested in folk music to be trained through performance instruction. Presentation of traditional material was accomplished by these organizations largely by the pressing of records through Melodiya. What most impressed Rinzler in Moscow was the powerful style and delivery of the Soviet songs he heard on field tapes while visiting these organizations. He noted that it would be difficult to select contemporary American groups that could match that vocal power.

Rinzler met with Demchenko and Moscow festival director Tamara Gavrilova to discuss the American side of the exchange. The Soviets clearly wanted a delegation to represent the participation of the United States as one of many nations in the festival—and a most prestigious one at that. The group's performance should address the stated festival theme, they said. Beyond that, they would leave the internal structure of the group up to the Smithsonian. Our concerns about mediated and stylized performance, traditionality and authenticity were not issues for the Moscow festival.

With Demchenko as key anchorperson, Rinzler and Mazo set up relationships with several folklorists and ethnomusicologists to serve as specialists who would help identify and document musicians who might then travel to Washington to participate in the Smithsonian's festival. Demchenko agreed to rely upon such specialists, although several suggestions for including some youth ensembles were lightly made. The ministry and the specialists agreed to develop preliminary recommendations for the Smithsonian to look at by January.

In the spring, the Smithsonian did receive such recommendations and some tapes, but little other documentation. Nonetheless, the groups represented the genres originally suggested, and from what we could ascertain, they seemed to be appropriate for participation in the Smithsonian festival. We anticipated that there would be some battles in the USSR over the groups to be presented.

We later found out that we were correct. Some people in the ministry took the position that the Smithsonian could not possibly want "real peasants" to perform in Washington. They were sure we were trying to embarrass the Soviet Union. While other nations would be represented at the Smithsonian's festival by superb, highly trained, artistic troupes, the Soviet Union would be made to look foolish by having peasant women and Siberian tribesmen. The Soviet folklorists and ethnomusicologists countered that the Smithsonian's festival was more ethnographic and had as participants only authentic, traditional folk practitioners.

Apparently Demchenko and Nalepin, bolstered by Alexeev and other scholars, prevailed. In the end the Soviet contingent was indeed composed mainly of people from the represented communities who had maintained their traditions and their local aesthetics without benefit of formal training or schooling. There were, however, cases that were harder to classify, and later Nalepin intimated that the selections represented a "middle level" of community-based groups. A women's choral group from southern Russia was traditional and developed locally in the rural village of Podserednee. But the Azeri group played *mugam,* a regional genre that is locally and historically supported by a schooled and formal tradition. The Yakut *homuz* (jaw's harp) player had become a professor in his native Siberia and wrote about the instrument; he was not a shaman, but he used the drum in some of his performance. The Estonians played a bagpipe type of instrument made from a fox, had learned traditionally through their family, but were also fairly active on the amateur folklore festival circuit.

Upon Rinzler's return to the United States, Smithsonian Folklife staff continued to work on the selection of an American contingent. We wanted to send a diversity of American groups to Moscow to present traditional, community-based material, as we had indicated to Demchenko. Rinzler, Folklife staff—Peter Seitel, Diana Parker, Nick Spitzer, and Tom Vennum—and Joe Wilson, director of the National Council for the Traditional Arts (NCTA), contributed ideas about our delegation of performers. We finally ended up with a group larger than the Soviets wanted, but we successfully argued that the size was justified given the diversity of material to be presented. Included in the group were Piedmont bluesmen Cephas and Wiggins, the Sioux Indian Badlands Singers, Los Pleneros de la 21, a Puerto Rican *bomba* and *plena* band from New York City, the African American a cappella group Sweet Honey in the Rock, bluegrass performers the Johnson Mountain Boys, Washington, D.C.'s H. D. Cooke Girls Double Dutch Jump Rope Team, and Cajun musicians Eddie Lejeune, Lionel LeLeux, and Bobby Michot.

Discussions about the composition of the American group among organizers in Washington paralleled discussions about the Soviet group in Moscow. Just as there were disagreements in Moscow, so too did Americans argue with each other. Rinzler suggested that we select American groups with strong, "strident" sounds to match the vocal quality of the Soviet groups. Rinzler, influenced by his wife, Kate, also particularly liked the idea of having a children's group demonstrate a nonmusical form of folklife like jumping rope. This would attract the participation of Soviet children and audiences and also illustrate a genre not generally presented as folklore in the USSR.

Several Folklife staff and advisers felt that the choice of Sweet Honey in the Rock was problematic, since they were "too stylized" and "less traditional" than others in the group. This might send the wrong message to the Soviets about what we meant by folklife. Other staff countered that Sweet Honey in the Rock grew out of the contemporary Civil Rights Movement and the Women's Movement as an expression of larger, more diffuse nonlocal communities. Sweet Honey's repertoire was indeed broad-ranging—from traditional sacred music to contemporary styliza-tions. Sweet Honey illustrated the living, adaptable, and transformable element of traditional music. The group respected received African American traditions, and by using and adapting them in contemporary circumstances of community struggle and advocacy, made them their own. Its members were very conscious of their music and its social im-plications, and they could not be easily placed in such other categories as entertainers, revivalists, or hobbyists. Sweet Honey was also quite ex-perienced in performing in a wide variety of circumstances around the world and in local communities throughout the United States. Its pres-ence in the group, its versatility, and its experience would help as we faced uncertain performance situations in the USSR.

Just as we were able to appreciate the arguments and issues facing our Soviet colleagues, so too did they become aware of ours. In Moscow, Sweet Honey's inclusion provoked discussion among Americans and So-viets about the defining features of folklore and how to assess tradition-alized expressions of contemporary social movements.

In addition to sending the American contingent to Moscow, we de-cided to mount a small music stage program featuring these groups at the 1988 Festival of American Folklife. That way they could meet not only each other but also the Soviet musicians at the festival, whom they might see again in Moscow.

Soviet Music at the 1988 Festival of American Folklife

The Soviet groups recommended and selected by Soviet and American scholars arrived in Washington one day before the beginning of the fes-tival. The contingent consisted of the Georgian men's choir Elesea, an Uzbek group from Fergana, Tuvan throat singer Genadii Chash, Lithua-nian and Ukrainian women soloists, and the aforementioned Russian women from Podserednee, the Azerbaijani *mugam* ensemble, the Esto-nian instrumental duo, and the Yakut *homuz* player from Siberia. They were accompanied by Anatoli Kargin, a folklore theorist with the Ministry of Culture's scientific wing; Alexander Medvedev, head of the Russian Folklore Commission; and Izali Zemsovsky, a renowned ethnomusicologist and student of Vladimir Propp.

Presentations were made on two stages: a large one with seating for five hundred under a tent, and a smaller, more intimate outdoor platform with bench space for about one hundred. Each group in the Soviet contingent had blocks of stage time, from twenty minutes to an hour, to present material several times a day, depending upon its needs as negotiated by the performers, Soviet and American scholars, and Smithsonian staff. The smaller stage was used more for demonstrations, workshops, and discussions. American scholars of Soviet musics Ted Levin, Margarita Mazo, Zev Feldman, and Marjorie Balzar helped present the performers by supplying background and historical and biographical information to audiences and translating questions and answers. Sometimes they would demonstrate musical techniques, as, for example, when Levin showed the audience how to produce the sounds of Tuvan throat singing. Since Zemsovsky knew English, he also served as a presenter to the American audiences. Stuard Detmer, a fluent Russian speaker, aided by other staff and two dozen volunteers, looked after the daily needs of the Soviet musicians.

Presentations were supplemented by phototext sign panels and maps that provided background information on the peoples and cultures of the Soviet Union, types of musical genres, music and the life cycle, music and ritual, and other topics. Program books with articles by Mazo and Levin were also available for sale to the public. These provided further information on Soviet musics and cultures and on the performers. Finally, we also sold a Smithsonian Folkways cassette, *Musics of the Soviet Union,* with documentary notes.[12]

Presentations at the festival are fairly informal, characterized by largely spontaneous choice of repertoire, announcers and presenters that the audience can see, openly viewed set changes, gaps in the program, and considerable interaction between performer and audience. Whether or not the Soviet groups were prepared for this, they adapted exceedingly well. The biggest exception was with costuming. Most had quite elaborate costumes. We asked about these costumes and their appropriateness, as well as the contexts back home in which they were worn. Some would be worn on special celebratory occasions, others in performances for out-group audiences. Given the hot, humid Washington summer, we indicated that the costumes (particularly the Siberian furs) were not all that necessary, especially day after day. The clothing they would wear back home to perform for each other or to sing together was fine with us. Indeed, because of the Washington weather, observations of other festival performers, or our suggestions, the Soviet costuming progressively lightened up over the course of the festival, becoming less uniform, less complete, and more casual.

Other types of presentations took place as the Soviet contingent assumed a measure of control over the festival program site and the festival format. One day the Russians from Podserednee set up a wedding feast under some trees, appropriated staff and volunteers, and sang wedding songs and danced, somewhat for the public, somewhat for themselves. Similarly, the Georgians made use of several vats of wine they had brought with them. They coerced some local Georgians to help them cook and prepared a marvelous wedding feast table. A festival aide who was fluent in Russian and our housing coordinator were roped into playing bride and groom. The Georgians used the mock wedding event (at which the bride and groom basically just remained seated as props) to toast, sing, and drink. Visitors to the Mall came upon this as marginal guests, observing others quite busy indulging in wine, song, and oratory.

Various types of cross-cultural performance also occurred at the festival. For the Massachusetts program—also part of the 1988 festival—Italian and Portuguese Americans enacted a Saint's Day procession, similar to those mounted in Boston's North End. Four Saint's Day societies from the Boston area participated. They trucked the sacred statues of their saints to the Mall in Washington to be carried, worshiped, and honored in the procession. Each of the saints was installed in his or her shrine—a wooden structure also transported to the Mall from Boston. On the plot of land devoted to the Massachusetts program, we erected the 30-foot-high and 50-foot-wide decorated cardboard-and-wood band shell used by Italian Americans for Saint's Day concerts in the North End. We installed street decorations and hung lights from jury-rigged scaffolding along a Mall pathway. More than two hundred band members from the four different societies came to the Mall for the event, to play their music and process with their saints. Some 10,000 people joined in the parade of the saints down the Mall and through the festival site.

At one point, the procession—consisting of the carried statues of Saint Anthony, the Madonna, Cosmas, and Damian, four marching bands, and thousands of people—moved past the Soviet area on the Mall. Festival staff were unsure how the Soviet musicians would react.

At the 1988 festival, participants treated the public and Smithsonian staff members to a Georgian wedding feast. Of course, such a feast demanded a wedding; a Folklife staffer and a volunteer obliged. There have been several real weddings at the festival. Photo by Dane Penland, courtesy Smithsonian Institution.

The women from Podserednee broke into traditional Russian songs used to greet the saints. They hadn't sung them for quite some time, and no doubt the Italian and Portuguese Americans had never been greeted in such a fashion. Some of the Russian women prayed and asked for blessings, touching the statues. The Russians sang, even the folklorists sang, and everybody danced and hugged and cried.

Similar interactions ensued as Russian women danced to the music of Greek Americans and sang during our semiprivate clambake, hosted by Massachusetts Quakers. Intimate interchange also occurred, as when musician Mike Seeger, who had been filming Yakut mouth organ player Ivan Alexeev all day, was asked to join him on the small stage for a Siberian-Appalachian version of dueling jaw's harps.

Americans at Moscow's 1988 International Folklore Festival

The American contingent that traveled to Moscow for the International Folklore Festival included performing groups and a support staff. The

Cultural resonances may transcend historical and geographic distances. Russians have a repertoire of traditional greeting songs for saints, but they are rarely used. At the 1988 festival, when Italian and Portuguese Americans from Massachusetts paraded their saints past the Soviet program, the Russians broke into appropriate song and festive dance, then some cried and embraced the paraders. Photo by Laurie Minor, courtesy Smithsonian Institution.

support staff was organized to help frame presentations, provide translations for audiences, and look after the technical and housekeeping needs of the group. The staff included Smithsonian deputy assistant secretary for public service James Early, who served as spokesperson for the group and presented an overview of American cultures at performances; myself; ethnomusicologist and Soviet specialist Ted Levin, who translated, coordinated our participation, and made presentations during performances; Simon Carmel, a folklorist who knew Russian and Russian sign language and interpreted for deaf audiences during performances; Elaine Hyman, a Russian speaker who helped translate and coordinate the group; translator and logistics coordinator Stuard Detmer; sound engineer Pete Reiniger; and Smithsonian scholars Bernice Reagon (who also led Sweet Honey in the Rock) and Nick Spitzer, who documented our presentations and experiences through photos and recordings for a Radio Smithsonian program.[13] In addition, we carried with us 40,000 flyers with program notes in Russian describing the groups and traditions represented and Masonite signs, in English and Russian, presenting photos and text material on American cultures. Short of building our own context-sensitive performance sites, we were equipped with a full complement of techniques for presenting, framing, and interpreting the represented traditions.

Our group stayed at the Olympic Village, on the outskirts of Moscow, with other groups from capitalist countries. Socialist-country delegations and those of Soviet republics and "fraternal" nations stayed in a downtown hotel. Given our distance from downtown Moscow and the central festival venues—Gorky Park and various concert halls—we generally left the Olympic Village early in the morning and returned late at night. This meant we had to carry our instruments, signs, brochures, and equipment with us all day. During his previous trips to Moscow Levin had negotiated with festival organizers to ensure that we would have venues where our whole group could put on an uninterrupted performance of several hours on our own stage with our own equipment. We would also have to participate in the various ceremonial parades, the opening and closing concerts, and special events. We had very little prior knowledge of these events and almost no control over their conceptualization and the structure surrounding our participation. The larger framing of the festival, and hence how we were presented, was not in our hands. We also learned that CIOFF was working with the Soviet Ministry of Culture to organize the festival. CIOFF is a federation that presents and promotes folklore internationally. It is recognized by the United Nations, with each nation entitled to one membership. Most memberships are centered in ministries of culture, some reside with various types of national organizations, with some or no governmental affiliation. Its folklore festivals have as their stated goals the encouragement of brotherhood among and understanding between cultures. CIOFF festivals tend to be large spectacles of a theatrical character that reify notions of national culture and make grandiose claims about humanity and art. Their pageantry is similar to the opening and closing ceremonies of the Olympics.[14]

This was made apparent on the first day of the festival. We were told to "dress in national costume" and then report to buses for the journey to Gorky Park. When we saw the costumes and the youth of the participants from France, Spain, the United Kingdom, and other nations, we realized that we would be in the midst of a theatrical event, involving amateur folklore clubs, dance academy people, and the like—as a Soviet musician said, it was a festival for "souvenir folklore." When we got to Gorky Park and saw a large sign announcing our participation in the festival, this became even more certain. The sign indicated that we were the "Smithsonian Folk Ensemble," representing the United States, and that Ted Levin was our "artistic director."

At Gorky Park we were asked to take our place for a rehearsal of the opening ceremonies parade of participants. We were given a standard to bear as we marched in the parade. The standard had a cloth banner, decorated with a northwest coast American Indian eagle motif, and the letters "США" (Russian abbreviation for "USA") inscribed on its top. We didn't bring an American flag, so our Russian hosts provided one. Along with the other twenty-five nations, contingents from the Soviet republics, and local groups, we rehearsed our march into a large plaza in Gorky Park.

Later that afternoon, we participated in the opening promenade, some of our musicians playing percussion instruments as we marched up onto a large stage and were announced to Soviet television cameras, assembled officialdom, and the other participants. The show featured stylized performances of Soviet youth groups backed by prerecorded music. In front of the stage, water plumes in the Gorky Park fountain rose and fell to the beat of the music. A well-known Russian "folk" singer sang salutes to the event, and officials, including Minister Zakharov and Politburo member Ligachev, gave speeches. Each national and republic contingent stood in an assigned space in the Gorky Park plaza. The arrangement of groups in lines and columns suggested to me the symbolic orderly arrangement and containment of national cultures under the rubric of international folkloric understanding, an example of what many have seen as folklore's being used purposefully, and cynically, in service of the authoritarian state and, now, the global order.[15]

At the end of the ceremonies the orderly array of the groups broke down as literally hundreds of musicians played their instruments, people sang, and members of different groups intermixed in a myriad of dances. From one perspective this display could be viewed as programmed spontaneity—a demonstration of the disordered "folk" prone to happy celebration. From another, it allowed individuals and groups of artists to control their own participation, to be curious and to explore the art of numerous others. Our girls' Double Dutch Team, for example, demonstrated various rope-jumping routines, an art unfamiliar to participants at the festival. They soon had many others from Siberia, Eastern Europe, and Russia trying their feet at jumping rope, observing the girls' skills, and asking questions about the tradition.

On that first day we also found out that we were to provide a five-minute performance for the televised three-hour opening concert on a large stadium stage. Festival organizers wanted our "whole troupe" to make a brief appearance. We suggested instead that the Badlands Singers, representing the first "Americans," perform at the powwow drum, since we were not a singular troupe. The six members of the Badlands group demonstrated their beating of the drum, calls, and the dancing of Ben Gray Hawk in the rehearsal. The Soviet artistic director for the opening concert found this performance problematic. It did not have the choreography and the theatrical air of performances by the other, larger troupes, and it failed to fill the stage. A Siberian Yakut troupe had rehearsed its very stylized performance just before the Indians went on, and the artistic director suggested that that troupe stay onstage to provide background to the Badlands group. They did and we tried it. There was still not enough movement to please the artistic director, who then suggested that the Yakuts, dressed in their stage outfits, sway to and fro in background, waving their hands. This he liked.

The opening concert was tightly organized, strongly choreographed, and visually impressive. The 10,000-seat stadium was populated by festival participants and constituted a "backstage" to a performance for television cameras. Various troupes processed on cue to the stage, which was framed by the festival's emblems and decorated with snowflake-patterned backdrops derived from traditional textile motifs. The show was run with directions and theatrical presentations developed for the concert stage. Traditional artists were used occasionally as props or tokens. An older Russian woman was set to one side of the stage to weave on an old loom and was, at intervals, the subject of a panning camera. Another presentation used about thirty seconds of jaw's harp performance and throat singing to help identify the home region of the troupe and then made way for a large ensemble and Moiseyev-like production. Indeed, any doubts we had about the character of the festival were dispelled when Moiseyev himself appeared onstage to deliver salutary remarks about the importance of folklore and the festival.

We were included in various other outdoor and concert hall presentations and asked to do five-, fifteen-, or thirty-minute performances. Almost always we identified one or two of our groups for such performances and insisted on verbal introduction and presentation, sign language trans-

The Badlands Singers, a Sioux group from Montana, played powwow songs for Soviet audiences during the opening of the 1988 Folklore Festival in Moscow. Native peoples of Siberia are in the background, as requested by the Soviet artistic director. Photo by Nick Spitzer, courtesy Smithsonian Institution.

lation, and distribution of our program notes. The one exception was for the closing concert, for which we were to present, as a troupe, a performance reflecting the theme. We chose the peace theme and, guided by Bernice Reagon's tutelage and experience, managed a group rendition of "Study War No More" for an appreciative audience. This particular performance was framed by large video-screen projections of a collage of American images—Bob Dylan in concert, civil rights marches, and touristic views of American cities—prepared by our Soviet hosts.

On the whole, our experiences in fitting into the concert-stage format, as defined in terms different from our own and discounting our ability to exercise control, were quite trying. We continually ran into the constraints of being initially perceived, mistakenly, to be like the other choreographed ensembles and of having to adjust to the demands of television production and a concert-hall ethos of theatrical production. This even extended to technical requirements, as sound systems were geared not to bluesmen or gospel singers but to theatrical productions, for example, with omnidirectional hanging microphones that had no onstage monitors.

We did have several venues where we had a stage to ourselves and put on a half-day's performance as we might do at the Smithsonian's festival. In these cases our groups had time to develop their material and exhibit a selection of their repertoire. Presenters and performers talked, explained, interpreted, and otherwise conveyed—through audience participation, for example—some sense of the history and social context of their art. Informal bluegrass and blues jam sessions, jumping rope, drumming, and other activities often occurred offstage with interested Soviet visitors and festival participants from other groups.

Our most successful venue was a low-tech, lengthy, and gripping performance at a "house of culture" in Leninski Prospekt, a collective farm town some forty miles outside of Moscow. When we arrived, we were met by local resident members of an amateur folkloric troupe and greeted with Russian song and the traditional gift of bread. Led by Bernice Reagon and Sweet Honey in the Rock, we reciprocated in song and gifts. We toured the farm during the day, viewed the home of Lenin, ate with community leaders, and in the evening gave our performance in the equivalent of a school auditorium.

Townspeople had either seen some of our previous performances on television, heard us on the radio, or read about the U.S. group in the newspapers. The turnout of perhaps a thousand people overflowed the auditorium—uniformed guards had to lock the front door. Our group was energized by the attention from local working-class people and the homey feel of the place. Program notes were snapped up, the audience hung on every word of the background presentations, studied bluesmen Cephas and Wiggins, stomped their feet to the Cajuns, cheered the Double Dutch girls, and danced to Los Pleneros. The event was emotionally moving and culminated with townspeople dancing onstage and in the crowded aisles with each other and with members of the American contingent.

In addition to the performances, members of our group met on several occasions with Soviet scholars and officials. A formal conference on folklore failed to materialize, since the Soviet Folklore Commission pulled out of the event, its scholars arguing that the Moscow festival was too theatrical, too disconnected from the city's populace and the people represented. Alexeev, among many others, found little in the festival that suggested his own ethnographic experiences and was critical of the festival's attempt to "put folklore on the concert stage." These Soviet folklorists and ethnomusicologists found the festival's presentation of culture to be a diversion from the more serious issues of cultural identity,

The Johnson Mountain Boys, a bluegrass group from the Washington area, played to rapt audiences during a performance at a local house of culture outside of Moscow as part of the Smithsonian folklife exchange program. Photo by Nick Spitzer, courtesy Smithsonian Institution.

human and cultural rights facing the larger society. Nonetheless, some small meetings and demonstration workshops were held in Gorky Park, as, for example Cephas, Wiggins, and Spitzer giving a workshop on the blues, demonstrating aspects of the tradition and discussing issues of style, repertoire, and performance context with Soviet folklorists and ethnomusicologists.

While the festival was clearly not organized on the same principles as our own, we did manage to communicate to many people the power and diversity of American grassroots performance traditions. We received a great deal of attention from the media. And while we might have been uncomfortable with the spectacular and theatrical nature of the festival, its lack of framed educational presentation and intimacy, we could not deny that folklore occasioned significant government support and occupied significant cultural space in the USSR. How often in the United States are traditional musics aired on television to reach mass audiences, and how well are they presented? U.S. network television's treatment of traditional culture is extremely limited, and programs like *Hee Haw* have presented awful stereotypic refractions of regional culture as entertainment. The Soviet festival and the infrastructure upon which it was based represented the mobilization of massive resources in the service of regional, ethnic, and cultural heritage. U.S. government resources for such purposes seemed quite meager in comparison.

Some of us reviewed our thoughts on the Moscow festival with Demchenko. Many of our criticisms resonated with those heard by the ministry from Soviet audiences and scholars. U.S. participation, intimated Demchenko, had served as a catalyst for more discussion about alternative models of inclusion and presentation under the folklore rubric.

Continuing the Festival Presentations

Following these public performance programs, both the Smithsonian and the Soviet Ministry of Culture explored other forms of collaboration. Anthony Seeger, director of Smithsonian Folkways Recordings, and I visited Moscow and Kiev in May 1989 to discuss joint research and recording possibilities with the ministry, Melodiya Records, and the Folklore Commission. This led to the issue of a recording titled *Tuva: Voices from the Center of Asia* (1990) on Smithsonian Folkways, based on work by Levin, Alexeev, and Zoya Kirgiz.[16]

We also visited Kiev to review planning for the 1990 International Folklore Festival, which was continuing along the Ministry of Culture plan of biennial folklore conferences and festivals. We were assured that the Second International Folklore Festival would host traditional performers in addition to theatrical and amateur troupes, but we were surprised when asked to attend "auditions" by the local organizers.

During the summer of 1989, Alexeev and Kargin visited the Smithsonian's festival in Washington to work on the contours of a joint research project between the two nations. Kargin also wanted to secure American participation in the Kiev festival. In exchange, the Smithsonian's Folklife office endorsed the proposal of the National Council for the Traditional Arts to have a Soviet contingent participate in the 1990 National Folk Festival held in Johnstown, Pennsylvania. In December 1989, Kargin and ministry liaison Vladimir Selivestrov came to Washington to firm up agreements on research and festival exchanges and to visit the site of the National Folk Festival.

The Second International Folklore Festival was held in Kiev in May 1990. A symposium, cosponsored by the Ukraine Academy of Sciences and UNESCO and titled "Folklore in the Contemporary World," was held in conjunction with the festival.

The Smithsonian sent an American contingent to Kiev that included Philadelphia tap dancer Lavaughn Robinson, Allison Krauss and the Union Station bluegrass band, dancers and chanters of the Kanakaole Hula Halau, a Tex-Mex duet of Jimmy Santiago y su Conjunto, and the New Orleans Young Tuxedo Brass Band. Performers were aided by presenter Joe Wilson, coordinator Richard Kennedy, sound engineer Reiniger, translator Detmer, and myself. Scholars of Soviet cultures Mark Slobin (Wesleyan, president of the Society for Ethnomusicology), Margarita Mazo (Ohio State), Bill Noll (Harvard), Richard Dauenhauer (Alaska), and Ruth Thomasian (Project Save) would participate in the symposium and help develop a longer-term collaborative research project proposed by the Smithsonian and the Ministry of Culture.

Although some of the Americans had written papers and wanted to formally present them to the symposium, they were left out of the program. The symposium was largely of uninspired quality. Despite the stated theme, there was a general lack of coherence to the papers. The presentations were rather staid and poorly translated, and they rarely generated discussion. The final plenary session, ostensibly scheduled to sum up results, was used to host a men's choral group wearing tuxedos and performing medieval chants. It was rather bizarre for me, but as several Soviet colleagues confided, it was considered rather normal. Many conferences were held, expectations were low, argument and substantive results infrequent.

The Kiev festival seemed to be a replay of the Moscow festival, with the same types of domestic and international groups. Again the American contingent was the exception. Unlike other groups, we were internally diverse, did not have choreographed and highly stylized performances, insisted on interpretative presentations to frame our performance, had program notes to give to audiences, and were composed of people from the societies or communities bearing the traditions represented.

Unlike our accommodations at the Moscow festival, in Kiev we were housed in a nicer, downtown hotel, had more and better food to eat, had greater flexibility in participating in the festival schedule, and seemed to be listened to when we complained. There was more effort to be nicer to capitalist-country delegations than in Moscow two years before. We did cause our hosts some trouble because we were more egalitarian than expected. The Soviets had arranged for scholars to be treated differently than performers were—the former got single rooms facing the main street, the latter got double rooms facing back streets. Scholars and performers were supposed to have separate buses for tours, separate tables for meals, and so on. The American contingent ignored these distinctions, causing problems for Soviet festival personnel and hotel staff.

In Kiev we had come prepared for the type of marching and Olympic-like spectacle that we expected to encounter in a CIOFF-produced festival. We had seven members of the Young Tuxedo Brass Band, who generally performed while parading in the streets of New Orleans. Their renditions and remarkable presence led the rest of the American group, which fell in behind them on the parade route through downtown Kiev, much to the delight of several hundred thousand spectators. As we began to enjoy the parade and get into the spirit, Edward DiLima, one of the Hawaiian hula dancers, lifted an umbrella and danced in front of the band, as is done in New Orleans. We did have an American flag this time, but alas, festival organizers had asked us not to fly it. They wanted the festival to be "nonpolitical" and were apparently worried about the flying of the Ukrainian national flag (as opposed to the state, Communist flag) and the flags of the Baltic Republics. We acceded to their wishes. As we later saw, the Baltic Republics did not.

We marched into a stadium where the eighty or so international delegations and the Soviet republic and Ukrainian folklore contingents were assembled. A crowd of about 20,000 cheered, the stadium scoreboard sent out messages, television cameras were everywhere. It was an impressive spectacle, with each group parading around the stadium track, sections of the audience cheering on cue and displaying various stylized patterns with hand-held cards. The music we played or the traditions that members of the group had nurtured did not seem important to the audience or the organizers—we could hardly be heard. We were cheered for being American and for being in Kiev to participate in the festival.

After taking our assigned seats, we heard and watched the opening ceremonies. We saw rock musicians described as "folk artists," heard "folk music" composed by professional and renowned composers, and witnessed a wonderfully costumed, beautifully choreographed depiction of Ukrainian folk culture involving a cast of thousands, several orchestras, massive fireworks, horses, riders, and hot-air balloons. It was the height of folklore as theater, displayed to millions over Soviet television.

Our stay in Kiev involved a lot of sight-seeing, and while our group liked and appreciated this, we were frustrated by not having the opportunity to play our music, sing our songs, and dance our dances for the people of Kiev. For our first performance we were given five minutes onstage after having waited for several hours.

Our second performance was to be in the town of Kanyev, three hours south of Kiev. We thought this would be a great opportunity to bring American musics to the people of rural Ukraine. In Kanyev, after lunch downtown, we were told by the Ministry of Culture official that we would be taken ten miles out of town to an exclusive Dnieper River site to perform for amateur folklore groups from Finland, Latvia, and Ukraine. We were in the center of town, there were plenty of people around, why not just play right there? our musicians asked. Despite the reluctance of ministry and local officials, the Young Tuxedo Brass Band, then Allison Krauss and Union Station, then Jimmy Santiago y su Conjunto played their music on the pavement of a downtown street corner. We attracted a large, if surprised, crowd and passed out notes explaining the music.

We later did go to the out-of-town site. The audience consisted solely of three other folkloric groups also participating in the Kiev festival and Mrs. Silkova, the deputy minister of culture of the Soviet Union. She left, however, before a stunning presentation of Hawaiian chant and hula and an intimate join-in-and-dance bluegrass performance.

On our return to Kiev, Joe Wilson and I met with the Soviet festival organizers. We wanted enough time to frame and present our material so that Soviet people would know or understand who in America does these things and why. We wanted to engage our audiences and effect an intimacy with them so they could appreciate the artistry of the traditions represented in the group. The organizers told us to perform on a stage in a Kiev park the next day.

The next morning it was drizzling, so we were forced to perform indoors at a park pavilion, which was, alas, hosting a numismatic show and market. No one was expecting us. Across the street was a complex of very tall apartment buildings. Big Al, a member of the Young Tuxedo Brass Band, suggested we "march through the projects" with the jazzmen in the lead, making music and drawing a crowd. We took up Big Al's suggestion. People in the apartments looked out their windows and came out on balconies. Some tossed down coins and flowers. During pauses, Detmer yelled up to people and told them to come to the pavilion for a full performance. We were enacting the anti-spectacle of the opening ceremonies, a low-tech, do-it-yourself, capture-the-audience performance. It was difficult, but it worked.

Following this, many of our group's musicians decided to "just do our stuff on the streets" of Kiev. We set up an area outside our hotel for jazz, string, and *conjunto* sessions. I don't think the festival organizers knew what to make of us, and we stopped traffic down Kiev's main boulevard several times. But we reached audiences and engaged people who stayed for hours to get a sense of the aesthetics and texture of several American musical traditions.

Our performances on subsequent days in Kiev's central park and on the factory floors and in the social halls of the Leninski Shipyards were more in this style. Each of the American groups had adequate time to present its performance. The audiences were close up and intimately involved. Performers or presenters were able to talk about the traditions and pass out explanatory material. We did not, however, participate in a "costumed street carnival evening" (which featured large air-filled cartoon characters on floats) or in the festival's closing ceremonies.

At a dinner celebrating the closing of the festival, Richard Kennedy, upon being publicly asked by the minister of culture of Uzbekistan if the United States would participate in the next International Folklore Festival, scheduled for Tashkent in 1992, replied most appropriately and ambiguously, "Insha Allah" (God willing)—a phrase well known among Muslims and others in central Asia. It might mean "I hope so," or also "perhaps," "it's out of my control," or "I don't know."

We did discuss the festival with Demchenko and Deputy Minister of Culture Silkova and informed them that the participation of the Smithsonian was unlikely if the festival was going to follow the same model. I had covered the ground previously with Demchenko—the Kiev festival had many of the same problems as the Moscow festival. I was somewhat angry and frustrated by the Kiev experience (as were others in our group) and was quite direct in speaking with Silkova. The festival located folk culture in a fictionalized and disembodied yet idealized past. It avoided any serious treatment or presentation of the culture of contemporary people, even Kiev's urban street culture. It was too big and too diffuse, and it had no educational value. It failed to address real issues of identity, cultural continuity, control, and practices bearing on various cultural policies. The presentational mode was an entertainment spectacle with no attempt at interpretation, intimacy, or educational engagement.

Almost all the delegations were made up of dance academy personnel or amateur enthusiasts who bore little relationship to the carriers of the traditions represented—or, more likely, misrepresented through stylization.

Silkova first argued that "every nation had the right to present folklore in their own way." Surely the United States was not telling the Soviet Union how it should deal with folklore. Later she proposed that the festival was successful because it offered a "good time for everyone during a difficult period of transition in the Soviet Union." It was a happy, entertaining, diversionary spectacle. Authenticity, scholarship, and presentation were not really their concerns. Finally she said, Soviet organizers were "not yet ready for the real folklore."

In our conversation I did not want to discount the fact that the festivalization of "traditional culture" was meaningful to many people. I did, however, want to stress that forms of folklore were to be found in the daily life of Kiev's people. We discussed contemporary forms of Soviet urban folklore—stories about standing in line and occupational folklife—as examples of cultural expressions that had no place in the festival but were, nonetheless, types of folklore that might resonate with and address broad social concerns. The ministry, I argued, needed a new policy of "cultural *perestroika* and *glasnost.*"

Joe Wilson, the director of NCTA, did want the "real thing" in folklore, and he spent some time in Kiev and Moscow trying to make sure that the ministry would send performers to the United States who would be suitable for participating in the National Folk Festival in Johnstown, Pennsylvania, August 31 to September 2, 1990. Wilson, in conjunction with the Smithsonian's Folklife office, had requested that the ministry compose and send a contingent of authentic, traditional performers from a number of specified genres. Again, enforcing our own notion of folklife and trying to be clear in signaling what we wanted from the ministry, we had written, "As you know from last year, we are not like Western Europeans in our appreciation of folk arts. We prefer the real folk to folk imitators in every case. So the artists you suggest to us do not need to be young, pretty and wonderfully costumed. It's okay if they are older and have lines of experience in their face."[17]

I confirmed arrangements for Soviet participation in the National Folk Festival during a subsequent trip to Moscow in August. NCTA welcomed a Georgian men's choir, a Russian vocal group, Tuvans, and others to its festival, where they performed admirably and fit in quite well, helped by translators, presenters, and festival organizers.

Soviet-American Folklife Research and Presentation Project

Based upon the success of the performance programs and their continu-
ation, scholars and officials associated with them were able to generate
enough interest, and funds, to initiate a long-term collaborative research
project. This project grew out of possibilities foreseen from the very first
contacts, to in-depth discussions between Smithsonian staff and Soviet
scholars, to gatherings of folklorists and ethnomusicologists from the
two countries and the signing of a formal protocol in Kiev.

The Soviet-American Folklife Research and Presentation project was
built on the facts that approximately 10 percent of the U.S. populace has
its roots in regions of the Soviet Union and that both the United States
and the Soviet Union are modern, technologically advanced nation-
states with populations that exhibit considerable cultural diversity. The
project sought to examine how various root traditions, having their origin in the Soviet Union, have continued and been transformed both in
Soviet society and in the American context.

The first phase of the project joined Soviet and American folklorists,
ethnomusicologists, cultural anthropologists, and scholars from related
fields in teams to carry out field research and analyses on American communities that had their origins in the Soviet Union and on cognate Soviet communities in the USSR. In the two pilot projects, Ted Levin
worked with Atanazar Matyakubov of Tashkent State Conservatory to
study Bukharan Jewish musical culture in long-lived Jewish communities of Bukhara, Uzbekistan, and in a more recently formed Bukharan
Jewish immigrant community in Queens, New York. Margarita Mazo
worked with Serafima Nikitina of the Soviet Academy of Sciences and
Irina Pozdeva of Moscow University to examine language use, narrative,
and music among Molokans in Stravapol, Russia, as well as in Oregon,
Los Angeles, and Fresno, California.

Other studies involved research on Ukrainians in Boston and in
L'vov, and Native peoples in Siberia and in Alaska. Future studies were
being developed for Armenians, Russians, and others. The research was
to result in scholarly articles and monographs, documentary recordings
and videos, and a living cultural exhibition to be mounted in Washington at the Festival of American Folklife one year and in Moscow the
next, assuming that funding could be found.

The project also revealed institutional considerations in the two
countries. While a formal protocol did exist between the Smithsonian

and the Soviet Ministry of Culture, neither was able to implement it without the cooperation and expertise of other institutions and individuals. The Smithsonian lacked any scholar or curator with expertise in Soviet or Soviet American cultures and had to call upon Mazo, Levin, Slobin, Dauenhauer, Thomasian, Noll, and others for advice and participation. The Folklife office also had to raise funds for the project through internal Smithsonian grants, external grants, and in-kind support. These limitations made the Folklife office painfully aware of the difficulty of conceptually occupying itself with another country without the scholarly presence necessary to understand not only the folk cultures of the place but its official, bureaucratic, and academic cultures as well. The project's potential for generating intriguing research and policy ideas did enable the Folklife office to successfully justify Smithsonian support for a position and funds to support the project, though final congressional appropriations never materialized.

The project necessitated similar actions in the former Soviet Union. The ministry had to call upon some of the scholars and organizations under its general purview to work on the project and provide fiscal support, e.g., Kargin and the Russian Research Institute, Alexeev in his capacity at the Cultural Institute, Melodiya Records, and others. The ministry also had to team up with the Academy of Sciences, the Composers Union, and others in coordinating, funding, and supporting project scholars and other costs. While this occasioned some reflection within the ministry about its own limitations, it also led to increased flexibility and greater awareness of research-based cultural exchange activities.

Post–Cold War Folklore

In July 1990 the new minister of culture of the USSR, Nikolai Gubenko, asked for the resignation of ministry staff and reappointed those whom he felt would help to realize his vision of a new ministry. Motivated by *perestroika* and attendant democratic movements in the USSR, this new ministry would encourage and support the cultural creativity of grassroots organizations rather than dictate a cultural canon. The new ministry would seek out a diversity of ethnic, regional, religious, and other groups previously excluded from support and encouragement. It would encourage internal and external collaborative efforts and seek to firm up financial support of cultural activities through self-financing and other "entrepreneurial" means. Among the changes effected at the ministry was a reorganization that took folklore out of the realm of theater and associated it with cultural policy concerns and issues of ethnic and national identity.

This new orientation and the impact of our cultural exchange program were made explicit when Minister Nikolai Gubenko visited Washington in November 1990. In a meeting at the Smithsonian, the folklife exchange was summarized and reviewed. In my remarks, I noted how American folklorists have attempted to define their field in relationship to cultural policy concerns, particularly the encouragement, understanding, and public presentation of cultural diversity. I noted that the question of national culture and ethnic diversity was a major historical and continuing issue in the United States and of obvious major contemporary importance in the USSR. Minister Gubenko agreed and thought that our joint program could help in dealing with the issue, as it was so large, complex, and vital to the future of his nation.

Minister Gubenko also presented an interesting proposal for joint large-scale, yearlong, multi-venue, artistically broad-ranging festivals (on the model of the Festival of India in the United States) in both countries. One component of the Soviet festival would be devoted to traditional culture. As indicated in Minister Gubenko's proposal, "this would consist of various programs to show the folklore of the peoples of the U.S.S.R. (*previously they showed pseudo-folklore, staged by state controlled choirs and groups, now we can show authentic folklore groups*)."[18] Minister Gubenko also indicated that the programs should show "multinational culture and the fate of cultural traditions during the Soviet era. It is important to show the unvarnished truth of our cultural reality and to reveal the drama of our national culture."

Our own language for presenting folklore and folklife had returned to us. The negation of the ministry's previous state support for folklore activity may overlook real achievements in the conservation of culture, as Alan Lomax has reminded me and Soviet colleagues on several occasions. The encouragement of amateur groups has inculcated people with a sense of regional, ethnic, and national identity, brought folk aesthetics into mainstream consciousness and public view, and nurtured an interest in and respect for traditional culture among a sizable segment of Soviet youth. Yet the shift, away from theater and folklore as entertainment to folklife as real life, entwined with contemporary issues of identity, style, cultural and political rights, seemed both timely and well grounded.

Our joint research projects continued. But the backdrop changed. In December 1991 Secretary Adams met with the ministers of culture of the various republics on the eve of the dissolution of the Soviet state. They warned Adams that America should beware, that the cultural diversity that undermined the Soviet Union will lead to the downfall of the United States as well.[19] They had finally seen the power of people's culture, the culture connected to identity and real life, and their attempts to construe a state-controlled folklore had failed to suppress that culture.

After the dissolution of the Soviet Union, we signed protocols with the governments of Russia and Ukraine. We continued the dialogue with numerous organizations and went on with our collaborative work. In 1995, at the Smithsonian's Festival of American Folklife, we produced a program that included Molokans—spiritual Christians—from Russia and from the San Francisco area, and Old Believers from Russia and from Erie, Ohio. This program brought together communities long separated by decades and by thousands of miles to explore and examine dimensions of their cultural practices—particularly religious ones. Members of Molokan and Old Believer communities found expected similarities and parallels. Some American Old Believers, listening to their Russian counterparts, rediscovered sacred songs from their youth. And interestingly enough, Russian Old Believers were invigorated by the American Old Believer preservation of the ancient neume notational system, *kriuki,* for singing *znamennyi* liturgical chants.[20]

The program also had other, somewhat unpredictable effects on those who participated. The Old Believers from southern Russian had to travel through roadblocks in Chechniya and even fend off an attempt to hijack their caravan. The Molokans from Russian came early, stayed in San Francisco, and shared with the community there. For the Americans, too, there were dramatic, even surprising results. Consider the effect of the festival experience on Edward Samarin, one of the Molokan leaders, who noted in a letter to us:

> I grew up in a very Russian, very Molokan community in San Francisco. I never really thought of myself in any other way other than as a Russian Molokan. I guess we were very insular, and did not see our connections to anyone else. The Festival has now changed all this. Standing on the Mall, seeing the wealth of cultural heritage under those beautiful trees in the midst of Washington, I had the realization, and the feeling for the first time in my life that I too was an American. That I had a place here. And that my Russian, Molokan heritage made me part of America, not separate from it.[21]

Our program had now come full circle. What had begun as a binational governmental exchange to stage presentations of each other's cultures to large audiences had become a matter of individual self-discovery about one's own transnational culture and its relationship to the broader society. A superpower had fallen, folklorists and officials on both sides had learned some lessons, and the world seemed to get a bit smaller. And if Edward Samarin was right, the Soviet ministers of culture were wrong: Diversity could be a strength for America, not its undoing.

CHAPTER 11

AMERICA'S REUNION ON THE MALL
A PRESIDENTIAL INAUGURAL

N egotiating the idea of national culture and ways to present it with the Russians was good practice for dealing with officials, leaders, and politicians in the United States. Mass events, offering either implicit or explicit visions of national identity and culture, give insight into policy orientations. The Soviet and Russian festivals indicated how some organizations of governments and how particular leaders imagined their country at a crucial time. The Festival of India provided feedback for government leaders about how Indian culture could be seen and how internal policy might change to support the artistry of impoverished performers and craftspeople. In this chapter, I discuss America's Reunion on the Mall, an event produced for the inauguration of President Bill Clinton in January 1993. America's Reunion on the Mall became a way of articulating a vision of American culture through a presentation at the inception of a new presidency. It came at the end of a rough election in which the politics of culture—termed the "culture wars" in the media—occupied a major role in public discourse. This inaugural festival had to be brokered both within the Smithsonian itself and between Smithsonian curatorial staff and presidential inaugural staff.

Background

Within days following the 1992 election of Bill Clinton and Al Gore over President George Bush and Vice President Dan Quayle, the Presidential

Inaugural Committee (PIC) announced plans to hold an event outdoors on the National Mall of the United States. To be called America's Reunion on the Mall, the event would bring together a range of American cultural forms—music, dance, performance, crafts, food. Hundreds of artists, musicians, and others would be brought to the Mall for a day or two to demonstrate, perform, cook, and do their thing for an audience of about 500,000 people. The idea was initiated by Hillary Rodham Clinton and apparently modeled after the rather culturally eclectic "open house" celebrations organized for the gubernatorial inaugurations in Arkansas.

The intention was for this event to be open, free and accessible to the public—a kind of "people's inaugural festival" in contrast to the "invitation-only" restricted events. Conceptually, the PIC saw in the reunion theme the chance to express in its first public act the idea of political inclusion that formed the centerpiece of the Clinton campaign rhetoric. "Everyone was welcomed back," "the American people—diverse as they are—are nonetheless one," "the culture wars are over." And, as one staffer said, "Just as President Clinton wants an administration that looks like America, so too should this festival sound and taste like America." The reunion would capitalize on the symbolic use of the National Mall that would help validate and legitimate the understandings encoded in the event.

The organization of the inaugural festival was given to a group of campaign advance people—mainly White middle-class political operatives in their twenties, with some background in law and political science. For them—an intelligent, well-meaning, and nice group—the event was a party, a celebration of victory. And as they started to plan the event it became evident that the festival would reflect their notions of what constituted American culture and which genres of representation would be appropriate.

The PIC asked the Smithsonian's Center for Folklife Programs and Cultural Studies to help these organizers. This was consistent with our previous work in aiding the Carter and Reagan inaugural committees in planning programs for the Smithsonian museums. In initial meetings we heard inaugural festival organizers run down a variety of ideas about things that might occur on the Mall. These included a Ferris wheel, great ex-pro hockey players staging demonstration games, an ice-skating rink, a fancy outdoor restaurant, an ice sculpture of the Golden Gate Bridge spanning the Mall, the world's largest cheesecake, a petting zoo, mimers and portrait painters, a variety of craftspeople such as one might find at a suburban shopping mall, a food court with funnel cake makers, pretzels, and the like, a variety of pop music groups, Disney and *Sesame Street* characters, the Tennessee or Arkansas symphony, a Broadway show or two, and the Goodyear blimp overhead.

The kind of event described in these ideas would require a budget of about $4 million; it would require erecting and heating about 400,000 square feet of tent space on the Mall for a six-hour event in the middle of January. In addition, the Smithsonian was asked to connect its museums to the tents by covered passageways and bring out some of its exhibits from the museums and from storage so they could be mounted outside.

Reunion as a Model of American Culture

Clearly the model of a reunion here was not the same as that done by Southern Black families, or by Indians going to regional powwows, or even by my high school classmates. In their search for a genre, organizers came up with a combination of county fair, Rockefeller Center, and shopping mall, and the forms they picked tended to be those commercial and public entertainments quite popular with many Americans. It would not offer an inaccurate snapshot of cultural life in the United States in the 1990s. But would it speak to the ideological purpose of its directors, the incoming president and the first-lady-to-be?

With a few weeks of time that no one really had, we worked with the PIC group to eliminate the logistical and conceptual nightmares. A 200-foot-high Ferris wheel on the Mall in the middle of January with potential high winds and winter storms seemed unwise. It also didn't have much to do with providing a context, model, or idea of American cultural diversity or its inclusion within a nation-state. We molded the inaugural festival more toward the purposes for which it was intended and talked a good bit about American culture outside of Hollywood, Disneyland, Nashville, Madison and Fifth Avenues. If the PIC was serious about its purpose, then the reunion of American cultural diversity had to be represented in something beyond Michael Jackson singing with or embracing Barbra Streisand.

Our attempts to represent the diversity of American cultural communities, to make the event somewhat educational through verbal presentations and publications, to lengthen the event (so as to minimize the risk of bad weather), and to scale down the scope and cost succeeded with PIC officials. The organizers, familiar with the use of entertainment and large-scale public events, started thinking more carefully about how ideas could be represented. "Culture" became a category of discourse lying somewhere between, and mediating between, politics on the one hand and arts and entertainment on the other.

The idea of the inaugural festival and the request for Smithsonian help was interesting in yet another way. S. Dillon Ripley, a former Smithsonian secretary, had taken great delight some three decades earlier in turning the Smithsonian inside out. When the March on Washington occurred and his assistants warned him to close the museums lest the marchers damage the place, he moved in the other direction, asserting that the Smithsonian belonged to the marchers, it was their museum, and if by chance in going to the rest rooms or using the fountains they wandered through the halls and learned something or became intrigued, so much the better.[1] Having the festival associated so closely with a new administration made it a powerful affair. Some museum directors worried that event goers would track mud into their museums. Others wondered if they should close their doors. The naïveté of the organizers about exhibits—"just bring them outside"—made many directors nervous. In short, the inaugural festival subverted the normal order of cultural power along the Mall. As James Boon suggests, museums (and museumlike events) can conjoin contradictory desires, the mature or propertied and the youthful (less propertied), the serious and the voyeurs, the child and the adult, the subversive and the reactionary. In this case, the outside—usually associated with the lower class, the young, the nonpropertied, the less than serious—was where the power was. The inside became just some exhibits, decorations, and possible overflow venues for performance—the staid, the entombed.[2]

In the end, we did work closely with the PIC and with Quint Davis and his company, Festival Productions, Incorporated (which produces the New Orleans Jazz and Heritage Festival) to define, program, and produce America's Reunion on the Mall. Held on two thankfully unseasonably warm days, January 16 and 17, 1993, the event drew somewhere between 500,000 and 600,000 visitors. The inaugural festival filled the center of the National Mall with huge tents stretching between the Washington Monument and the U.S. Capitol.

Thousands of musicians, actors, writers, craftspeople, and cooks, volunteers, staff, and contractors were involved in its production. Enormous

For the 1993 presidential inaugural, the Mall was covered with people, tents, and activities to celebrate "America's Reunion on the Mall." Photo courtesy Smithsonian Institution.

food tents hosted scores of stalls featuring Cajun, deli, Thai, Chinese, African, Ethiopian, Southern, and Mexican food. A football field–long tent hosted a variety of traditional crafts and was always overcrowded. Large music tents were devoted to Broadway shows, rock 'n' roll, jazz, blues, gospel, regional, ethnic, and traditional community-based musics. We at the Smithsonian provided overall advice, technical, design, programming, and logistical assistance and took responsibility for programs in a number of venues—a community music tent, a traditional crafts tent, a children's tent, and auditoriums in three museums—American History, Natural History, and the Ripley Center. The Anacostia Museum also held a program featuring musicians, writers, poets, and dramatists from Washington, with buses shuttling to and from the National Mall. This last program represented a unique undertaking—holding an inaugural event east of the Anacostia River in an African American neighborhood.[3]

Some strong tradition bearers and cultural spokespeople from communities across the country participated. And they said their piece. Members of Halau O'Kekuhi, for example, talked before, through, and after their performance about Hawaiian sovereignty and their governor's

Although some in the organizing committee wanted a petting zoo, an ice sculpture of the Golden Gate Bridge, and a Ferris wheel on the Mall for the inaugural festival, performances highlighting the cultural traditions of the American people—like double dutch jump rope—proved to be highly popular as well as more appropriate, given the theme. Photo courtesy Smithsonian Institution.

decision to take down the American flag from the state capitol building in Honolulu the day before. Folks talked about their music in the contexts of cultural survival issues, the Civil Rights Movement, binationalism and biculturalism along the U.S.-Mexico border, and so on. An Arab American embroiderer from Dearborn demonstrated her craft next to African American quilt makers and Hmong embroiderers, discussed comparative styles, and fielded questions when people asked her, "How come you're here? Are you American?"

The Clintons and the Gores signed on to a widely distributed statement about American cultural identity that would probably please most scholars, politicians, and Americans:

> From Kamuela, Hawai'i and Ketchikan, Alaska; from Ponce, Puerto Rico and Rangeley, Maine; from the rural heartland of Kansas, Missouri and Tennessee; from our major cities of Los Angeles, New York and Chicago, they have come to our Nation's capital. From the glamorous world of popular entertainment and from the neighborhoods of local communities they have come to the Nation's front lawn. Craftspeople, representing the long-

lived arts of America's cultural past have come, along with new immigrants whose artistic and cultural traditions will make their place in the history now being written. Cooks and storytellers, musicians, dancers and artisans have come to this Festival on the Mall to tell, to sing, and to weave the story of America. Their artistry, skill and talent, as immense as it is, is but a sample of the cultural diversity that exists throughout our land. That this diversity can be united, together, in the symbolic center of our nation tells us much about who we are and what we dream.

The enlightened founders of this country conceived of a new nation in which the many could be united. We have always thrived as a nation of nations. This has not been easy to achieve. We have overcome many travails to forge ideals of tolerance, mutual respect, and human dignity. We are still engaged in the pursuit of these ideals, yet America stands as a beacon of hope. Here, cultural difference can be a source of strength not weakness, hope not despair, joy not sorrow.

A nation comprised of a diversity of people, communities and cultural groups is a flexible and adaptable one. Ideas, inventions, songs, arts, even foods developed by some can be enjoyed by all. Never before in the history of humankind have so many different people from so many different places joined together in one nation. And never before has a nation accomplished so much politically, economically, socially and culturally as ours. Our form of democracy, our freedom of expression, our concern for human rights and for the rights of the minority grow from our recognition of a diversity of origins, perspectives and interests. The diversity of American lives has enriched our souls, our minds, our institutions, and even our senses.

We Americans are proud of who we are. We take pride in our own regional, ethnic, religious and family identities, for these give us a sense of self. But we are all Americans first. Being American means bridging differences, not stamping them out. It means learning from each other. It means including everyone as "us," rather than excluding some as "them." It means we can sing our own song, enjoy the singing of others, sing together, and even make up new songs. Some of the distinctly American forms of jazz, blues, gospel and rock 'n' roll heard at the Festival arose from just such a creative combination of cultural styles. Just as our recognition of the uniqueness of each and every individual does not detract from our sense of a common humanity, so too, the recognition of our diversity need not stand in opposition to national unity and identity. Indeed, just as the creativity, genius and generosity of individuals enlarges our sense of humanity, so too can an appreciation of our diversity increase our sense of national accomplishment.

It is fitting that we rededicate ourselves to joining together at this time and in this place. The Mall is the place where Americans talk to each other.

It is where we celebrate and enshrine our national understandings. It is the place where some 30 years ago the Reverend Martin Luther King, Jr. informed the nation of his dream—of a nation in which children of different backgrounds, races and creeds could walk hand in hand. Where the bells of freedom would ring and be heard by all. Where the differences that divide could one day be used to unite. It is thus fitting that in the same place on this day, and on Martin Luther King day, for the inaugural and for the first public event celebrating a new administration, the American people gather here, to reunite with each other, to reunite with an American ideal, and to reunite with a national dream that all of us can help realize.

BILL & HILLARY CLINTON
AL & TIPPER GORE[4]

Now there was still the world's largest cheesecake somewhere on the Mall, and Big Bird did show up. But crowded with local people and visitors from across the nation, sometimes muddy and messy, nonchoreographed and popular, the juxtapositions of people and traditions from different communities and from different walks of life made this first-ever inaugural festival indeed feel like some type of American get-together. It was a moving event for those who came—one Smithsonian assistant secretary in charge of museums (not someone given to overstatement or particularly enamored of these types of events) wrote to me that it was "the highlight of my life." And it was empowering for those who performed and displayed their art—because they were included. As Tanya Osadca, a Ukrainian egg painter from Ohio, said afterward to her hometown paper, "They gave me a tag to wear that said 'talent.' There is something to be said for that when Linda Ronstadt and Big Bird are wearing the same tag."[5]

CHAPTER 12

O JERUSALEM!

The Clinton inaugural festival was an event intended to signal a philosophy of national identity and policies of inclusion on behalf of a new presidential administration. It offered popular entertainment to carry an ideological message. Brokering between and among organizers involved a silent partner—the American people—who ultimately had to, and did, accept the event's portrayal of American culture.

Another contemporaneous project, on the cultures of Jerusalem, also joined cultural presentation with politics, albeit in a different way. Jerusalem is a place in which conflicting ideologies coexist in uneasy juxtaposition. In the Smithsonian's Jerusalem project, the attempt to develop a cultural presentation at the Festival of American Folklife served as a means of political arbitration and mediation. It defined a process of discussion, debate, negotiation, and representation through which Israelis and Palestinians were enabled to speak with each other about the character and significance of Jerusalem and her populace.

Background

The idea of representing the folklife of Jerusalem on the National Mall as part of the Smithsonian Festival of American Folklife originated with a visit to Washington and to the festival by Jerusalem's deputy mayor, Ornan Yekutieli, in 1991. At that festival, he was struck by the cultural interchange between audience and participants, and among participants from several different cultural groups. Yekutieli thought this might be a good vehicle for enhancing communications between Israelis and Palestinians, and between both of these peoples and the American public. Additionally, the idea of producing such a living display on Jerusalem's folklife in Washington, on the Mall, would give it the advantage of neutral, yet symbolically endowed, land—an item in short supply in Jerusalem. If successful, the program could be remounted back home and serve as a model for Palestinian-Israeli dialogue.

Obviously there was a lot at stake, and many divergent stakeholders were involved in how Jerusalem might be represented in this format. We at the Smithsonian had to go to and through many people in our own organization, in Washington, in Tel Aviv, Jerusalem, and Tunis to describe the festival genre of cultural representation and the process that would guide the development of the program.

Planning the Project

From the beginning, we were very clear with all parties that the Smithsonian's Festival of American Folklife had its own set of needs, standards, and institutional practices. The festival would seek to represent the diversity of communities in Jerusalem, would be based upon ethnographic research, would be collaboratively developed with local scholars and specialists, and would foreground community-based culture bearers in the public presentation. In the period before and during the peace talks we met with Jerusalem mayor Teddy Kollek and Palestinian leader (and son of the last Arab mayor of Jerusalem) Faisal Husseini. Both gave their blessings to the project and through immediate subordinates engaged the issues of how the city might be represented.

In consultation with scholars on both the east and the west sides of Jerusalem, we organized two teams of about fifteen researchers each, one at Hebrew University led by folklore professor and department head Galit Hassan-Rokem and the other at Bir Zeit University led by Suad Amiry, a professor of vernacular architecture, head of a Palestinian cultural research organization, and member of the peace talks delegation. Through our own curator, Amy Horowitz—a folklorist and specialist on music in Jerusalem—these teams participated in both joint and separate activities and meetings over a two-year period.

Local community members and scholars jointly carried out research for the Jerusalem Festival project. Serene Hleleh interviews a Palestinian *oud* player, Abu Gharnam, at his home. Photo by Yacub Arefheh, courtesy Smithsonian Center for Folklife Programs and Cultural Studies.

Much of our ethnographic research involved documentation and examination of local forms of cultural expression. There was a strong emphasis on the sacred arts and their profanation and transformation in modern Jerusalem. For example, Armenian tile makers in the old city, who came to Jerusalem from Turkey during the genocide in order to repair ancient tiles for the Al-Aqsa mosque, later made tile street signs for the city and now make tiles for tourists with such sayings as "Shalom, have a nice day." Much of the research also concerned the ways in which particular traditions expressed, reinforced, established, or challenged people's sense of identity as Muslim, *sefardi*, Israeli, local, *sabra*, and so on.[1]

Brokering Representations

But beyond the kind of normal ethnographic documentation was the issue of how to represent Jerusalem writ large. Jerusalem is a complicated city. Everyone—not only those who live there but others in the Muslim, Christian, and Jewish worlds as well—owns a piece of it. Needless to say, our work involved talking to many, many different groups, leaders, and institutional representatives and finding out how they represented Jerusalem, officially, semi-officially, unofficially, personally. This was no simple matter given the ongoing peace talks, the issue of the deportees on the Lebanon border, the Israeli elections, and the secret negotiations.

The biggest task was to deal with the divisibility and indivisibility of Jerusalem. From a political policy standpoint Israelis, Palestinians, and other concerned parties were most interested in how we would divide up the program. Official Israeli and Palestinian positions are that there is one undivided Jerusalem. In political-military terms, Jerusalem has been undivided, divided, and undivided again over the past fifty years. Socially and culturally there are at least several Jerusalems—some distinct, others overlapping, some hierarchical. Spatially, the old city is walled. At the time of our research the green-line boundary between the former East and West Jerusalem was being buttressed with a highway and dividing walls. Simply stated, all sides were interested in the way that the perceived neutral and scholarly Smithsonian might draw boundaries and divide up or not divide up their city. Our site map for the festival became an object of interest, a metaphor for the real Jerusalem, and a vehicle for speaking about what could not yet be addressed at the peace talks table—i.e., the status of Jerusalem.

Alternative schema for representing Jerusalem were proposed by many involved in the project. The U.S. consul general, herself a specialist in the area, suggested dealing just with the old city, which is bounded and problematic enough, rather than dealing with the issue of the surrounding parts of the city, which would raise issues of where the city begins and ends, who made the boundaries, and for what political purposes. Another proposal was to represent the geographic layout of the city in scale literally on the Mall in Washington. Another was to join all artists, craftspeople, musicians, cooks, and others, by genre in a series of concentric circles with the sacred at the center and the more profane arts on the periphery. Another proposal, from Faisal Husseini, was to have completely separate sections for East and West Jerusalem, one Palestinian (Arab Christians and Muslims) and the other Israeli (Jewish). Another, Teddy Kollek's, was to represent the city as a cultural mosaic, with neighborhoods and ethnic groups. And yet another was to have two separate spaces for East and West, with an area of overlap between them representing the conjoined but contested old city, all surrounded by a fence signifying one city.

As can be imagined, each of these plans had supporters, opponents, and flaws. Negotiating and considering the various site plans for the festival led researchers, scholars, politicians, and others to argue about the cultural and political realities of Jerusalem and the framework for its future. For example, Teddy Kollek's long-articulated idea of a united Jerusalem as a cultural mosaic did not resonate with Palestinians. The idea of representing East Jerusalem as a mere neighborhood of the city, and Palestinians as just another "ethnic group" was politically untenable for Faisal Husseini and his colleagues. Indeed, even the issue of terminology was problematic. Is it "eastern and western Jerusalem," with lowercased adjectives indicating direction in a city, or is "East Jerusalem" a proper noun deserving of capitalization on a Smithsonian sign or as published in the Smithsonian's festival book?

The process of negotiating cultural representation also had its penetrating insights and moments of humor. Fearful at one point that the whole project was a plot by political operatives unsympathetic to Israel, the Israeli foreign ministry was assured, "No matter what we do, the distance between Arab Jerusalem and Israeli Jerusalem will be less on the Mall than it is in real life." A Palestinian researcher, reflecting on the ethnographic fieldwork, intimated, "We are so consumed with getting political rights for our people, we sometimes forget who our people are." Confronted by the absurdity of one of his own proposals, another Israeli cultural official offered a parody song title for his site map: "This Land Is Our Land, Their Land Is Our Land." A Palestinian scholar, negotiating for parity in the numbers of participants for the festival yet mindful of the balance of power, agreed to an even split—"50 percent for East Jerusalem, 60 percent for the West."

With a great deal of hard work, we did arrive at a final site map and program plan for Jerusalem that was agreed to by the parties involved. We were not, however, able to produce the program on the Mall in 1993. We were saddled with demands for consultations with various officials, which, while appropriate, consumed a great deal of time. We were also unable to identify and raise the requisite private funds needed for the program—despite a heroic try.[2] We did, however, produce an article for the annual festival program book that detailed the research effort.[3] The following year, events, including the Hebron massacre, forestalled production of the project. Given the uncertainties associated with the peace process, the assassination of Prime Minister Rabin and its consequences, it is unsure when, if ever, a Jerusalem program at the festival might be attempted.

Whether that site map would work in the present is unknown, for much has changed. Jerusalem has a new mayor, and the Israeli nation has a new prime minister. The forces both for and against peace in Israel seem to have hardened and become more extreme. So, too, on the Palestinian side the advent of the Palestinian National Authority, divergences within the leadership, and the power of Hamas and other groups make it considerably harder to broker agreements—for the parties involved are neither singular nor fully authoritative. Additionally, as Jerusalem comes onto the table for formal discussion and resolution of its status, the stakes get even higher. The festival as site metaphor might not be seen so metaphorically anymore.

The Jerusalem project still, however, continues, in less dramatic form. The project has produced a book manuscript about the cultural life of Jerusalem, the documentary film *Jerusalem: Gateways to the City*, and a continuing exchange of scholars and cultural producers.[4] The 1996 Festival of American Folklife included two groups of singers from Jerusalem—one Jewish, the other Muslim—within a topical "Sacred Sounds" program. They successfully presented their music and a discussion of the religious and social foundations of their respective musical traditions to interested and appreciative audiences on the Mall. Given the extraordinary circumstances, these are no small accomplishments. The project did not bring peace to the conflict, but it certainly allowed for thoughtful, committed people on both sides to share their understandings of the city's people and their traditions, and to try to broker their differences by using a cultural presentation as a means for doing so.

CHAPTER 13

WORKERS' CULTURE IN THE WHITE HOUSE

I n 1991 the Smithsonian Folklife Center was approached by the White House Historical Association and White House staff to come up with an idea for celebrating the 200th anniversary of the White House in 1992. Many events were planned—symposiums, books, lectures (mainly on its architectural history). But given our penchant for living culture, what would we suggest?

With our proclivity for exploring the oral tradition, the cultural expressions at the grassroots, we suggested a program at the Festival of American Folklife that would focus on the workers of the White House. Enough had been done by presidential biographers and institutional historians on the presidents and first families who lived in the White House, as well as the politically appointed staff who moved through it. Instead, we would interview butlers, doormen, cooks, maids, ushers, and others and develop a program around the occupational culture or worklore of the institution.

At the time this seemed like an iffy proposition, since the coming year was an election year. "Kiss and tell" books were hot, and no one running for president, especially an incumbent, wants his staff to reveal potentially embarrassing, intimate information about the first family's lifestyle. Having only retired workers participate in the program seemed a good way to avoid this pitfall and also to take the pressure off current employees who, fearing for their jobs, might otherwise gloss over important issues.

There was another issue. Many of the White House service staff, some ninety-six employees, were African Americans. Some appointees and former political staffers thought that the program might run into trouble, depicting African Americans in servile roles. This would draw attention to racial issues at the nation's center and cause political problems for the president. Yet among the White House staff were people who thought that the story of the workers should be told and that the bicentennial was the logical time to tell it. Rex Scouten, the curator of the White House, brought the idea to President and Mrs. Bush, and they agreed, against the recommendation of others on their staff.

Marjorie Hunt, of the Smithsonian Folklife Center staff, was assigned as curator for the project. She interviewed some fifty former workers in their homes to review their life's work, their experiences, and their thoughts on the White House. She, aided by assistants Ann Dancy, Craig Stinson, and Liesl Dees, reviewed historical records, documents, and diaries and conducted background and photographic research. In the end, some three dozen former workers appeared at the festival in 1992. They told stories of their first day on the job, their poignant moments, the skills and knowledge they needed to do their jobs, special events, the giving of state dinners, their relationships with first families, their experiences with fellow employees, the impact of social change upon work routines, first family transitions, and so on. Some demonstrated job skills at the festival—chef Henry Haller, who cooked presidential dishes; Sanford Fox, who used calligraphy to create elegant invitations; Rusty Young, who demonstrated floral arrangements;, and stone carvers, who worked on the restoration of the White House.[1]

The festival program was immensely successful and well received by the public. Audiences on the Mall sat on benches in the heat and humidity listening with rapt attention to the workers. Workers, too, took great pride in their performances. While some, like maître d' Alonzo Fields, doorman Preston Bruce, and seamstress Lillian Rogers Parks, were experienced storytellers who had published books about their White House years, others were somewhat reticent at first.[2] But most, like head butler and maître d' Gene Allen and plumbers Bonner and Howard Arrington, warmed to the role of telling their stories.

The program on the Mall was filmed and subsequently edited into a documentary, *Workers at the White House,* that aired on television.[3] The sign text panels from the festival were turned into a traveling exhibit, "Workers at the White House," that with the video documentary toured the Ford, Eisenhower, Truman, Carter, Reagan, Johnson, and Bush presidential libraries and centers with the cooperation

At the 1992 festival, retired employees shared stories and reminiscences of what it was like to work in the White House. Photo by Richard Strauss, courtesy Smithsonian Institution.

of the National Archives.[4] Another version of the exhibit and video was mounted at the Shaed Elementary School in Washington, D.C. In that school, students and their families recognized many of their neighbors who had served in the White House. Workers were invited to a special program at the school and were honored by Hillary Rodham Clinton, who spoke of their service to the nation.[5] The exhibit was also hosted at the White House Visitors Center with the cooperation of the National Park Service.

The success of the program in certain quarters was somewhat surprising. Hillary Rodham Clinton asked that the video be shown to all White House staff over a three-day period. Secretary of State Warren Christopher has ordered several copies of the video to give as gifts to, among others, Vice President Al Gore. Former president George Bush wrote us a personal note about the project. Why should a president, a first lady, and a secretary of state be so taken by a display of White House culture that features not them but their workers? Would George Washington, Abraham Lincoln, Teddy or Franklin Roosevelt have been so engaged if such a program had been produced in his time?

First Lady Hillary Rodham Clinton addresses students and teachers at the Alice and Ernestine Shaed Elementary School in Washington, D.C. The school hosted the "Workers at the White House" exhibit and honored several longtime workers. Photo by Richard Strauss, courtesy Smithsonian Institution.

To be sure, we had facilitated and produced the festival program, exhibit, and video on the White House workers. But what struck me was the reflexiveness of the workers, especially the more articulate ones, and their understanding of their own roles—not so much as maître d's and butlers but as culture brokers within the White House.

The White House, like other institutions in American life, is at the confluence of varied cultural streams. Most commonly, we think of the presidential ones. But there are also others, of the professional staff who bring with them the beliefs, values, and practices of their occupational roles—soldiers, statesmen, secretaries, spokeswomen, Secret Service agents, chiefs of staff. There is also another cultural stream, quite out of public view, much more informal, that is daily crafted and enacted by the workers on the domestic and service staff.

The two key variables in brokering culture are difference and distance. The greater the degree of cultural difference, and the greater the social distance between people, the more exacting is the task of brokering some form of agreement, compromise, or conspiracy for mutual interaction. Both in their specific jobs and historically as a staff, White

House workers are engaged in the cultural extension of political democracy, bridging the distance between the presidency and the people, finessing the difference between one person and all others.

Presidential Culture

Most Americans are familiar with the symbols of White House culture: the televised image of the president speaking to the nation from the Oval Office, the view of the south portico, the Marine Band striking up "Hail to the Chief," the presidential seal on a podium, a crowd gathered in the Rose Garden, the first family arriving by helicopter on the lawn, a visiting dignitary toasted at a state dinner. The presentation and display of White House culture awaken the public consciousness and make people take notice. The rituals and trappings of the White House command attention, if not respect.

George Washington would recognize their purpose, though not their form. The first president was keenly aware of the importance not only of being president but also of performing as president. Insisting on ceremonials such as twice-weekly levees (social audiences), and traveling in a handsome horse coach with grand retinue, the first president took these not as empty gestures but rather as means of conveying the grandeur and seriousness of the presidency and encouraging its acceptance among the populace of a new nation.

The official culture of the White House is largely determined by the style of its presidential occupants, the social mores of the times, the technologies available, and how these are practically enacted and symbolically articulated. Presidential style is at the intersection of personal life and public institution. It has always been discussed and debated. It is a continuing source of tension in a democracy that so singles out one of its citizens as president.

Historical Developments in Presidential Culture

In the early days of the presidency, some saw the chief executive as a kind of elected monarch. Debates over presidential style began with the architecture and proposed plans for the building of the President's House, as it was first known (though nicknamed "the White House" early on, that did not become its official name until 1901).[6] George Washington and original planner Pierre L'Enfant wanted a presidential palace some five times its current size. They wanted a building constructed of cut stone to mirror the grandeur of older, established European capitals and great cities. Thomas Jefferson and others argued for a smaller, less pretentious brick house.

As president, Jefferson saw that his style of living in and entertaining at the executive mansion would reflect and reveal his political principles. While he adopted plainer and more egalitarian measures than his predecessors—he walked to his own inauguration, cut back the haughty levees, instituted open seating at his dinners—he nonetheless realized the importance of presidential continuity for the new republic and use of the President's House as a symbol of authority.

Furnishing the White House was a political statement, and James Madison invested in buying American, albeit in imitation European styles. James Monroe's was the first of the imperial presidencies, and French food, high European style, powdered wigs, and a full and elaborate social season followed. Management of the White House became a campaign issue between John Quincy Adams and Andrew Jackson, and again between Martin Van Buren and William Henry Harrison. Harrison's widely published campaign poem to unseat the incumbent makes clear the alternative styles for living in the White House:

> No parties exclusive, no minuet balls
> No Levees a la Royale shall flout in his halls
> The string of his door shall ne'er be drawn through
> Always Welcome the world with Old Tippecanoe.
> No banquets he'll give a la mode de Paris
> No Wines of great price on his board you will see
> But Sirloin and Bacon and Hard Cider Too
> Shall be the plain fare of Old Tippecanoe.[7]

By the mid-1800s there was no real fear that the United States would establish a ruling aristocracy. Still, the tension between appearing presidential enough and appearing too regal remained. This was reflected in food, clothing, ceremonial pomp, and even music and dance. It was in Polk's imperial White House that the Marine Band first played "Hail to the Chief" to announce the president to distracted visitors who danced the waltz and quadrille; Andrew Johnson's more egalitarian receptions hosted square dances, polkas, and Highland flings.

The post–Civil War White House was relatively grand, reflecting stability and the good life. Information about the presidents, their families, and life in the White House reached a large American public through the newspapers. Nellie Grant's wedding occasioned big coverage. And it was during the 1870s that the title "first lady" came to be used. But it was really Teddy Roosevelt's presidency that gave rise to contemporary White House style. The Roosevelts reshaped the physical building, the social organization of the staff, and the character of White House activities. They stressed state splendor at a time when the United States sought a major place in international affairs. White House receptions and dinners were imperial in order to project the status of the president as a world leader and public personality. Affairs of state were well orchestrated, full of ceremony, formalized and codified by an increasingly permanent professional staff.

Roosevelt's formula has largely stayed with all the presidents who have followed, modified by personal choice, family tragedy, and war. The content of presidential display has changed, adopting popular forms of entertainment and new styles of cuisine, for example. And audiences for presidential display have become more diverse at the White House itself, and much larger through the media. Yet presidents find themselves, far more than their nineteenth-century predecessors, bound by an elaborate system of operation and code of behavior that prescribe how to be presidential.

Public Accessibility

Much of the tension over how to be president revolves around the issue of public accessibility to the White House. Presidents and first families have varied considerably in their ideas about access and means of achieving it. When John Adams first occupied the mansion, he was continually in contact with workers finishing its construction and living on its grounds. High-society lady visitors with the appropriate passes wandered its rooms. Adams continued the tradition of levees and initiated a New Year's Day "open house."

In 1801 Jefferson ordered the doors opened daily for the public to visit the state rooms, displayed artifacts and curiosities of the West gathered from the Lewis and Clark and the Pike expeditions, held audiences for American Indian leaders, and started a Fourth of July public celebration fair with tents on the grounds, handicrafts, food, horse races, tests of skill, cockfights, and military drills. Madison started Wednesday drawing rooms, during which two hundred or so guests from society would show up, uninvited, at the White House to engage in open, informal discussion. Through most of its first fifty years, office seekers, petitioners, and visitors would regularly come by the executive mansion and expect a meeting with the president. Still, however, the public openness of the White House was largely restricted to "high society" under the norms of its postcolonial formalities. An early exception was the raucous inauguration of Andrew Jackson. Friends, visitors, and well-wishers—commoners, children, and Blacks—stormed the White House in a popular celebration of his accession.

By the mid-1800s weekly Marine Band concerts were held for the public on the White House grounds. President Lincoln continued these, as well as the customary open houses, even during the Civil War. He signed the Emancipation Proclamation after the New Year's open house in 1863, met Sojourner Truth, and hosted a large group of African Americans at the 1865 open house. Andrew Johnson revived the levees in his White House, holding numerous boisterous meetings that he viewed as important for the functioning of democracy.

By and large, though, despite public events, such as open houses, concerts, and the Easter Egg Roll begun in 1879, access to the White House and the president was restricted to members of White high society. Mrs. Teddy Roosevelt developed musicales and teas for hundreds as a means of engaging this group. And when Booker T. Washington became the first African American to be invited to dine at the White House as an official guest in 1901, it caused a storm of protest. Mrs. Hoover met with a similar reaction almost thirty years later when she invited the wife of a Black congressman over for tea.

Eleanor Roosevelt broadened participation in White House events by expanding the list of those invited beyond Washington high society to people from all walks of life. She held her teas for hundreds of people at a time, and in shifts. Her attention to social causes brought into the White House a broader range of people than heretofore had been involved. At the same time, increased security for the president, growing out of historic assassinations and threats arising from the Depression and the New Deal, coupled with the desire to shield President Roosevelt's disability from public view, made the president less personally accessible. Indeed, the days when citizens could innocently run into the president shopping in the market or strolling on the grounds were long gone.

Tourism to the White House was encouraged by a number of presidents and now amounts to more than 1.5 million visitors annually. Still, though, in the twentieth century, the White House, its life, customs, and ways have become more broadly accessible to an American and even a worldwide public mainly through the media. Teddy Roosevelt started the tradition of press conferences for the nation's newspapers. Hoover first used radio broadcasts regularly, but it was Franklin Delano Roosevelt in his fireside chats from the White House who used radio to build an intimate link with Americans across the nation. Television access to the White House began with a tour of the renovated building by Harry Truman for Walter Cronkite but hit a high mark on February 14, 1962, with Jacqueline Kennedy's renowned televised tour. Today, immediate, real-time access is taken for granted; we expect presidential spokespeople, network correspondents stationed at the West Wing portico, and wire services to inform us about the president and White House happenings.

Technology, Infrastructure, and Historicity

As does any culture, that of the White House relies upon a technological infrastructure. The first occupant, President John Adams, insisted on a kitchen garden and had outhouses moved to less visible places on the property. President Jefferson installed the first water closet–operated toilet. For much of the nineteenth century, presidents contended with a functioning stable of horses, milk cows, and even sheep (used to keep down the lawn). Running water came to the lower floor of the building in 1833. The White House sometimes provided the exemplary model for technological innovations in American life; sometimes it followed. Gas lighting and central heating were first installed in the Polk White House; the telephone was installed for Rutherford Hayes. Air conditioning was developed in 1881 by R. S. Jennings, Simon Newcomb, and John Wesley Powell as they experimented to make the remaining life for the wounded President Garfield more comfortable during an awful Washington summer. Electricity came in under President Benjamin Harrison; the automobile was in and horses out for the large William Taft. Personal computers came to the White House under George Bush, the World Wide Web with White House home page under Bill Clinton.

Parallel to the development of technology has been the constant desire of White House occupants to renovate and redecorate a building and grounds often seen as inadequate for the times. Under the direction of the original architect, James Hoban, the White House was rebuilt after it burned in 1814. The south portico was put in under James Monroe, the north portico under Andrew Jackson. Numerous presidents and first ladies devised schemes for enlarging, renovating, and refurbishing the White House. Plans developed in the 1860s called for building a whole new building in another location. Chester Arthur's plans for rebuilding the White House anew on its site came to naught but enabled a redecoration by Louis Tiffany. Caroline Harrison's ambitious plans for a major expansion of the building as palace failed but were revived by Edith Roosevelt and ultimately led to another major renovation. Truman's renovation was a major structural one, causing his family to relocate to Blair House. Familiar architectural and landscaped features that often symbolize the White House are of relatively recent origin—the first Oval Office was built in 1909 under President Taft, the Rose Garden was established in 1913 at the Wilson White House, though many other ornamental and botanical gardens preceded it. The situation room was added in 1958.

While innovation and modernity have driven plans to improve the status and functioning of the White House, so too has a sense of tradition, historicity, and national aspiration. Dolley Madison's saving of the Gilbert Stuart painting of George Washington became a story told and retold over the years and symbolized the role of the White House in protecting and preserving the national patrimony. Questions of whose furniture to buy and in what style to decorate the White House became issues for several presidents, including Madison, Coolidge, Kennedy, and Reagan. The idea that the White House contained national treasures that needed care and documentation was elaborated with the formal development of a curated White House china collection under Edith Roosevelt and Edith Wilson. Grace Coolidge and Lou Hoover both showed great interest in the furniture, paintings, and decorative arts of the White House, the latter seeking to develop an inventory and also move toward period interior design. The Kennedys and Nixons added appreciably to the collection, care, and refurbishment of White House art consistent with a congressionally mandated development of a museumlike quality for the building's public rooms and spaces. The Clintons added to this with a collection of White House crafts and sculpture in the garden. Nancy Reagan's attention to the living quarters and upper floors added to the idea of the White House as a fine residence and a national place of distinction.

Social Organization of Work

The White House was built and modified in its early days by a variety of tradesmen and laborers—Italian and Scottish stonecutters, Irish and African American workers. There was no government appropriation of funds for any staff until the 1840s, so presidents hired their own, brought their slaves, and used family members to run the White House. Presidents were responsible for their own expenses, most of their entertaining, and much of the considerable cost of maintaining and operating the White House. Many family members, hired servants, and slaves lived and worked in the White House. And their children were born there. Jefferson's grandson was the first in 1806, followed by the son of slaves Fanny and Davy.

Though John Adams first established divisions in the White House between private and public space, they have often become conflated. Visits to residential spaces have long been used to foster intimacy, personal and political. Roles of family members have also been conflated. Family members—wives, daughters, and other female relations—generally served as hostesses for dinners and receptions and overseers of the household, while men served as secretaries and other functionaries of the president. For example, Priscilla Tyler, the president's daughter-in-law, filled out invitations, wrote menus, drew seating charts, and served as hostess. John Tyler served as his father's secretary. Some women, such as Sarah Polk, Roslyn Carter, and Hillary Rodham Clinton, have crossed established gender lines, sitting in with their husbands in Cabinet meetings or other substantive discussions. Stewards and housekeepers, first hired by the Adamses, oversaw the household, were responsible for getting food, cooking, and servicing events. They tended to be French well into the nineteenth century.

From the beginning to very recently, presidents brought their own private servants to work in the White House. Zachary Taylor was perhaps the last president to bring slaves to work there, in 1849, given the sensitivities of a nation and a capital approaching confrontation over the issue. Many free Blacks and emancipated slaves worked at the White House through the nineteenth century in a variety of personal and household capacities.

Some became quite close to the first family and played trusted roles. Witnessing the British victory at Bladensburg on August 24, 1814, President Madison entrusted a free African American, James Smith, to ride to

Washington to warn Dolley Madison to flee the White House in advance of the invading troops. His actions ensured the survival of valuable White House possessions. Another African American, Paul Jennings, a slave of Madison's who was later manumitted, wrote the first of worker memoirs about his time in the White House, titled *A Colored Man's Reminiscences* and published in 1866.[8] And while for years later Dolley Madison functioned as the doyenne of Washington society, advising the White House on proper conduct, it was Jennings who, behind the scenes, arranged for her care with key officials. Another ex-slave, Elizabeth Keckly, served Mrs. Lincoln as a White House seamstress, later becoming a confidante and friend, sharing as they did the loss of their sons.

White House servants wore livery well into the twentieth century. Those who have greeted and met visitors have worn blue coats with brass buttons and breeches, imperial blue, black suits with lapel ribbons, summer whites, green jackets, and other outfits designed by first ladies and others. Maids and others wore long white aprons or variations thereof. African American servants lived in the basement and later in the attic of the White House. The 1840s saw the beginnings of professionalization of the staff, with congressional appropriations for a doorman, two gardeners, and a guard, and the transfer of responsibility to the Interior Department. Still, servants and family members carried the major responsibilities of making the President's House work.

The White House staff expanded after the Civil War. Julia Grant formalized rules of behavior for workers in the White House, specifying responsibilities and expected conduct. The division of White House staff into office and household workers occurred under President Hayes, who also appointed Frederick Douglass as marshal of the District of Columbia, to serve as master of ceremonies for the city, Congress, and the White House. Formal rules and tables of organization and duties were again promulgated in the Teddy Roosevelt White House, given the increased orchestration of presidential presentation and the growth in staff. At the beginning of the nineteenth century, when Abigail Adams first moved into the White House, she had a staff of six to run the entire White House operation. She envisioned a need for about thirty people. Indeed, by the time of Teddy Roosevelt's presidency a century later, the White House staff numbered some twenty-five household help and another forty to fifty people associated with the executive office. By Truman's time, the staff stood at more than forty for the household and another seventy to eighty or so for functions connected with the office of the president. For the last several administrations, approximately ninety people have been on the household staff, with hundreds more serving in various capacities relating to the office. This reflects increased complexity in the functions and duties of the president and a more complicated world, necessitating professional specialization.

With the growth and professionalization of the staff came a diminution of the everyday work roles of family members. Family members from the Civil War on have become involved in a variety of projects. But they have increasingly moved away from housekeeping, accounting, secretarial, and support functions. Stewards, assistants to the president, chiefs of staff, spokespeople, florists, calligraphers, and others took their place. Thus presidents have had an opportunity to establish more firmly the roles of first ladies and the lives of their children in the public eye. Public weddings such as those of the Nixon and Johnson daughters, births, Christmas, and other celebrations have helped millions of Americans identify with the humanity of their presidents. Family crises, funerals, illness (for example, Betty Ford's breast cancer), and tragedies have similarly led Americans to sympathize with members of the first family and to see in their travails common points with their own.

Workers' Culture

Official presidential traditions are not the only ones established at the White House. The people who have worked at the White House have also invented their own traditions and developed skills, practices, and stories that account for their role in a powerful and historical institution. Just as at other workplaces, workers at the White House develop an unofficial culture of beliefs, practices, wisdom, knowledge, and skill that grows out of daily experience and that is shared and passed down orally from one generation of workers to another.

Most of the White House domestic staff is now African American. African American workers have a long history there, going back to the Jefferson White House. Paul Jennings's diaries of his time in the Madison White House are the earliest that remain. Questions of White House staffing were raised leading up to the Civil War, with President Buchanan deciding in favor of an all-British staff with no Blacks. This changed under Lincoln and others. In 1866, Congress created the federal position of steward of the White House. President Andrew Johnson appointed an

African American, William Slade, with the responsibility of maintaining the well-being of the property and grounds, operating as the fiscal agent for the White House, managing the president's and congressionally appropriated funds. Winston Sinclair, another African American, continued this tradition under Grover Cleveland. And for most of the late nineteenth and early twentieth century there was a mix of Blacks and Whites on the domestic staff, helping to run the place on a day-to-day basis.

In 1909 the Tafts hired a housekeeper, Mrs. Jaffray, who imposed segregation upon the household staff. Strong objections were voiced, but Blacks and Whites on staff were made to eat separately. In 1910, with segregation in effect and African Americans excluded from presidential guest lists, Black workers launched the Chandelier Club and an annual ball, which was then held for some years. Lillian Parks, a ninety-eight-year-old former maid and seamstress who started working for President Hoover in 1929 and served through the Eisenhower administration, remembered the White House back in 1909, when her mother, Maggie Rogers, joined the staff as a maid for President Taft. At the festival in 1992 she recalled:

> There was a club organized by the butlers, housemen, and doormen at the White House—named the Chandelier Club after the big chandelier in the White House. It started in the Tafts' time and went to about the Hoovers' time. Every year they had a ball. I couldn't go until I was 18 and that was in the Wilson administration. That's when I first went to the Ball.[9]

This ball featured music by the Marine Band and was the social event of the year for the staff, supported and even attended by White workers and even some close to the president. The Chandelier Ball demonstrated the "class" of the Black workers and their ability to participate on a par with White high society.

The segregation that greeted African American workers at the White House sometimes shocked them. Alonzo Fields, who started at the Hoover White House, notes:

> They had separate dining rooms—Black and White. We all worked together, but we couldn't eat together. . . . Here in the White House. I'm working for the President. This is the home of the democracy of the world and I'm good enough to handle the President's food—and do everything—but I cannot eat with the help. Well, I was a little miffed over that because I'd come from New England where in the service we would all sit down at the

same table together. And I thought, "Well, in the White House of all places, this is where it should start—at the White House."

Ideas about segregation permeated the operations of the household through the Roosevelt and Truman days. Mrs. Nesbitt, housekeeper under Eleanor Roosevelt, felt that a "one color" domestic staff worked best. White domestic workers were released and Black ones hired. Eventually the White House was integrated by President Truman, with both Black and White domestic, maintenance, service, and support personnel.

Like the culture of presidents, that of workers seems to have several key themes around which tensions, stories, and aspirations are construed. Workers emphasize the importance of work skills as performance, strategies for instructing, surviving, and resisting presidents, and ways of preserving mutual respect and politeness—achieving intimacy without servility.

Work Skills as Performance

Each job at the White House—butler, doorman, messenger—has a unique set of challenges, skills, tasks, and responsibilities. Workers take pride in their abilities—the mastery of special techniques, the knowledge of work processes, the exercise of proper decorum. For a butler, serving a state dinner requires not only precise timing and efficiency but the ability to conduct oneself with social grace. "It's the presentation," says former butler Norwood Williams. Doormen take pride in the way they treat people, prizing their ability to remember names and make White House guests feel comfortable. "I had my own style of receiving guests," said doorman Preston Bruce. "I remembered everybody. I greeted all the guests when they came to a State Dinner. If a person came more than one time, I didn't have to ask his name." Bruce gives a good indication of the subtle skills needed for his job at the White House:

> We had many people coming to the White House, coming to the White House for the first time, and many of them were scared to death. They were nervous. And I decided that I would try to improvise a way to settle these people down before they got to the president. And I would talk to them and many times I'd stop them on their way and show them various things. And by the time I was ready to present them to the president, they were calm and certainly in greeting form.

For Bruce, a sharecropper's son, to work at the White House was to serve as a guardian of the national honor, to show the president and the nation in the best possible light:

> We would receive diplomats to present their credentials about every two months. . . . They would come in every seven minutes. That was their schedule and the schedule that I was holding. Well, the first diplomat that would come in I would usually stash him somewhere not far from the grand stairway where he could go right up and no one would see him. But the problem would be, with some of our presidents, they would be late and there was a problem because I'd sometimes have as many as four or five diplomats stashed from one place to another and I'm about to run out of places. But then someone would make a fast dash over to the Oval Office and tell the president, he'll have to come because the diplomats are coming in and they're piling up! But you know, each diplomat who was presenting his credentials that day, he thought he was the only one coming because I could keep them from seeing each other.

Strategies of Instruction, Survival, and Resistance

"When the old family goes out, you felt lost for just that flash. And then at 12 o'clock when the other family comes in, you took on a new perspective. You just had to turn over; you had to forget those folks and start over," noted Lillian Parks. On Inauguration Day, workers must say farewell to a family they have served for years and begin adjusting to new ways of doing and acting, new likes and dislikes, new routines of work. "You had to adapt. That's the thing that's paramount," said Alonzo Fields, who experienced the dramatic shift in the White House from the formal elegance of the Hoovers to the exuberant informality of the Roosevelt family.

Maître d' Eugene Allen, who served eight first families from the Truman through the Reagan administrations, had similar experiences: "I've seen the time that certain things we did in one administration and they thought it was wrong, we should never do it. Then another administration would come in and it was perfectly all right." For example, in the Eisenhower administration,

> when we had State Dinners or any dinner, Mrs. Eisenhower forbid us to pick up plates until everybody was through eating. And she would sit there and look and if we did, she would tell us about it. And so we learned and

we decided that we would not pick up a plate until everybody had eaten. So then the next administration comes in and sometimes they would want to rush things. I can recall once that President Johnson told me, he says, "Why don't you pick up?" I said, "Mr. President, your guests haven't finished eating." And he said, "Well, if you'd start picking up, they'd rush to get through!" That was just one of the little things that from one administration to the other, the differences, that one liked and the other one didn't.

White House workers are in a difficult position. Having been permanent or long-term employees, they are likely to know a lot more about how to be presidential than the president or his family. But how to convey this to the president? According to Parks, "They have to ask you different things, but you don't ever tell them the other first lady did so and so. You don't tell them what the other first lady did. You let them ask you questions."

White House workers continually depend upon each other to help out, improvise, and do what's needed. Sometimes creative strategies have to be developed. As workers, Alonzo Fields and doorman Arthur Jackson concocted an interesting scenario for Eleanor Roosevelt in order to secure an eight-hour day and rightful compensation for their work:

We talked to them [the Roosevelts] about it and we carried on campaigns undercover, you know. But it didn't work. So Arthur and I came up with a solution. We started a rumor. He'd go to someone in the kitchen, someone who was very talkative, and say to him, "Have you heard of organizing? Did anyone say anything to you about organizing the White House?" And they'd say, "No." And that person would go to someone else and in no time it was back to the housekeeper. So the housekeeper calls me in. She says, "What's this about John L. Lewis, the CIO's gonna organize the help in the White House?" I said, "I don't know anything about it. You know they wouldn't come to me." Then Mrs. Roosevelt and she talked it over. And Mrs. Roosevelt asked me to come up to talk to her. She says, "Do you have any way of finding out?" I said, "Well, perhaps I could get the doorman, Arthur, to find out for us." . . . So he went to the meeting and he came back and told us that they would organize us if 75 percent of the people would sign up. So I told her that news. And she said, "Well, that mustn't happen. Tell me, what do they want?" I said, "Well, they'd like eight hours a day, and compensatory time off; when they work overtime, they want pay for it." So she said she and the President didn't think it [the matter] should go up to the Hill [to Congress]. And so everybody then got eight hours a day.

Intimacy without Servility

In an age in which access is power, closeness to a president and intimacy with a first family can be a charged experience. White House workers developed ways of dealing with the intimacy without feeling overcome by presidential power.

One strategy is to humanize the president and his family. "We took care of the family—breakfast, lunch, and dinner. We were the first people to see them in the morning and the last at night," said Eugene Allen. Allen points to an appreciation, but also a leveling, of president and servant. "After working so closely with the presidents—it's just like any other person. I come to know these people are just flesh like we are." Says Fields, "Presidents are just as human as we are." Most staff generally pride themselves on retaining a respectful and polite attitude, and expecting that in return.

Another way of approaching the relationship is to know a lot about them. Fields noted, "You have all kinds of rumors about the incoming family. When they come to the White House the servants will know quite a bit about them. In fact, I made it my business to even go out and get books, read about them—their religion, what part of the country they come from, their viewpoints. And you would apply that."

Workers also have to earn the trust of presidents and their families. Qualities of discretion and loyalty, the ability to adapt to the different styles of successive first families, and a willingness to perform multiple duties were key work skills. "Hear nothing, know nothing, see nothing, and keep everything to yourself! That's the best quality of a good butler," said Fields.

> When a new president goes in there, he doesn't know his way around, and he's watching you. And you must assure him—you must assure him by body language—that you have no interest other than in him, in the presidency. You don't care who's president—you're working for the public.

The Culture of Public Service

What then connects the official culture of the presidency and the unofficial culture of the domestic staff? How are differences of culture and distances of social status brokered?

One way in which the culture of the president and that of the workers are joined is by reducing the social distance between their lives. This is done, quite literally, through events and stories that demonstrate a shared residence and participation in a shared household. Consider, for example, the well-told tale of Armstead Barnett. Barnett worked as a butler in the Roosevelt, Truman, and Eisenhower White Houses, lived and slept in a room on the third floor from 1938 to 1941. Coming home late one night by taxi, Barnett told the driver to take him to 1600 Pennsylvania Avenue. The cab driver was amazed. "He said, 'To the White House at this time of night?' He thought I was telling a story." Barnett went through a similar experience when asked to list his home address on his Washington, D.C., marriage license:

> I got married when I was in the White House. I went down and got my license and they asked me my address. I told them I lived at 1600 Pennsylvania Avenue. So they looked at one another. And they must have called the newsmen, because when I got back to the White House, they said to me, "Barnett, they had it on the news—Armstead Barnett giving Franklin Delano Roosevelt's address—1600 Pennsylvania Avenue." So Mrs. Roosevelt went out and told them, "That's the only address he's got, he had to give that address!"

One means of reducing distances of power and status is for workers to name things in the White House. Just as there is the Lincoln bedroom, so too is there Bruce's table, named for longtime doorman Preston Bruce, who designed it with carpenter Bonner Arrington in order to hold escort cards at formal events. The ability to name and thus exert conceptual power over things and people, just like presidents, is undertaken by staff. For example, workers dubbed President Hoover "Smiley," President Roosevelt "Charlie Potatoes," and President Truman "Billie Spunk." And while to most of us "the Chief" might refer to the president in his role as the nation's commander, for those inside the White House, it referred to Alonzo Fields, maître d' and a commander in his own right.

Another strategy to bring workers' culture and presidential culture into sync is to find key similarities of practice and value. Both presidents and their staffs share ideas of the public performance of the presidency. Both recognize the symbolic importance of their actions and their relation to history, both of the past and as it is made. But the central theme that connects these cultures in the modern White House is the idea of public service. Service to the president, the presidency, and the nation.

As Alonzo Fields said so eloquently, "I didn't feel like a servant to a man. I was doing the same thing the president was doing. I felt I was a servant to my government, to my country."

For Fields, giving good service had its own intrinsic value. It was not a betrayal of a larger struggle for recognition but rather an act of dignity in itself. It illustrated a striving for excellence, everything he felt the White House should stand for. Fields was a remarkable individual, well known and recognized by generations of White House workers as an inspirational, guiding force for African Americans on the staff.

The idea of public service as informing the work of the White House was not always or necessarily associated with the president or his staff. Historically many people had labored at the White House under coercion or contract, out of personal loyalty or hope for gain. Some occupants believed it was their due, given their station in life. In the 1870s, during an age of privilege, excess, and scandal, President Rutherford Hayes had made a case for the idea of public service. Hayes saw the need for good and just government service, even in the White House. No doubt influenced by his outspoken cook, Winnie Monroe, who called herself "the first colored lady of the land," Hayes reformed the practice of disguising White House domestic workers as laborers and clerks, recognizing them for their service to the presidency. Hoover, Fields's first presidential employer, also saw himself as a longtime public servant, bringing good, efficient management to the people's work, in wartime relief, food administration, at the Department of Commerce, and in the White House.

At a time of segregation within the White House, when distinguished African Americans were denied full participation in the political and social life of the nation, it was a powerful formulation for Fields to make, equating the public service of domestic servants with the public service of the president.

With this service came a certain ethic of responsibility, illustrated in a story that Eugene Allen, a Fields protégé, tells about houseman George Thomas:

> President Truman used to come over for lunch and he used to go into the Oval Room on the second floor and do some work at a desk in there. So when he'd leave and go back to the office, we had a houseman named George Thomas, and he would go in and look around and make sure the place was tidied up. So George looked around and, of course, President Truman was neat and everything was in order. So George decided that he

would sit down. So he got in the president's chair—he had one of these big leather chairs, you know—and sat down. And who comes in the door but President Truman. He looked at George—he had forgot something, you know—he looked at him and said, "George, I'll tell you one thing, you're in a mighty hot seat!" He picked up his papers and went back to the office. That was the end of that.

The connections, even parallel duties, of president and staff extend to conducting affairs of state. Literally. As Alonzo Fields recalled of state dinners, rather pensively a year before he died at the age of ninety-three:

When a dinner table was set and the president and his guests were seated at the table, I stood behind the president's chair and would give a nod to the butlers in the dining room and then everyone would move forward and serve. And with that action I pictured myself as being in charge of my orchestra. I was playing a big symphony. I had my winds and my strings and my reeds and my percussions in the back. And I was directing the biggest symphony playing any overture that made me happy. And people would watch and they'd marvel at it, they really did. I enjoyed being at the White House, maybe it's the only place I ever should have been.

CHAPTER 14

WHAT
IS IT?

THE AMERICAN
SOUTH
AT THE
OLYMPICS

How do you represent the American South to the rest of the world, to the millions of people who visited the Olympic Games in Atlanta and the billions more who watched the sports and snippets of other events on television?

In 1993 I and my colleagues at the Smithsonian were asked to advise on and help produce a free outdoor festival in Atlanta as part of the larger Olympic Arts Festival for the 1996 Games. The Cultural Olympiad for the Atlanta Committee for the Olympic Games (ACOG) was interested in using our work with the Festival of American Folklife as at least a starting point. We agreed to help, believing that this offered an unparalleled opportunity to represent cultural themes to a huge audience. What eventually emerged was a three-way partnership of the Smithsonian, ACOG, and the Southern Arts Federation to produce Southern Crossroads: A Festival of the American South, held in Atlanta's new Centennial Olympic Park from July 18 to August 4, 1996, concurrent with the Olympic Games. The festival included almost five hundred music and dance performances, crafts demonstrations, a marketplace for the sales of Southern music, crafts, books, and foodstuffs, evocative signage, and a supporting publication.[1] Some 100,000 to 150,000 people a day visited the festival—about 2.5 million people over the three weeks of the Olympics. Millions more saw at least some images of the festival through television coverage.

Despite the limitations of the overall event, the cacophony of the Atlanta Olympics, the world-shattering terrorist bombing in Centennial

Olympic Park, the overbearing nature of the sponsors, the awful design of the park, and the ambivalence of ACOG itself, the festival succeeded, but only just barely. The festival overcame the cultural insecurities of Olympic organizers, the elegance of contract designers, and the planning of park supervisors to become an arena within which at least some shred of human festivalization occurred. Within the tightly scripted world of the Olympics, its corporate sponsors, and media partners, the festival did take on some characteristics of the people's space and became a place, at least occasionally, where the numerous imposed boundaries and categories broke down. To understand the festival, it is necessary to understand its history and the tensions that led to it.

No Bubba Olympics

Billy Payne, former University of Georgia quarterback and real estate lawyer, had the vision to bring the Olympics to Atlanta. He and colleagues formed the Atlanta Committee for the Olympic Games and eventually won the bid to stage the Games. Payne, as president and CEO of ACOG, thought the Olympics offered a great opportunity to show the "new South" to the world, to showcase Atlanta as a cosmopolitan, world-class city and the region as a transformed, modern, wonderful place to live, work, and play. The Olympics would make the point to the rest of the world that Atlanta, as the unofficial capital of the South, was a magnet of commercial and cultural wealth freed from the past and racing into the future.[2]

As had Barcelona and other cities, Atlanta made the case with the International Olympic Committee (IOC) that in hosting the Olympics it would offer cultural events that would highlight the distinctive character of its region. The American South occupies significant territory in the cultural consciousness of Americans and, indeed, people around the world. Popular images of the South abound, as a scene from *Gone with the Wind,* as rural crossroads for the blues, as the battleground of the Civil Rights Movement, as backwater bayou, as lifestyles as extreme as those portrayed in the television series *In the Heat of the Night* and *Mayberry RFD.* Whatever the South might be, whatever contradictions, variations, and tensions it might contain, it is strongly imaged and imagined; holding the Olympics in the South did appeal to the IOC.

The tension over how to culturally represent the South was apparent from the beginning. For one thing, Atlanta had a Black mayor, a majority Black population, and was a key city in the Civil Rights Movement, the birthplace of Martin Luther King, and the site of many organizations important to Black Americans. How to deal with representations of Black and White in the South? Could the Civil War and Georgia's Confederate-looking flag (up for debate in the early 1990s) be written out of Olympic cultural presentations such as the opening ceremonies? Would the culture of the South be sanitized when it came to the history of racial relations? Second, how would the Atlanta Olympics deal with the rural hinterland of the South—the peoples and cultures of the mountains, the bayous, the plantations, and small towns of the region. Southern culture was largely defined in terms of rural roots—would these get in the way of ACOG's desire to demonstrate the new, cosmopolitan South?[3]

ACOG did not want to embrace a rural-based, historical Southern heritage. This it perceived as problematic and low class. Billy Payne and his colleagues were repelled by the thought of presenting the "Bubba Games," as they were called. They wanted instead a higher-class, sophisticated affair that would show the South in a good light to the rest of the world—that would announce the South as a player in the global business, sports, and cultural/entertainment arenas. At the same time ACOG understood the need to appease the Black community and recognize past sins and history overcome. It understood the need to mollify other parts of the region that were less willing to recognize Atlanta as the capital of the South. And it was continually reminded by the local and regional media that something had to be done to recognize the grassroots culture of Southerners who would be hosting world visitors and the international media. ACOG could not run away from local and regional culture or shy away from the pride that people felt in being Southern. In the end, the committee chose a strategy that would honor and celebrate the South in a nice, clean, and expensive way.[4]

The tension over the cultural representation of the South was expressed early on in the development of the Olympic mascot. ACOG paid a computer animation company to develop a mascot. No Br'er Rabbit or Georgia Peach emerged. Rather, the company came up with a cartoon character from some new, invented celluloid species with blue skin, large eyes, and no tongue. Lacking a good name for the mascot, ACOG sponsored a contest and decided to go with the moniker "Izzy," short for "What is it?" Later on, in response to an unenthusiastic public reception, a tongue was added to make the creature more personable.

In a region rich in folklore and imagery, to come up with the techno-cultured Izzy was viewed as a travesty by several commentators. John Shelton Reed, a distinguished scholar of the South and Olympics programs adviser, excoriated ACOG for its decultured view.[5] The mascot exemplified the cultural tension and insecurity of Atlanta, ACOG, and the South. Instead of going with something homegrown or rooted in Southern experience, organizers picked something from outside the culture—made up, manufactured, imposed. As the Smithsonian's Diana Parker noted, the South has a long history of investing in other people's "mediocre" instead of in the strength of its own people. Izzy—techno-cultured, manufactured, state-of-the-art high tech—was elevated above any hand-produced, antiquated symbols of the South associated with rural, low-tech, agrarian life.

But what did Izzy say? If the question is, What is the South, then Izzy or "What is it?" gave the ACOG answer. ACOG was in the midst of a complex identity crisis with no simple answer. It could not choose a traditional mascot and thus comfortably embrace an old vision of the South. But the South had not yet developed new cultural symbols that resonated widely with the regional populace. Just as Atlanta was not sure about whether it was a Southern city or a global one (that happened to be located in the South), so too was ACOG unsure of how to read the cultural compass.

This tension was manifested again and again during the planning period in Atlanta. For the 1994 Super Bowl, Atlanta brought in French chefs to help cook for visitors to the city. This despite the fact that Atlanta not only has hundreds of down-home traditional Southern eateries but is also a leader in the emergence of nouvelle Southern cuisine. As we developed plans for a Festival of the American South, we continually heard jokes about not having tobacco-spittin' fiddlers, toothless ladies sitting on porches making baskets, and festival front lawn re-creations with beat-up or wrecked automobiles, trailers, and satellite dishes.

As ACOG developed its cultural plans, Billy Payne was able to signal that this was no Bubba Olympics in announcing appearances at the Olympic Arts Festival of Itzhak Perlman, the Miami City Ballet, and an art exhibit curated by J. Carter Brown. But, smarting from the implication, Payne also told *Time* magazine: "All those people calling us the Bubba Games—we're going to have the last laugh bigtime. We're taking all that Yankee money, and we're spending it to put on the Atlanta Olympic Games. Well, who outfoxed whom on this deal?"[6]

Planning the Walk-by Festival: No Grits 'n' Gravy

While the idea of a free, public, outdoor festival celebrating the culture of the American South emerged early on in the planning of the Atlanta Olympic Games and was, indeed, included in ACOG's proposal to the IOC, conflicts among the Cultural Olympiad staff called into question the commitment of ACOG to the concept. In 1994 articles and editorials in the *Atlanta Journal-Constitution* warned ACOG organizers about reneging on their commitment to the people of the South. One editorial suggested that ACOG should arrange for street corner performances, an overflowing of Southern music, craftsmanship, and food throughout Atlanta to show off for visitors.[7] Other newspapers were not so laudatory of such a program. A *New York Times* reporter supposedly tweaked ACOG plans of a "grits and gravy" festival, playing back into the insecurity about traditions perceived by the cosmopolitan press as rural, traditional, and lower class.

The ACOG officials with whom we worked—Linda Stephenson, managing director for Olympic programs; Sherman Day, managing director for the Olympic Legacy; Jeffrey Babcock, the director of the Cultural Olympiad; Leslie Gordon, Cultural Olympiad humanities producer; and Rebekah Jones, Cultural Olympiad technical director—were committed to producing a festival they could be proud of. There were, however, differences between producing staff and ACOG officials as to how that should best be done. This divide was characterized as a tension between "glitz and heart." ACOG did not want to imitate the Smithsonian's Festival of American Folklife, although they liked its scale, scholarly base, institutional standing, and educational mission.[8] It was too raw-looking with its tents and vernacular architectural constructions, too traditional and unstylish in its representation. At various points, ACOG leadership toyed with the idea of contracting with Dollywood, the Grand Ole Opry, and even Walt Disney World to produce a well-organized, fancy festival.

ACOG goals were varied and ever-changing, given the uncertainties of funding and other arrangements. At first, the leadership wanted the festival to be in Piedmont Park, which is the usual venue for open, free outdoor arts festivals in Atlanta, including the National Black Arts Festival, the Arts Festival of Atlanta, and others. The park was not near Olympic event venues, however, and thus was somewhat off the beaten path of Olympic visitors. As plans for the new, downtown Centennial

Olympic Park developed, so too did the need for some programming within it, and it would seem redundant to allocate funds to a festival in Piedmont Park as well.

Centennial Olympic Park was clearly a more prized location. To pay for the creation of the 21-acre park and to leave it as a legacy to the people of Atlanta after the festival, ACOG came up with a plan for financing its construction. First, an area of abandoned warehouses, parking lots, a halfway house, and Thelma's restaurant had to be bought and cleared. Opposition from the local-area community was relatively minimal. The construction would cost about $45 million. A planned hotel would be built on the site and would pay for much of the park. The rest would be made up from the sale of red bricks made by Home Depot, an Olympic sponsor. The public would order bricks with the names of loved ones engraved on them for $35 each. When the hotel fell through and brick sales failed to reach their goal, ACOG began to look for other sponsors to "buy" pieces of the park. Thus the need to program the park with a free festival for visitors was juxtaposed against the need to gain corporate sponsorship through advertising or sales operations in the park.[9]

Putting the festival in Centennial Olympic Park necessitated that it look good. It had to blend with the overall "look of the Games," which entailed a certain style, color palette, use of banners, fonts, and so on. It had to look good on television. It had to look good for corporate sponsors. Given the emphasis on the visual elements, the festival could not be built out of unfinished materials and have a lot of ropes and hanging plastic and jury-rigged structures. Most tents, even the relatively fancy ones used at the Festival of American Folklife, would not do. The Olympics, we knew, could not afford to build elaborate structures to meet the needs. Yet, as we argued strenuously, and repeatedly, the festival needed to cover performance venues and a good part of the audience in order to protect them from rain and Atlanta's 90-degree-plus summer sun. Without coverage, festival performances could be washed out, midafternoon crowds would not linger, and many visitors would face heatstroke and other discomforts. ACOG's leadership was quite clear about its priorities: It was more important that the festival look nice than that it provide creature comforts.

Officials were also justifiably concerned with the safety of visitors. ACOG planners figured they would get about two million out-of-town visitors to the city. The venues around the park—the Omni, the Georgia Dome, the World Congress Center—would host 250,000 ticket holders each day of the Olympics. Given the location of downtown hotels and the logistics of the bus dropoffs and the Atlanta metro transit system, these visitors would have to walk through the park. Moving that many people each day would require an easy system for walking from one location to another. A festival in the park would provide an impediment to rapidly moving that many walkers. People might tarry to hear a musical performance, watch a craftsman, get something to eat. Thus the festival might create congestion in the park as attendees lingered and blocked the easy and direct egress of others scurrying to an Olympic event, their hotel room, or their bus. This concern led one ACOG official to say, "We want a walk-through festival." To Smithsonian and Southern Arts Federation advisers, this became known as "the drive-by festival."

The need for a walk-through festival prompted ACOG organizers to suggest that all music sets at the festival be twenty minutes in length, with ten-minute breaks in between. Other presentations should be tightly scripted—like "shows," presumably at Disney and Epcot. Further, they shunned any seating, so people would have to stand and would literally walk through the festival. They even argued that if not much cover was provided for the festival audience, people would be discouraged from staying. Food vendors would be limited, so that people would seek meals elsewhere. Signage pointing and prompting people through the site would be very clear.

At the same time that the festival's parameters limited its impact, ACOG's leadership continued to insist that it would be an educational and entertaining event. The festival would correct old stereotypes about the South while affirming other aspects of the South's heritage. Some ACOG officials wanted everyone who went through the festival to have a singular orientation session—an idea that directly contradicted the walk-through festival concept. Initial ideas to have narrative and "workshop" stages that would be highly discussion-oriented—and educational—were nixed by ACOG as being too boring and too chancy—despite the Smithsonian's positive experience with these formats.

ACOG wanted the "real South" to be highlighted at the festival. The team working on the project—Diana Parker and myself from the Smithsonian, Peggy Bulger from the Southern Arts Federation, Leslie Gordon and Rebekah Jones from ACOG, and contract program director George Holt—suggested a festival that eventually came to be called Southern Crossroads. The festival theme was "Southern Expressions/Global Connections," illustrating the richness and diversity of Southern cultural expression and how it has reached around the globe, in the past, and now, through modern technology. The festival would have several components. The Dance Hall (initially called Talking Feet) would be a section in which bands played dance music of the South—particularly those forms that tie the South to other areas of the nation and the world. The dances would be demonstrated, and the audience—as many as two to three thousand visitors at a time—would join in dancing to a Southern beat. Among the traditions represented would be country line dancing, zydeco, step dancing, square dancing, blues/juke joint dancing, Native American powwow dancing, western swing, rock 'n' roll, salsa, hip-hop, and others. The original intention to build a large, vernacular dance hall fell by the wayside, as it was too expensive to do so—and would indeed hold audiences and lead to crowd congestion.

A second area of the festival would be Savor the South. Here, Southern regional cuisines (Upland South, Deep South, Coastal South) from traditional to nouvelle styles would be sold to the public in meal-size and sample portions. A Family Picnic area would impart the idea of dinner on the grounds. This would be a large area with long tables covered by oilskin cloths for "world family-style dining" for two thousand visitors an hour to sit and eat together. Additional space would be available for picnic blankets. Photo banners of various scenes of Southern picnics and dinners on the grounds would surround the area. There would also be strolling "impromptu" performances by a cappella quartets, old-time string bands, Piedmont bluesmen, and others.

A Southern Marketplace, operated by Olympic Services, would feature retail sales of Southern items. Merchandise would include traditional and contemporary Southern crafts, recordings of the musics of the South, books and videos about Southern history, food, art, and culture, packaged food items, e.g., beef jerky, preserves, astronaut food, barbecue and hot sauce, Southern care packages. The idea was for Southern musicians, craftspeople, authors, and others to benefit from the visiting consumers at the Olympics. All items, for example, would have provenance cards, provided by the Smithsonian, to encourage follow-up with the artist and the conveyance of educational information with craft purchases. The marketplace plan also included an on-site UPS station for sending items back home and such activities as demonstrations by Southern artists and craftspeople every day and book signings by authors.

Another section for the planned festival, Southern World Music, would feature performances of a diversity of music that grows out of

Southern experience and has now gone around the world. Large audiences would hear country and western, blues, soul, gospel, rockabilly and rock 'n' roll, jazz, bluegrass, Cajun, and *conjunto*. We also planned for Southern Celebrations—parades and movement of Mardi Gras floats, *comparsa* dancers, second-line jazz bands, fife and drum trampers, and the like. These moving performances would help animate the site, and in appearing to be spontaneous would sweep visitors up in the excitement—getting people to "join in."

ACOG wanted the high-tech South to be represented. So did we, but we wanted to find a clever way to accomplish it. While ACOG officials thought in terms of industrial trade show or fair, we suggested ways of joining high technology with cultural performance and demonstrations. We developed the idea of a Studio Stage, eventually called the South on Record. Southern recording studios, radio programs, and television provided the means for Southern expressions to reach beyond the region and the nation to the whole world. At the festival, a re-created studio for TV performances, radio shows, and musical recordings could give visitors a "behind-the-scenes" glimpse into the South's entertainment and information industries. Included would be televisionlike shows on Southern cooking, talk shows featuring the Civil Rights Movement and Southern poets and writers, and shows on Southern oratory—for example, a preacher, a politician, a football coach, and a tobacco auctioneer. Radio shows might include stories and verbal performance by public radio personalities, Black radio shows, samples of broadcast evangelism, and live performances of on-air programs. Recording-studio performances would include Atlanta record label showcases, rockabilly from Sun Studios, and sample recording sessions of R&B, soul, and country from Memphis, Nashville, and Muscle Shoals studios. There were complications in implementing this planned area because ACOG's network sponsor was NBC-TV, not the Atlanta-based CNN and Turner Broadcasting Network. Later, when NBC made a deal with Turner, this changed, but the idea was abandoned.

Another section of the festival was planned as Byways and Skyways, with demonstrations and performances on a culture and transportation theme. This area would examine trails, roads, railroads, trucking, buses, barges and boats, airlines, and spacecraft and the forms of cultural expression associated with them. Thus, we would program stories of the Trail of Tears, blues associated with crossroads, songs of the bayou, songs of railroading, the songs of the rivers, Civil Rights songs of the freedom rides, country-and-western truck-driving songs, and the occupational lore of airlines (like Delta and American, located in the South), and the work culture of the space industry—as found in Cape Canaveral, astronaut school in Huntsville, Alabama, and NASA's Mission Control in Houston. Overall, we would set up a cutaway airplane, a spaceship or two, rail cars, a freedom ride bus, and so on, and have everyone from astronauts to gandy dancers, the Freedom Singers to Cajuns on the bayou demonstrating the songs, worklore, and cultural traditions associated with various forms of transportation. Transportation itself would become a symbol of the movement of cultural expression across distances and boundaries—from within the South, across the region, and around the world.

While our plans in general were accepted, the response from ACOG officials was largely "we don't get it." The idea of a participatory festival, rather than staged entertainment, did not resonate very well. ACOG officials could not understand how a large-scale dance party would work. Concert stages made sense, but generally in a highly produced way. The idea of featuring demonstration programs, more-intimate performances, worklore, and so on seemed far afield from what they were used to—which was a more set, timed show or a trade-fair type of event. There was a general feeling among these ACOG officials that our scale was way off. Yet our attempts to define venues that would accommodate a thousand or two thousand people at a time were met by ACOG's attempts to limit coverage, seating, and space to only a few hundred. Our efforts to define the festival in a contiguous space, with an identity of its own, were also undermined by ACOG's need to parcel out space in the park for the purposes of sponsors and for other uses beyond those that we could control.

Corporate Takeover Plans for Centennial Olympic Park

The compelling interest in the park was taken by the Olympics' corporate sponsors. Coca-Cola was going to build a theme park across the street, advertising its product. McDonald's considered building its largest store in the world across the way. In the park, Budweiser, somewhat paralleling our idea of a dance hall, planned a Budweiser Beer Garden and sports bar, serving its brew and pretzels and munchies to entertainment, not much of which had anything to do with the South.

Indeed, most of the corporate partners were little concerned with

Southern culture and even wanted to run away from it to broader national and global identifications. AT&T, for example, was approached when it appeared that the name-a-brick program would fail to generate enough cash to pay for the construction of the park. AT&T agreed to come up with $12 million above its already sizable Olympic investment to support the park. In return, it would get one acre of the park on which to construct a 70-foot-tall modular building (looking like Battlestar Galactica) that it would call Global Olympic Village. AT&T would take over what had been our transportation and communication theme, but would execute it in its own way. The AT&T pavilion would feature high-tech communication equipment that it produced. It did not want to show its regional base—after all, that was a matter for its putative competitor, Bell South. Rather, AT&T wanted to stress its reach across the globe to visitors in Atlanta who had come from afar. If there was any cultural emphasis in the pavilion, it was on the grandeur and exclusivity of the technological and corporate culture of AT&T. The pavilion featured a three-story-high stage for televising the re-presentation of medals and hosting concerts nightly during the Games. It included an exclusive dining and viewing terrace (under hard cover and air-conditioned) for Olympic athletes and their families, and a massive video screen for showing Olympic Games highlights, transmitted over its lines. The building also featured actual NBC-TV studios set under the base of a globe 70 feet in diameter. There was nothing Southern about the Global Olympic Village. It could have been anywhere, and in fact, AT&T planned to put up the same structure for the Sydney Olympics in the year 2000.

We had been under pressure to develop some type of presentation dealing with high technology in the South. Our pavilion, which would have cost ACOG a few hundred thousand dollars, was discarded relatively quickly when in the funding crunch it became clear that AT&T was willing to provide the cash for the park. The months of scrutiny to which our plans for a culture and transportation area were subjected didn't mean much when AT&T came in. And the AT&T rough architectural plans with no proposal for public presentation or exhibitry were immediately accepted. When you can pay for it, no one has to "get it."

So too did Swatch gain a half acre in the park, not because it had anything to say or do particularly about Southern culture. The corporation came up with the money to rent land in the park and proceeded to show off and sell its watches as products to park visitors. Included in the

Swatch pavilion—again, hard-walled and air-conditioned—would be an exhibit of Annie Leibovitz photographs and a "conveyer belt–like" Swatch museum. At one point we were told that General Motors, another Olympic sponsor, was considering putting up $32 million for the park. In return, the whole festival might have to be scrapped and the park made into a car lot, advertising GM's product line. Talk about brokering culture! Eventually GM did buy some of the park in order to install a pavilion and show off its model cars.

Even in areas where rampant commercialism did not have to intrude, it did. And sometimes for convenience rather than money. For example, the initial plan was to encourage local and regional participation in the festival through food vendors. Many mom-and-pop enterprises and other small businesses serve outdoor festival-type events in the South. We thought the space could accommodate a rotating group of about thirty-six different vendors at a time (in three- or four-day shifts) serving snacks and meals at the festival. In this way, visitors would get some home-cooked foods, a feel and taste of the South. The concessionaires would come from various regions of the South, cook and serve traditional and nouvelle cuisine, and take home some money and benefit from the Olympics. This would spread the wealth around and broaden participation so that they could feel that they too helped to represent the region to the world.

This plan was scrapped. Too complicated, said ACOG, which fired its knowledgeable and experienced food concession manager and instead signed a master contract with Delaware North, a stadium concessions management company, to produce and serve all the food for the park. This decision had the benefit of simplifying things, managerially and financially, for ACOG. But it also left visitors bereft of more interesting culinary experiences—particularly Southern ones, as the contractor planned to serve mainly prepackaged hamburgers, hot dogs, and Italian food. When pushed, it agreed to carry some Southern items. But by and large, this arrangement excluded a whole group of people who could have participated and benefited, and it also transferred the responsibility for representation from the people to its corporate imitators.

Ironically, the planned Centennial Olympic Park began more and more to resemble the mall.[10] Not the National Mall in Washington, but the shopping mall in suburbia. Large corporations had purchased space to anchor the park and to advertise and sell their products—not the South. In buying space they had to conform to the Olympic look at a ba-

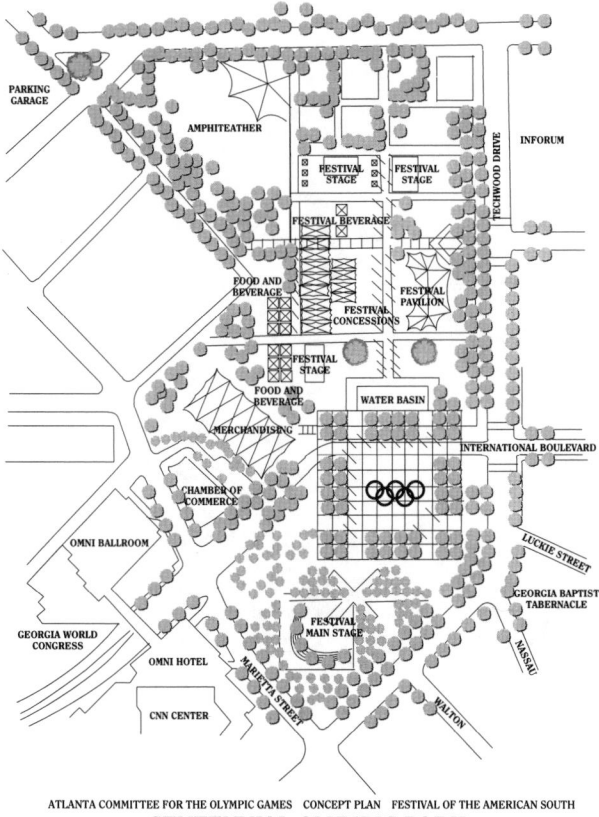

ATLANTA COMMITTEE FOR THE OLYMPIC GAMES   CONCEPT PLAN   FESTIVAL OF THE AMERICAN SOUTH
CENTENNIAL OLYMPIC PARK

Preliminary drawing of Centennial Olympic Park in 1994.
Notice the numerous trees, the grassy lawns, and the spacious,
tented site plan. Based on drawings by EDAW and ACOG.

sic level, but having provided the leverage money, they could pretty much do what they wanted. Once secure in their space, they could turn inward and regulate their own affairs, much as they might do as tenants of a shopping mall. Park space, designed as the gathering place of a large international public, had now been privatized, to be owned, regulated, and controlled by companies with something to sell. What had been envisioned as a free, open, and educational festival was now shopping mall entertainment in ever-diminishing open areas. One ACOG official recognized "the sellout" but argued that it was unfortunately necessary in order to afford building the park and supporting the free festival that did

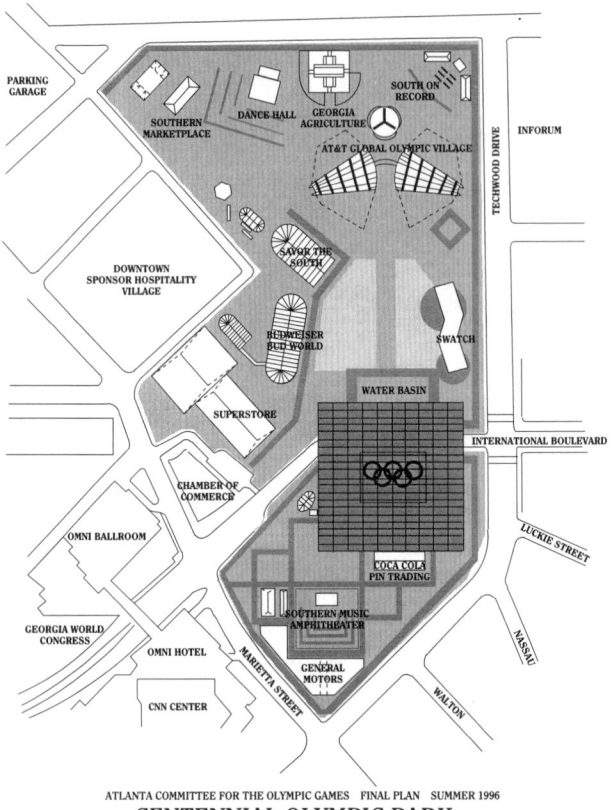

ATLANTA COMMITTEE FOR THE OLYMPIC GAMES   FINAL PLAN   SUMMER 1996
CENTENNIAL OLYMPIC PARK

Drawing of final plan for Centennial Olympic Park in 1996.
Notice how the formerly pastoral park has been transformed
with locations for corporate sponsor pavilions, stores, shops,
and other activities. Few trees or grassy areas remain. Based
on drawings by EDAW and ACOG.

remain. Another colleague was more blunt: "The message is that the
South, like the Olympics, like Atlanta, is for sale. We're just doing what
we've always done and for some reason felt we always had to do."

The Park Is Built: Where's the Festival?

In reality, Centennial Olympic Park was uglier than I expected it would
be. It was largely paved over with green-colored asphalt. As we had pre-

dicted to ACOG, the few grassy patches were worn away within days. The ugliness of the park resulted from its being carved up by its sponsors. While a shopping mall has an overall look and design and rules to preserve its architectural and operational order, Centennial Olympic Park had little. It was a nonzoned frontier. Budweiser, Swatch, AT&T, and General Motors garnered their own space and, by the looks of it, did what they wanted—irrespective of each other. Their pavilions were garish, boring, industrial, and uninviting. Much of their programming was worse. Budweiser offered Bud World, where, after waiting in line for half an hour or so, one could enter an air-conditioned bar and watch scores of continuous Budweiser commercials projected onto the walls, ceiling, and floor—while drinking overpriced brew. AT&T did provide some high-quality and interesting evening concerts. But its Global Olympic Village offered long lines of people a free phone call and commercials on a video wall. General Motors offered a car ballet—dull chromelike automobile sculptures poised on 10-foot-high pedestals, rocking this way and that. The popular press had it right: Centennial Olympic Park was one big commercial, a corporate theme park, where the aesthetics of experience was a commercial of shorter or greater length.[11]

The problem extended beyond the park to a whole swath of downtown Atlanta. The city, to the chagrin of ACOG and the IOC as well, sold rights for vending on the downtown sidewalks. Makeshift booths sprouted on every available inch of real estate—selling T-shirts, shaved ice, pizza, official and pirated Izzy dolls, pennants, banners, and other merchandise. These vendors were doing nothing different than the larger corporations were in intruding on the partnership rights for the Olympic Games. Samsung opened its own Olympic Expo blocks from the park, and in signs and banners gave the public the false impression that it was an Olympic sponsor. So, too, did Nike buy an old parking garage adjacent to Centennial Olympic Park and open a highly touted Nike World—which turned out to be yet another commercial. And Coca-Cola, though an Olympic sponsor, opened Coca-Cola World across the street from the park, hyping its product in a simulated sports-themed attraction.

Southern Crossroads struggled against this cacophony. On opening day, the *Atlanta Journal-Constitution* ran a lead story for a special section devoted to the park with the subhead "The Southern Crossroads festival opens today, giving visitors a taste of the region's music, crafts, and food—without big-name corporate sponsorships or promotions."[12] And

Children play in the fountain in Centennial Olympic Park. Photo by Brad Parker, courtesy Diana Parker, Smithsonian Institution.

the next day, the same reporter found the festival overshadowed, writing a story titled "Crossroads Talent Loses to Flash."[13] Though its stages were relatively large, and its 24-foot-high signs were sprinkled throughout the park, Southern Crossroads was virtually invisible in the midst of the corporate presence. It could not compete with the size and mass of the AT&T building, the seven-story Coca-Cola can, the overall ragtag and incomprehensible stretch of downtown Atlanta. Indeed, even the park itself became indistinguishable from the non-park, the Olympic from the non-Olympic. It all became just one big commercial.

Billy Payne defended the need for sponsors, citing the lack of taxpayer support—at the national, state, and local levels. Olympics, if they were going to be privately supported, needed corporate funds. And corporations needed something in return—advertising, marketing, and promotion. He decried nonsponsors' taking advantage of this, including some in the city of Atlanta who were, by their commercialism, cheapening the Games. Some members of the International Olympic Committee were more outraged. The Canadian vice chair of the IOC opined that Atlanta would be the last U.S. city to host the Olympics if the ACOG model of private sponsorship without full local government cooperation prevailed. The Atlanta Olympics were generally derided in the national and international press as being flagrantly commercial.

There were exceptions. There was some noncommercial, festival-like behavior in the park, but it had little to do with ACOG or Smithsonian design. The dancing fountains near the park's center became the people's space. Children and adults would run under the spurting water geysers to cool off in the summer heat. Thousands would play and soak in the water, watched by thousands more. This was the plaza that the people made their own.

Southern Crossroads

A festival that is orderly, rigorous, and controlled is not destined to be much of a festival. For it is in the ritual nature of experiential spillage that festivals take on their partylike character, their counterstructural features, their density and layering of activities.

Within the tightly planned Atlanta Olympics script, Southern Crossroads only occasionally realized its festival nature. For the most part, it provided a daily schedule of musical concerts on three stages and a few crafts demonstrations in front of the marketplace.

In the effort to make the park look nice and to accommodate sponsor privilege, we had to surmount some difficult problems. The Southern Music Amphitheater was hampered by poor acoustics and sound bleed because of its proximity to the General Motors pavilion. Though General Motors had nothing to do with the program per se, because the corporation had "bought" a share of the park, its signs, logos, and advertisements were strewn around the stage area. Its car ballet indeed ringed the audience. Staged musical presentations had to stop when the ballet began. Another stage, the South on Record, was cut off from park crowd flow because of a fence covered by opaque AT&T banners. Musicians performing onstage could not in the first few days attract crowds because visitors could not see the stage or find their way to benches. We finally got park staff to remove the banners.

A third stage, the Dance Hall, was nicely set, but the audience had absolutely no shade. To sit baking in Atlanta's afternoon summer sun was asking a lot of the audience—even if they did have benches. After several days of performances to empty benches, Southern Crossroads staff examined the possibility of covering the audience. The expense and impracticality of the idea mitigated against doing so. Diana Parker came up with the idea of using beach umbrellas to at least provide shade for several hundred people at a time. Staff contacted Coca-Cola, which had many such umbrellas, used in various venues for eating and lounging. Coca-Cola agreed to provide scores of umbrellas that could be used for the Dance Hall audience. But AT&T objected because the umbrellas had the Coca-Cola logo on them. Since the park was "AT&T's," it would not allow the the Coca-Cola umbrellas to be placed there. We could use AT&T-logo umbrellas—but, alas, there were none available.

This level of corporate competitiveness and blind pursuit of perceived self-interest at the public's expense was mirrored in other ways. In the days leading up to the opening of Southern Crossroads, the AT&T public relations liaison complained that AT&T wasn't getting enough recognition—even though its logo was emblazoned on just about every banner, fence, and sign in the park, its Global Olympic Village dominated the scene, and every publication displayed its name as sponsor or presenter. I was incredulous.

But my incredulity reached new heights at the press conference on opening day. Everyone who worked or volunteered for the Olympics received a free Coca-Cola card that when slipped into select soft-drink-dispensing machines allowed one to get a free Coca-Cola product. I, like many others, wore this card (about the size of a dollar bill) around my neck with my Olympics credentials. The card had "Coca-Cola" printed on it. As I, Jeff Babcock, and an AT&T vice president were walking toward the dais on a stage to begin the opening day press conference for Southern Crossroads, the AT&T person stopped in his tracks. Grabbing the credentials hanging around my neck, he turned the Coca-Cola card over so that the big print was now facing my chest and said, "You don't want them to see that. Coca-Cola isn't sponsoring the park. We are."

The opening ceremony, with Smithsonian secretary Heyman, Billy Payne, and Georgia governor Zell Miller, went much better. And performances over the course of the Olympics were quite good. Southern Crossroads included some of the best Southern groups in a variety of musical genres—from deeply rooted and traditional performers to contemporary innovators in those traditions. Old hands like rockabilly original Maggie Lewis participated, but so did Ulali, a contemporary American Indian group. Visitors heard the gospel of the Blind Boys of Alabama, the Birmingham Sunlights, and the Georgia Mass Choir; the blues of W. C. Clark and Cephas and Wiggins; the zydeco of Geno Delafose; the Cajun music of D. L. Menard and of Steve Riley and the Mamou Playboys; a variety of jazz, from Kermit Ruffins, the Treme Brass Band, to J. P. Torres and His Orchestra; the country music of Robin and Linda Williams, Don Walser, and the Vidalias; hip-hop and rap from A Night of Urban Poetry and Jack "the Rapper" Gibson; the soul music of Rufus Thomas; and the Tex-Mex music of Tish Hinojosa and Mingo Saldivar.

Thousands of visitors from around the nation and all parts of the globe danced to Cajun music, tried a salsa for the first time, joined in western swing, and rocked to the sounds of Memphis. Thousands more joined fraternity steppers from Atlanta, demonstrating a popular African American male tradition. Craftspeople like C. J. Meaders, Ernie Mills, Betty Mae Jumper, the Mississippi Crossroads Quilters, and contemporary kudzu artist Carol Stangler demonstrated their work and spoke with hundreds of visitors.[14]

The food for the public, was, as predicted, lousy. Discussions and workshops did not take place, though some of the presentations and introductions were extremely well done and instructive. Processions through the park were rare. Signage, with imagery of the South, existed on the edge of visitor consciousness throughout the park—though these kiosks were 20 to 24 feet high, they were lost in comparison with the size of the corporate pavilions.

Musicians and craftspeople endured a good deal of discomfort, poor accommodations (in a Ramada with a bar featuring an unavoidably large Confederate flag that was removed only just before the festival began), late buses, and awful food. The Freedom Singers captured the experience with their standby "We Shall Overcome." And, for the most part, everybody did—we had to. Camaraderie did develop, the staff came together. The ACOG program team led by Leslie Gordon and the technical crew led by Rebekah Jones solved problems and established an operational tempo. And so too did the festival. Though lost in the muddle of the park and downtown Atlanta, Southern Crossroads did, as the *Atlanta Journal-Constitution* reported, eventually find "its niche."[15] It became a place within the park and the Olympics to discover and even learn. Wrote the *New York Times:* "Here at Southern Crossroads it was possible to slip away from the crowds and sit for a few moments listening to prayerful, jubilant, protesting voices raised in song and to the softer sounds of conversations among strangers. Somewhere else in the city, men and women were competing for the highest honors in sports. But here too, it seemed, there was a quintessential Olympics experience to be had."[16]

The Shop Saga

It was my belief that if the Smithsonian had not pushed hard for Southern Marketplace, such a shop would not have been part of ACOG's plan for the park. Both the Smithsonian and ACOG recognized that Southern Marketplace would be a service to Southern craftspeople, authors, and musicians. Though estimates about its possible gross sales ran from $30,000 to $90,000 a day during the time of the Olympics, neither ACOG nor the Smithsonian projected it to be a big moneymaker. ACOG, with its master retail contractor, Eric M. Chandler Merchandising, had organized a one-acre Superstore in the middle of the park for the sale of Olympic merchandise from hats, pins, T-shirts, and Izzy dolls to commemorative prints and high-end jewelry. These items all had high markups and would generate huge demand and sales of $250,000 to $500,000 a day. Selling crafts and books was less profitable, and demand was much more uncertain. Neither ACOG nor Chandler wanted to invest the money or the time to assemble an inventory of Southern merchandise.

Nor did the Smithsonian's museum shops unit. Although they and ACOG tried to negotiate an arrangement, it fell through. The Smithsonian's own shops unit wanted profits from the operation. And while, like ACOG, it may have wanted to provide a service to Southern craftspeople, musicians, and writers, that was not its primary purpose.

Given the whole thrust of what we were trying to accomplish at the Olympics—giving local and regional people a cultural presence in the midst of an international extravaganza so that they could retrieve some benefit—the Smithsonian's Folklife Center agreed to take on the task. Our formal arrangement with the Olympics was for the Smithsonian to provide the inventory for a 4,000-square-foot Southern Marketplace in Centennial Olympic Park. We would acquire an inventory of Southern crafts, recordings of Southern music, books about the South, and nonperishable food items and transfer this merchandise over to Chandler, which would be responsible for the retail operations. We would also provide provenance cards for the crafts, with information about the items and the name and contact information for the artists so that potential customers or people interested in their craft could get in touch with them after the Olympics. Additionally, we agreed to produce a program book for the festival, to be sold in Southern Marketplace and at other locations. The program book, *Southern Crossroads*, contained the daily schedule of events, a map of the park and downtown area, listings of the musicians and craftspeople, greetings from President Clinton, Billy Payne, Secretary Heyman, and informative, substantive articles about the South by Julian Bond, Bill Ferris, Mary Hood, John Shelton Reed, Bill Malone, and others.[17]

Chandler would run the warehousing and retail operation. The Smithsonian would get a percentage of the gross sales and the cost of goods sold to be redistributed back to the craftspeople, presses, recording companies, and so on.

Gathering the inventory took a hectic six months. Claudia Telliho of our office contacted scores of craftspeople, cooperatives, presses, food manufacturers, and recording companies. She used a network of leads from the Southern Arts Federation, scholars, activists, community organizations, and others to establish contacts. While some of our suppliers would be university presses and businesses that operated according to normal commercial standards, most did not. They were craftspeople, often making their stuff out of their homes or workshops, running a family business. We did not have any advance funds to purchase inventory, and so we had to rely mainly on consignment. Negotiations were personable but ongoing, varied, and diffuse. In some cases, we needed to acquire a sizable part of their total craft production. They could not afford to give it to us on a consignment basis—so we bought their merchandise outright. In other cases we put down deposits against sales. In all, we obtained merchandise and built up an inventory from some 280 different suppliers.

The big difficulty with the operation arose with regard to pricing. At the Festival of American Folklife, we sell crafts at a retail price 40 to 50 percent above the price at which the craftsperson consigns them to us. Chandler was setting the retail prices at an average of about 250 percent of the consigned price. We gave Chandler a $400 quilt—they proposed pricing it at $1,000. Music CDs that we provided at $10 they wanted to sell at $28. We found this problematic on two counts. First, merchandise would not sell at these prices. Chandler was treating Southern crafts, books, and recordings as if they were Olympic-logo T-shirts. The markup for our kinds of merchandise was customarily lower than that of logo goods. Simply put, the stuff wouldn't sell; customers wouldn't buy the overpriced merchandise. Second, craftspeople and others whose items were being sold would be upset—and rightly so. They would regard the pricing as an exploitative attempt to rip off artists. And they would be vocal about it to the press—causing damage to the reputations of both the Smithsonian and the Olympics.

I informed Chandler representatives and Olympic officials of this problem, albeit to little avail. When the Southern Marketplace opened in the park the week before the Olympics, Chandler's prices were on the merchandise. To get the shop open took an intense effort by Smithsonian staff, who, though not contractually obligated to do so, nonetheless felt responsible for the adequate care and display of the items.

While the Southern Marketplace looked good and had enough customer traffic—even though the Olympics had not yet begun, sales were awful—averaging a paltry $1,000 per day during this first week. Most visitors were local Atlantans or people from the surrounding region. They knew what Southern crafts, CDs, and books sold for. They knew the prices were high, and few were buying. Indeed, by midweek the *Atlanta Journal-Constitution* ran a story, "Prices May Stun, But Folk Art's a Delight," about Southern Marketplace, its wonderful stuff, and the overly high prices.[18] The article noted how the shop's prices were likely oriented toward an international crowd.

Despite the efforts of ACOG Cultural Olympiad staff, Chandler could not be persuaded or pressured to reduce its prices—even for the most sensitive of items. With Southern Crossroads about to begin (the day before the Olympics opening ceremony), and craftspeople about to come and demonstrate their artistry directly in front of the Marketplace, we had to do something about the situation. As soon as the quilters showed up and saw how they were being ripped off, they would justifiably scream to the press. Indeed, I was already getting calls from a number of reporters about the "story"—how, in the midst of the overcommercialized Olympics, here were two great institutions also exploiting the very people they were supposed to be honoring.

With no other alternative in sight, and with the clock ticking, I made a risky offer to Jeff Babcock as a way of getting around what promised to be a terrible crisis: The Smithsonian would take over the shop. We would do this in a day. Contracts that had taken months to negotiate would have to be sorted out in hours. My staff, already stretched and stressed, would have to do more—like reprice 40,000 items, many of them overnight, and run a complex retail operation with virtually no preparation. The arrangement risked Smithsonian money, the well-being of my staff, and possibly my job. The Olympics and the Smithsonian bureaucracies would have to move quickly. Amazingly, they did. Billy Payne, Secretary Heyman, and Undersecretary Constance Newman backed the idea. Barbara Strickland, my administrative officer, with help from our accounting division and Robert Tanner and Linda Schryer, as well as Emily Botein, Karin Hayes, Bill Holmes, Philippa Jackson, Marcus Johnson, Heather MacBride, Khadijah Mann, Molly McGehee, Mary Monseur, Sheila Mooney, Ray Searles, and Claudia Telliho, rushed into action. Heroism takes many forms. But in the midst of the heat and rain, the commercialism and greed, the privilege and pretext that swirled around the Olympics, these people performed heroically, working eighteen-hour days in great discomfort to do what was right for the people we sought to represent and for the broader public.

In the end, the shop had its $9,000 days, $14,000 days, and a high of about $21,000 one day. It was closed for three days following the Centennial Olympic Park bombing. Funds of almost $300,000 were paid out to craftspeople, presses, record labels, and musicians. Like almost all vendors at the Olympics, we were hurt by the lack of a large international visitorship and the plain economic fact that there was just too much competition for visitor dollars to make any venture profitable. Though the shop would draw about 1,500 visitors an hour, twelve to fourteen hours a day, most did not buy.

Suppliers also had problems with the operation. Many were disappointed with the level of sales, given their expectations. And in the hectic effort to reorganize and reprice merchandise, take over the inventory management, and send items back to suppliers, we had a significant amount of missing and damaged goods. Doing all the accounting and processing the claims took time and strained our relationships with some suppliers. We lost money, lost some credibility, and learned a great deal. We also did the right thing. An institution like the Smithsonian operated in a personal, humane way—as did ACOG. Without any hoopla or contractual obligation, Jeff Babcock and the good people at ACOG helped to mitigate part of our financial loss.

The Southern Marketplace shop also stimulated our development of a new product, an enhanced CD called *Crossroads: Southern Routes*.[19] Pro-

Billy Payne, Andrew Young, Zell Miller, and others join hands in the ceremony on the AT&T stage to reopen Centennial Olympic Park. The scene is captured on the Panasonic video screen and broadcast around the world by NBC-TV. Photo by Brad Parker, courtesy Diana Parker, Smithsonian Institution.

duced with Microsoft, *Crossroads* played like an audio CD, but also as a CD-ROM in a computer, and as a World Wide Web site companion with an Internet connection. We sold and demonstrated the product in the Marketplace. And it earned kudos in the press—it was called the "best enhanced CD yet" by *U.S. News & World Report.* It generated royalties for artists and became a source of lesson plans and curriculum material on the Web.[20]

Though the end result of Southern Marketplace fell short of what was initially anticipated, we nonetheless followed through on our promise to help provide exposure for Southern cultural products. And indeed, some months after the Olympics we were approached by other organizations that had seen the Marketplace and were interested in its merchandise and the opportunities it presented for sales and support of Southern artists.

IN MEMORIUM:
ALICE HAWTHORNE
U.S.A.
MELIH UZUNYOL
TURKEY

A makeshift folk shrine in Centennial Olympic Park arises with flags, mementos, notes, and a handmade cardboard sign, at the site of the bombing and death of Alice Hawthorne and Melih Uzunyol. Photo by Diana Parker, Smithsonian Institution.

Back to the People

While the communal water fountain and the musical performances helped mark out some "people space" in the park, the most moving and dramatic event that brought the park back to the people was, of course, the result of the bombing. A bomb exploded in the early-morning hours of July 27. Tragically, the bomb, placed near the sound tower in front of the AT&T stage, resulted in two deaths. The park was closed for three days following the bombing, as the FBI combed the area for clues and ACOG put into place more rigorous security in the park. Centennial Olympic Park became the focus of international media attention.

Smithsonian staff spent the hours immediately after the bombing verifying the location of all the musicians, craftspeople, and others who were participating in Southern Crossroads. Smithsonian staff worked closely with their ACOG counterparts in holding together the spirit of the group in light of the bombing and the speculation and rumors of other acts of terrorism. Diana Parker, the senior Smithsonian official on the scene, determined that she had to stay in Atlanta to work on rebuilding the program—even though she was needed in Washington to help organize the Smithsonian's Birthday Party on the Mall. Though she and other Smithsonian staff had their problems with the park, the festival, Southern Marketplace, and everything else, they felt it important to stand by ACOG and our colleagues in recapturing the park for public use.

Indeed, much of the media coverage and many talk shows, interviews, and press conferences were devoted to the issue of the park. Here was a free and open place in the midst of the Olympics, the gathering point of the world's people. How could this place be desecrated in such a manner? Could the people be denied their place? Would the park reopen? Billy Payne and ACOG officials were determined that it would. Centennial Olympic Park, whatever its problems, had become a symbol of the Olympic committee, visitors to Atlanta, and even people around the globe. It stood for the ability of free people to gather in public, to celebrate a good thing. Ironically, the park overshadowed even the Games in communicating the Olympic spirit.

And it was this spirit that prevailed when the park reopened three days later. The overwhelming public feeling—inscribed on T-shirts, so we know it to be true—was that the people would not tolerate a terrorist attempt to take the Olympics away from them. People, including my own wife and children, walked into the park with the conviction that they had a stake in maintaining that most public of spaces. The park had become distinct from the cacophony surrounding it. To walk into the park was to have a purpose and make a statement; and to do it with tens of thousands of others provided a massive show of public force and will. And in the midst of all the overproduced pavilions, the slick advertisements, the logoed banners and signs was a simple folk shrine, made by the people. There on the site of the bombing deaths were flags and flowers, written messages and mementos, reclaiming that place in the name of humanity.

CHAPTER 15

CONCLUSION

THE NEW
STUDY
AND CURATION
OF CULTURE

In a world increasingly permeated with the mass cultures of Western capitalism, the drive toward homogenization seems relentless. If we cannot yet see a future with the planet being overrun by a single dominant global culture, we can nonetheless easily imagine it. Consider a rather insidious but telling example, a McDonald's television commercial broadcast during the Olympics. The commercial featured a teenage gymnast from Korea, first walking the streets of Seoul, I presume, looking for her favorite place to eat. She found it—a McDonald's. The scene shifts. She is now in Atlanta as part of the Korean national team, competing in Olympic gymnastics. She is somewhat homesick, but then relieved when she finds that she can get a hometown meal in Atlanta—from McDonald's. McDonald's seeks to have its food become everyone's hometown, standard fare.

At the same time, the world has never seen a more creative time; new and recast peoples and cultures are being formed on the basis of any one of a number of characteristics and interests, not over generations but within years. Indeed, consider McDonald's again: it recently opened stores in India that serve neither beef nor pork but rather mutton burgers, in order to make the product appealing to Hindu and Muslim consumers.

The social boundaries between populations have never been so porous. Cultural identity, once seemingly simple to determine, is now exceedingly complex. Without exception, human beings around the world find themselves caught in the tension of simultaneously moving closer together culturally and further apart. And if the world is caught between McWorld and Jihad,[1] scholars, curators, presenters, and brokers of culture are at its crossroads.

Grappling with and figuring out one's identity—personal, communal, racial, ethnic, occupational, national, regional—and how to represent it have become a major issue of the times. Scholarly disciplines, museums, and cultural institutions need to stand somewhere. Their publications, exhibitions, programs, and products offer a unique forum for the practice of cultural civics. They provide an important vehicle for cultural dialogue, democracy, and self-help, engaged in by those who stand both to gain and to lose by the way they are represented. Unfortunately, cultural scholars and curators are being outgunned and eclipsed by politicians, journalists, filmmakers, television producers, theme park operators, public relations firms, tour operators, corporate marketeers, novelists, and Webmeisters. Even community groups, native peoples' organizations, and grassroots activists are out in front of scholars and curators in terms of representing their cultures and brokering those representations with larger publics—witness, for example, the profusion of Web sites for such groups. Cultural scholars and curators have something important to contribute—the research-based understandings of culture that they generate and the prestige value of the institutions in which those understandings may be delivered. But until now, their contribution has been relatively minor, their engagement limited. A new map, on which the political and economic importance of culture is recognized, is emerging and with it a greater need for refocused, rejuvenated attention to cultural scholarship and curation.

Culture as Political: Culture and the State

Culture, understood as the values, worldviews, and identities that people construct for themselves, plays a major role in world events. Culture affects the coherence and viability of nations. This is not the "culture" of high society, the elite arts, or the commercial media. Rather it is the culture of ordinary people as expressed in daily life, on special occasions, and in trying times. Culture has emerged as a topic of public concern and political action.

Nations have been the dominant form of political organization over the past two centuries. Despite a common etymological root with the terms "native" and "nature," "nations" are not natural—they are historically forged and articulated, albeit often in mythic, naturalistic terms. By the nineteenth century, European nationhood was defined in terms of a physically distinct race of people, natively born of a particular land and speaking a language suited to them. This definition also led to invented traditions of peoplehood—of the folk—like forms of national costumes. Songs, ballads, and folktales were invested with stronger meaning as they came to stand both metaphorically and metonymically for the nation of the whole. And national destinies—generally the formation or expansion of the state—were sensed and articulated, often in reaction to the modernism of the Industrial Revolution.

Elsewhere, ideas of national culture developed from other sources and stimuli. In colonial India, Indonesia, Kenya, and Mexico, for example, an emergent or newly uncovered national culture expressed its identity against the state. Culture was used by nationalists to fight against colonial powers.

In the former Soviet bloc, there was a disjuncture between the culture of the state (bureaucratic state communism) and forms of state-created national culture like folklore. People nowadays rebel against this invented folklore, seeing in it the symbolic projection of state control over the expressive life of its people.

Currently, there are growing attempts to redefine national culture in religious terms. Hindu fundamentalists in India, Muslim fundamentalists from North Africa and across southern Asia, Jewish fundamentalists in Israel, and Christian fundamentalists in the United States are all pursuing new forms of statehood in a supposedly traditional response to states that have become too secular. These are not people, energies, or events of the past, however, but thoroughly contemporary movements threatening to undercut the authority of the state and reconstitute it in different terms.

The Culture of Diversity

Most Third World countries, emerging from colonial rule after World War II, had to contend quite centrally with the possibility of a culturally diverse state—that is, a nation consisting of a population speaking a variety of different languages, possessing a number of different religions, and coming from many ethnic and tribal backgrounds. India, Indonesia, Brazil, Kenya, and others defined the issue as "unity in diversity," "in one many," and other, similar ways. The maintenance of a central government, with an attendant core civic culture, has been a challenge in these fissiparous societies. As in the past, ethnic, religious, occupational, tribal, linguistic, and regional differences continue to rend the social fabric.

The industrialized European countries also had to knit their internal diversity into national form. Italy had to bring together various regional cultures; Germany assimilated populations of different religions; Great Britain unified nations with different languages, histories, and traditions. But because of traditions of governance and levels of literacy and education, these countries were thought to be more immune to centrifugal pressures.

The problem with this view is that some of the societies that supposedly successfully negotiated this transition have experienced a reemergence of state-threatening cultural identities. Many nations seem to be under cultural siege of a sort, threatened by the diversity of their people that results from persisting native populations, immigration, and internal divisions. A Native American nation and a Quebeçois nation may yet break off from Canada; Germany struggles with its immigrant Turkish populations and the very definition of what it is to be German—is it as national citizen or as ethnic native? Japan tries to come to grips with the way it deals with cultural minorities in its own and other societies. In the former Soviet Union, the cultural wars are literally shooting wars, over land, language, and religion. And the United States, Australia, Great Britain, France, Spain, and others struggle with the issue of where the cultural center is to be found and in what it should consist. More and more, the "advanced" democracies themselves ask the question, How is a culturally diverse state possible?

Cultural Policy

The question is not so much one of demographics—every nation will always have a populace with differing cultural characteristics—as one of policy. Is one way of dealing with cultural diversity to have a policy of eliminating it, as Skip Gates notes? For some, cultural diversity could be reduced through acculturation to a mainstream way of life. For others, elimination of cultural diversity involves a more coercive strategy of exclusion, cleansing, and oppression. Or should policies encourage diversity because it can be a source of strength?

National authorities exert influence over the cultural practices of people. States can and often do set up ministries and agencies to institutionalize culture. They may succeed in implementing their will to a greater or lesser extent, depending upon their power and resources. States can encourage the continuity of oral traditions and behavioral norms or their formal, literary, legalistic transformations. States can try to wipe out practices they regard as primitive and vulgar. States can promote majority culture or the culture of a minority.

State policy toward culture may even be officially neutral, but that is exceedingly difficult to effect in actuality. Use of official language, forms of adornment, even forms of entertainment offered at state functions encourage certain kinds of cultural expression and discourage others. Policy can also determine who has rights and privileges, based upon cultural criteria and the interest of the state.

The state often determines what is taught in the schools and who and what are to be respected. It decides who is eligible to be taught whose history. And state policy can include and exclude people from that history, defining some people as culture heroes, consigning others to oblivion. State policy may even decide what is defined as knowledge and what isn't. The state can encourage certain occupations with cultural roots and discourage others.

Should the state promote high culture, popular culture, commercial culture, or folk culture? Should it abstain from using culture as a tool for either national unity or the expression of personal freedom? Should the state foster a singular cultural identity among its populace or promote diversity? Should the state invest its own resources in culture, and if so, to what end, or should the state encourage participation in forms of global culture?

Subnational Cultural Representation

Though states are powerful, so too are the cultural communities that form parts of their polities. Members of these communities actively pursue strategies of forwarding their cultural agendas. They use political techniques that are quite conventional—running for elected office, lobbying power holders, going on strike, writing letters to the editor. But native advocacy groups like the Shuar federation in Ecuador are also setting up their own museums and cultural centers. Others are writing their own textbooks, producing them with desktop-publishing technology, and photocopying their own histories. In South Africa, townships use community radio. In New York, the gay community uses public access cable television. The low cost and wide dissemination of modern electronic technology—tape recorders, video cameras, computers, fax machines, and modems connecting personal computers to the Internet and the World Wide Web—have broadened the ability of even the most isolated and traditional communities as well as idiosyncratic microcultures to represent themselves to global audiences. Hundreds of documentary films are being made with low-cost Handycams. Thousands of recording companies have been spawned by dual-cassette boom boxes. And even new cybermuseums are being created. Home pages for individuals, communities, institutions, and even nations have within a year or two become a widespread electronic means of cultural self-representation, of people brokering themselves.

Globalism

Still, with all the internal difficulties, partitions, separations, and questioning based on or making use of cultural differences, there are new and growing unities. Global institutions, such as the United Nations, have moved in an unprecedented way to define a new global consensus. Global agreements and standards for ethical and legal conduct, human rights, and environmental policy have been forged and applied. A more united Europe has emerged, partially subsuming sovereignty and national identity for shared economic interest. New free trade zones in North America and other parts of the world are based not on identities of ethnic groups, language, religion, or kinship but on participation in regional and global markets.

Not all global unities and alliances are supranational. Many, as Arjun Appadurai notes, are transnational and involve nongovernmental organizations.[2] Voluntary organizations, advocacy groups, self-help networks, and others have joined the multinational corporation in working beyond, around, and through national boundaries to accomplish their objectives. They rely on neither governments nor a central, hierarchical form of organization. So alliances of Native American schools communicate with each other and pursue educational goals over the Internet without going through the Bureau of Indian Affairs in Washington. Various chapters of Greenpeace achieve their goals without sanction of the United Nations. And a host of right-wing, leftist, and radical organizations move people, goods, and ideas across the globe without national approval or direction.

Indeed, there is, as seminal sociologist Émile Durkheim predicted a century ago, a division of labor and interest that has produced its own new communities across the globe. These new forms of global culture are tied to the industrial and postindustrial world and made possible by telecommunication technologies. They are themselves diverse. There is not a single global culture or "new world order." Rather, there are various global—i.e., nonlocalized and transnational—cultures, with their own languages, codes, and worldviews.

Forms of global political and economic culture are neither so universal nor so entrenched as to preclude real or perceived threats. Some, supranational forms, are fairly widespread—international law and conventions with regard to moral conduct and human rights. Others are quite narrowly defined and make little claim to universality.

Though the cold war is over, the world, particularly the former Soviet bloc, continues to ponder the alternatives of capitalism and communism. In many parts of the world, neither of these alternatives has proved viable, and in questioning both their political and their economic dimensions, new alternatives have emerged. Often characterized as nativistic, though not necessarily homegrown, some of these options suggest their own universalism, their own globalism, which contrasts with the dominant supranational one. Thus, in the United States, and in parts of Europe, some analysts see in Islam an alternative and a threat to the new world order. Domestically in the United States, some Christian fundamentalist groups are regarded in the same way and, indeed, explicitly challenge the very notion of such an order.

How much multiculturalism can the new globalism stand? How are supranational globalisms, such as declarations of human rights, to be weighed against the values of multiple cultures that may not see humanity in the same light? How much of the global definition of women's potentialities, as delineated by the 1995 Fourth United Nations Conference on Women, in Beijing, is culturally appropriate to the varied societies around the planet? What do we do with alternative cultural standards that do not accept a global institution's framework? And what do we do with those who use instrumentally acceptable means to forward unacceptable goals? Do we face conceptual paralysis, as did the

U.S. government in light of the electoral victory of religious fundamentalists in Algeria who sought through the democratic process to institute a nondemocratic Islamic state?

We don't know the answers to these questions, nor, more fundamentally, do we have the research base to begin to figure out how to answer them. But debates over cultural policy issues, the relationship of culture to the state, and the desirability and processes of multiculturalism and globalism have emerged from current events and in public consciousness around the world.

Culture as Economics: Tourism

Cultural representation is not only of political importance. It has a strong economic dimension as well. Culture is increasingly commodified, packaged, and marketed for use in a rapidly expanding culture industry. The ways in which cultural production is exploited will be a key economic issue in the early twenty-first century. A huge amount of money is spent on producing and controlling the symbols, images, values, ideas, and beliefs of the world's people. Cultural production consists of everything from advertising about what you should eat and wear to cultural tourism, entertainment, much of the education industry, and the movement of information in books and over radio, television, and computer networks. At issue is who does the representing to whom, who makes money from it, and at what cost.

The largest single cultural enterprise in the United States is the Disney Corporation. Millions of Americans learn about world cultures at Disneyland and Walt Disney World. One does not need a highly developed theory of authenticity to recognize these as entertaining but misleading representations of culture. There is nothing wrong with entertainment, and indeed fantasies can have a wonderful effect of stimulating the imagination. It is only when fantasy and theatrics are confounded with history and ethnography that there is a problem. It was with only a slight sense of irony that former minister of culture Jack Lang, interviewed about Euro-Disney, said, "They claim to present our folklore and culture, but they have taken it and returned it to us in unrecognizable form. . . . Look, not even the french fries are French."[3]

Yet we continue to see a profusion and proliferation of commercial firms exploiting culture in the form of the cultural theme park. The

Japanese, having procured a Disney park, are now building their own, the clean and convenient Dutch town park. Hawai'i has long hosted a Polynesia Cultural Center, run by Mormon missionaries and featuring somewhat stereotypic depictions of exotic Pacific Island life. Indonesia's Taman Mini, with its formulaic representation of each and every province, and China's new cultural theme park are also examples of the genre. Even in a free and democratic South Africa, we see the growth of tribal shows and villages that freeze the "ethnographic present" in the more comforting 1890s or so, ignoring the living culture of townships, political resistance, modern life, various "mixed" immigrant groups, and even Afrikaaners.

Interestingly, such efforts use a notion of authenticity, sometimes taking great pains to re-create particular architectural or environmental features. Less thought appears to be given to the people who animate such theme parks. The biographies and enactments of those who perform in them may be only loosely connected to the social life and history of the communities being represented. Contemporary people may end up "playing" their ancestors, employees may be hired to act out someone else's ethnicity, people may be scripted to perform as someone they are not.

Nevertheless, the worlds of scholarship and commerce, education and entertainment, previously separated, are becoming increasingly conjoined. "Infomercial" is a new word in our vocabulary. Commercial representers of culture have been able to invest huge sums of money and apply new forms of technology that engage tourists. These techniques—multimedia stations, holographic images, robots, hands-on activities, telecommunications—are being adapted by museums and other educational institutions. Controversy also moves between these worlds. At the same time that conventional educational genres—textbooks, exhibitions—are challenged for the ways in which they depict history and people, so too are entertainment conglomerates being forced to take responsibility for the ways in which they depict peoples and cultures in their films, television shows, and even theme parks—witness the controversy over Disney's attempt to build a history-themed park called Disney's America, adjacent to the historic Civil War battlefields of Manassas, Virginia, for example.

Still, tourism, entertainment, and commercial displays will grow. How to assure that they do some good—that their representations do justice to those represented? How to assure that the benefits of tourism are not just exported or placed in heavy capital outlay for luxury high-rise hotels but actually reach the people? How to assure that such activities do not destroy local environments and settings for community culture? Consciousness and strategies have been increasing in regard to forms of ecotourism and cultural tourism. And despite what scholars, as purists, might like, local folks need money. Increased attention on how to achieve and balance three broadly desirable goals—cultural conservation, economic development, and environmental preservation—will be the concern.

Indigenous Products

Another growing arena of cultural economics is the exploitation of cultural property the world over. Paul Simon has benefited by mining the music of South Africans, Brazilians, and Cajuns. Many cultural producers use performances from around the world for their extravaganzas. Pharmaceutical companies are now working with shamans and healers to develop new drugs and treatments that one day may cure cancer or AIDS or lead to new, moneymaking biotechnology. Many of us make a living from and get tenure by writing about and displaying the wisdom and knowledge of "our" people.

The issues of how cultural property—intangible and tangible, individual and community, owned and used—is going to be handled will be with us for some time. Questions and tensions over the commercial and ethical use of cultural creations are going to continue to emerge as the industrial and postindustrial economy appropriates traditional knowledge, wisdom, and art. More and more, the cultural knowledge, wisdom, and products of tribal groups, folk communities, and other civilizations are going to be repackaged, made and marketed for profit, and distributed far beyond their traditional audiences. Some of this may even occur under the control of the very communities that produce that culture, if the technology, knowledge, and networks are available.

Such developments will occur increasingly as corporations find that the factory model of "one size fits all" tastes doesn't quite work. The market is just too big, too diverse, and too segmented to work that way for long. Consumer product companies look for niche markets—albeit large ones—and for products that will sell. In the United States of today, that old standby—ketchup—is being outsold by salsa; there is a need for

Hindi film rentals in New York, and *halal* grocers and butcheries in Detroit. In their search for new markets, producers have realized they have to be somewhat responsive to local needs. And they may have to compete with local, niche producers.

On one hand, the market has become more homogeneous—penetrated by internationally produced and widely available goods. IBM and Apple computers, JVC CD players, Toyotas, blue jeans, and CNN are available everywhere. Yet, at the same time, many products are increasingly customized for local consumption. Computer companies have developed a variety of script and language packages to serve different, non-English-speaking populations. Coca-Cola started a line of Goombay punch in the Bahamas, only to be followed by Pepsi's Junkanoo punch. What may have previously passed separately as either market research or ethnographic research is likely to become more entwined, as good marketing and needs assessment may also be good ethnography.

Among the subsets of these products are those that represent the culture and often pass as entertainment. The giants of the entertainment and media industry have the ability to produce images and products and send them around the globe to mass audiences, making money as they go. Their budgets dwarf those of local educational systems, museums, and other cultural institutions. How many more people will know, or think they know, about India from the movie *Indiana Jones and the Temple of Doom* than will learn about that country from a scholarly monograph on Indian cultural life? Or how many more people will learn about the Caribbean from going to the Pirates of the Caribbean ride at Walt Disney World than by reading a truthful scholarly book about the Caribbean—or even one about pirates?

There is money to be made by representing culture and using its resources. As Chuck Kleymeyer illustrates, grassroots development agencies and organizations are becoming increasingly savvy about the economics of cultural tourism, local handicrafts, traditional knowledge, educational and communication programs.[4] Folks are learning that economic power can be used to promulgate and preserve their culture and that their culture may be valuable for fueling their economy.

In order for people to achieve local-level cultural and economic viability, training and experience are helpful. Strategic enhancement of local-level institutions—sometimes families and clans, sometimes church groups, other times community organizations and cooperatives—may be necessary. Analyses and an understanding of previous cases and attempts to buttress local economies in culturally appropriate ways would likely be useful. Unfortunately, in this area, as in the political arena, there is a relative dearth of research and literature on the microeconomics of cultural development. There are few practitioners, little theory, and a poor base of useful research from which people the world over can draw.

Culture in Scholarship and the Museum: An Assessment

What is the state of cultural scholarship in this political and economic context? Is it positioned to provide curators and other practitioners with the knowledge, information, and linkages they need to adequately present culture to the public?

Cultural scholarship faces several problems. One concerns our own standing and that of our subject matter. Everyone knows something about culture, and a lot of people think they are experts—or can't imagine others as experts. It is, in the public consciousness, difficult to separate out folk sociology, folk history, and folk anthropology from their disciplinary counterparts. The same or even worse holds for the use of knowledge about culture in a museum. More than one member of Congress has asked something like, "What do you have to know to nail a painting to a wall, put an object in a vitrine, or put a performance on a stage?"

Understandings from scholarly disciplines have to a great degree failed to penetrate popular ones. The social sciences, the arts, and the humanities are largely marginalized and trivialized in our educational systems. Museums fare no better. While many museums can boast of sizable visitorship, we still have only vague ideas of how much learning really takes place in a museum through exhibitions. Seeing things on the walls or in the cases of a museum or encountering them in performances and other museum programs does not necessarily convey knowledge.

Where are we as academic departments, public institutions, professional societies, and practitioners in the contemporary debates about culture? We should be at the forefront of national and international debates on fundamental cultural issues. Yet we are not. Our failure is not because we are not consulted by others. It is rather because, with only few exceptions, we have shunned engagement. In the museum world, we are engaged only inadvertently, or in a reactive mode, when we have to answer the complaints of a constituency.

This general lack of engagement has a long history, expressed in the ideas of a museum as curiosity cabinet, temple, and attic. Since the origin and expansion in the nineteenth century of museums of natural history, art, and history, these institutions have been faced with the challenge of collecting remnants and samples of natural and cultural forms before such items are lost, diffused, or forgotten. As evidence of prehistoric species is dug out of the ground, recoverable bones and fossils find their way into museums. Art museums attempt to gather collections and evidences of artistic careers and visions, lest such be scattered beyond retrieval. Historical museums collect artifacts as symbols of events that are rapidly receding in the public memory.

Museum professionals generally define the challenge of museum work as how to understand and represent the whole by the part. How to represent the epoch of the dinosaurs from bones, the eye of Picasso from several paintings, the Civil War from guns and uniforms. Motivated by this challenge, museums collect and document before the specimens, creations, and memories disappear. The traditional curatorial concern is what can be brought into the museum, not what can be taken out.

As several recent studies and symposiums illustrate, innovative programs arising from many museums, some national, some local, suggest a more active approach to museum work.[5] In such programs, a biologist views her role not as that of a collector of dead specimens but rather as that of curator and conservator of the living rain forest and the ocean planet. An art curator sees his role as one of encouraging and supporting aesthetic innovation among young artists from diverse contemporary communities. A curator of Chinese American social history encourages the children of Chinese immigrants to help document the lives of their parents. In these cases, it is the living whole rather than the dead specimen that holds meaning. Curation is not limited by what is in the museum but is directed toward the living context—natural and/or cultural—from which the object, specimen, painting, or document is generated. Still, however, within the museum world, such efforts are often marginalized and defined as "non-core" or extraneous functions.

Limited engagement is also true in cultural economics. Economically, our efforts are largely marginal—sometimes assisting with local community self-help development through the use of cultural resources. Cultural Survival has a popular program in partnership with Ben and Jerry's Ice Cream to market rain forest crunch bars and specialty ice creams on behalf of the Amazon's Indians. Aid to Artisans, Pueblo to

People, the Inter-American Foundation, and many others have a range of local-level programs that encourage communities to use their cultural resources for economic development. But for the most part, these are on a very small scale compared to the need. And compared to the more extractive mode of the culture industry, such self-development projects are hardly even considered when it comes to talking about aid and investment policies.

This problem is not just one of scale or communication. It is also one of authority—partly, and honestly, a problem of our own making. The human studies disciplines have undercut their own legitimacy and worth. Cultural scholars have—rightly, I believe—displaced an objectivist, scientific ethnography. But good cultural scholarship is methodical, quite empirical, and still requires disciplined learning about the ways and thoughts of people. When my colleagues rejoice in finding that their work tells us more about the author (and his or her society) than about the people studied, we become a bit too narcissistic. This is an originally unintended consequence of a critique that rightly examined the questions of what constituted knowledge of a culture and who had the authority to speak for it. That critique, offered by the symbolic anthropology/cultural analysis movement in the early 1970s to better understand indigenous constructions of reality around the world, and by the "cultural studies" movement in England, which developed to understand contemporary working-class culture and its intersections with popular forms and political power, seemed a healthy corrective to more imperial, ethnocentric, objectivist approaches.[6] But the result has gone astray.

The problem is not only a methodological one. It is also a disciplinary one, driven, I believe, by overspecialization on the one hand and a failure to confront, deal with, and broker the participation of the people studied. In a sense, events and circumstances have overtaken the need and raison d'être of the conventional disciplines. And the disciplines have not responded very well to such shifting relationships of need, power, and geography.

Consider the current, albeit slow, changes in academia today. Geography departments, an outgrowth of an age of shipping, exploration, and colonialism, are being dissolved in U.S. universities. Few universities are establishing new departments of anthropology, sociology, history, political science, folklore, or linguistics. Yet there is a growth in new programs in cognitive studies, women's studies, and cultural studies, among others. The social science disciplines that developed largely as a consequence of the Industrial Revolution, rapid urbanization, nation-building, and colonial administration are being superseded by new ways of organizing and seeking knowledge and its applications.

Academia will be in foment as it adjusts to a new, postdisciplinary era. In some areas, specialization in the traditional disciplines has outpaced application and synthesis, and seemingly incomprehensible abstraction and examination of minutiae have replaced both the solving of concrete problems and reflection on larger, transdisciplinary issues.

It is not that the need for knowledge or research, or academic activity, has diminished—it is just that it has changed. For example, consider the post–World War II development of area studies. Though interdisciplinary, area studies—Asian studies, African studies, Indian studies, Latin American studies, and so on—arose to increase the available knowledge on world areas of importance to American political, military, and commercial interests in the context of the cold war. While taking a generally civilizational approach, area studies served both scholarly and practical interests well for some three decades.

But new factors arose that now entail the demise of area studies and progress in new directions. Massive movements of populations meant the dislocation of people from their geographic areas. Diasporas, migrations, and the exodus of refugees occasioned by wars, drought, and the 1965 U.S. immigration law meant that one could study Indians in New York, Jamaicans in London, Salvadorans in Los Angeles, Algerians in Paris. New forms of telecommunication and air transport reduced the consequences of geographic proximity on the social life of numerous area-based communities. And the ability of information and people to move rapidly around the globe called for a more trans-areal, transnational perspective than that rendered by the older organization of knowledge.

Encrusted archaeologies of knowledge and their slow change are even more obvious when it comes to museums. For in the museum categories of knowledge are carved into the walls, chiseled in stone, and constructed with brick and mortar. We continue to have natural history museums long after the idea of "natural history" has been superseded by systems of ecological relationships. We have museums of art divorced from culture, technology divorced from history, peoples and regions divided up in ways that seem anachronistic today. Yet in many cases there is not much that can be done about it, and so we must repeatedly defend a table of organization or institutional definition that we know from the outset to be flawed.

In the museum world, the encrusted may include collections themselves, which must be cared for, housed, conserved, and sometimes exhibited. Often our knowledge does not grow through inspection and analysis of collections. In some cases, they are totally irrelevant to the museum disciplines and research engaged in by their curators.

Another challenge to the disciplines comes from the fact that neither universities nor, certainly, museums monopolize intellectual and scientific energy—much of which is coming from outside the academy these days, from the corporate research laboratory, the think tank, the community hall, and the media. For example, the need for new knowledge in the communications technology and computer industries has driven much of the development in cognitive studies—bringing together work from linguistics, mathematics, computer science, engineering, and psychology—a congeries of departments rarely united in even the same university division.

But perhaps the most important development in the undermining of traditional social science and cultural disciplines is the growth of intelligentsias and institutions from the nations and societies of the represented. Politicians, leaders, writers, dramatists, media personalities, journalists, and others from these countries and communities do not necessarily trust scholars to represent them any more than Americans do. These intellectuals and cultural presenters have become brokers in their own right, with their own thoughts, voices, and genres of representation. The resentment between exogenous scholars and indigenous thinkers has generally been mutual, though disengaged. The political debate on culture issues will continue—but it will not be bound by the traditional social science and humanities disciplines. This situation is unfortunate, and it might have been avoided had recruitment, training, and opportunity within the scholarly fields been greater earlier on.

Cultural scholars and curators face a fundamental contradiction, one that is all too evident at the meetings of any of their professional associations. We claim a special empathy for, an understanding of, and an ethical relationship with the people we study and represent. Yet, if we are so close to the people and communities struggling with cultural issues, those people should be flocking to us for knowledge, wisdom, and insight. They—the studied, the represented, the brokered—should be coming to our meetings, enrolling their children in our courses, reading our books, and even joining our ranks. In the United States this is not happening. The participation of African Americans, American Indians, Hispanics, and Asian Americans in the cultural studies and curatorial fields is stunningly low. My guess is that this relationship also holds true in other parts of the world—low Aboriginal participation in Australia, low participation of lower castes (the so-called tribals and untouchables) in India, Koreans in Japan, Asians in Russia, newer immigrant groups in Europe, mestizos throughout Latin America, Blacks in Cuba, Pacific Islanders throughout the Pacific Rim.

Even more crippling is that instead of responding to this situation and finding new life and vitality in inclusion, the disciplines and their established scholars seem increasingly intent on defending their own diminishing turf and privilege. There is much disquiet among social scientists and humanists, a sense that the scholarly, disciplinary community is being lost. In some cases, that community is breaking into numerous subdisciplinary specialties. In other cases, it has deconstructed itself in a postmodern critique and seems to have lost its subject matter, its vitality, and its mission.

Tragically, because cultural scholars find themselves less a part of communities of researchers, they find it harder to see such communities in others. Since their own discipline, subject matter, or field has become de-essentialized, they de-essentialize everyone else's. Fortunately, others have their own intellectual, moral, and social feet to stand upon.

Emerging Professional Goals

What are scholars and curators going to need for a world in which increasing weight is put on culture? How do we go about studying and representing culture? What should be the role of museums, cultural institutions, cultural brokers, and scholars with regard to the people represented?

Simply put, museum curators, programmers, and cultural presenters have to rely on a much firmer and sharper focus on *situated* scholarship—that is, research and analysis located in contemporary contexts, presented to the communities, leaders, and polities affected. Gone are the days of singular, monological, acontextual studies of civilizations, countries, communities, villages, and cultures. Studies that fail to situate their subjects in a contemporary world of multiple, if not contending, cultural narratives and ways of communicating them are perilously misleading.

Research work will necessarily cross-cut the disciplines, populations, and genres that have usually bound our work. In this effort, we need the active involvement and engagement of community and lay scholars who can bring to the field new understandings, assumptions, approaches, and connections. We need research on the multicultural state, on compara-tive cultural politics, on cultural economics, on multicultural lives, on transnational cultural flows, on cultural processes associated with immi-gration, acculturation, urbanization, and the relationships between cul-ture, environmental preservation, and development. We need much stronger scholarship—not weaker scholarship—if our findings are to stand up under the scrutiny of the audiences who can seriously think about and use our work. This means students and professionals trained in several fields and methodologies. And it also means the sophisticated use of cultural scholarship to train professionals in applied fields—from lawyers who work on intellectual and cultural property rights issues to pharmacologists who will work with rain forest healers and shamans to discover new, illness-curing drugs.

We have to integrate research more thoroughly with education and public service. This means training producers and presenters of cultural performances, events, and programs who have a solid knowledge base for their work. And it means more-worldly scholars who can understand their own work—from lectures to written ethnography—as itself a form of cultural presentation. We have major work to do in developing teach-ing materials and upgrading teacher training to reflect the complexity of culture. We have to use fully the range of new media and forms of com-munication to transmit our ideas so that the young and broader publics may entertain them.

In the museums there is much to do. Given the massive destruction of traditional cultures in the twentieth century, transformations of cul-tures, and the creation of myriad new forms, museums are all the more important. Their lesser goal will still involve the effort to collect the arti-facts and document the lifeways of those cultures before they disappear.

But the greater goal for museums is to serve as gathering places and focal points for seriously examining the knowledge, accomplishment, and creativity, as well as the failings, of these cultural forms. The Smith-sonian Institution, for example, played such a parallel role at the time of its founding 150 years ago, not so much in collecting or researching but in establishing the idea that knowledge was a good, nationally important pursuit for the citizenry of a democratic country. More so now than when the Smithsonian was founded, communicating cultural subjects to broad publics is big, and serious, business. Museums—through public exhibitions, programs, performances, lectures, and products—offer a special experiential platform that can be used to represent cultures to broad audiences. Museums are empowered with a still potent discourse of scholarship, science, and legitimation. They offer an ideal crossroads for bringing together "us" and "them," the tellers of tales and the listeners, the scholar and the student, the spokesperson and the citizen, the expert and the tourist, the makers of history and its curators. They are in an ideal position to broker culture among a variety of constituents.

There is a great deal of consensus in the museum world for a new form of cultural curation. At a recent conference, "Museums in the New Millennium," held at the Smithsonian in September 1996, directors and curators of art, history, and science museums from around the United States and some twenty other nations discussed the status and future of museums. Though there are certainly differences in mission, resources, and circumstances, a paradigmatic shift in the nature of the museum when compared to the past century or even the past decade was evident. I summarized this shift in a presentation at the end of conference, with the following table:

What's In, What's Out—What's Hot, What's Not

Museum Feature	Out	In
Collection value	Just stuff	Value-added stuff
Curators as	Collectors	Stewards
Museum experience	Awful	Awe-inspiring
	Worn out	Attractive
	Exhibits only	Whole packages
	Low tech	High tech as vehicle
Audience orientation	Our needs	User needs
	Elitist	Communitarian
	Exclusivity	Connectivity
	Divorced from the community	Engaged with the community
Curatorial style	Authoritative	Helpful
	Demeaning	Meaning making
	Conformational	Informational
	Monologue	Multilogue
	Giving to	Sharing with
Institutional attitude	Rigid	Flexible
	Opaque	Transparent
	Reflect understandings	Generate understandings
	Outreach	Inreach
Institutional product	Hype	Trust
	Authenticity	Authenticity
	Material reality	Virtual reality

What's In, What's Out—What's Hot, What's Not (*continued*)

Museum Feature	Out	In
Institutional concept	The museum	Museums
	Museum as end	Museum as means
	Attic	Forum
Staff orientation	Curator director	General manager
	Thing skills	People skills
	Finite knowledge	New knowledge
	Market averse	Market aware
Survival strategy	Mission	Promise
	Government money	Earning money
	Philanthropy	Promotion/advancement
	Stand-alone	Partnerships
	We/they	We all
	(If it's broke, then)	(If it's not broke, then)
	Fix it	Break it

Curation for the museum of the new millennium is processual, not static. It relies on the idea of partnership and trust between community and institution, a proactive effort to serve the public, increase understandability, and use the museum as vehicle of inter- and intracultural communication. Helpful, skilled, and connected, the museum is enmeshed in the social and economic life of the people around it.

The new cultural curation will require a very modest public investment in the research, documentation, and presentation of human cultural knowledge, expression, and resources. Yet such seems necessary for the development of a knowledge-based, humanitarian, democratically oriented society. Conveying rich and accurate understandings of culture through public presentations, through the educational system, and by other means is vital for developing a healthy sense of self, community, nationhood, and humanity, and it strongly contributes to the maintenance of civil society. And the conservation, encouragement, and even enhancement of local cultural resources can be beneficial to the economy and well-being of people the world over.

We have to expand the ability of people—regular people, common people, people at the grassroots—to create, debate, and manipulate their culture, and to share it with others. When culture is not created, it dies.

When people cannot share, they fight. And where the cultural dialogue stops, it is replaced with violence, death, and destruction.

Cultural programs can address public knowledge, discourse, and debate with considerable care, expertise, and ethical responsibility. But the scholars and curators who labor in public cultural institutions have good cause to worry that their efforts will be eclipsed by those with greater access to larger audiences.

Cultural institutions can no longer be the preserve of the elite or the refuge of the scholar or curator. In a public institution like the Smithsonian, analysis needs to be coupled with action. As Tony Seeger, one of my colleagues, puts it: "Knowledge of any kind should be used in the real world—where theory is tested in the crucible of action, and where one's own actions can themselves become the object of theoretical reflection."[7]

Scholars who labor in the public interest should be attuned to the form of power increasingly shaping the twenty-first century's social order—the ability to produce (and control) meaning and disseminate it (some would say inflict it) upon others. The means of producing meaning, particularly about things cultural, are widely distributed. Yet at a time when commodified culture is emerging as the world's foremost economic industry and issues of cultural identity have become part of big-time politics, scholars have both an opportunity and a responsibility to participate in the public understanding of culture. We must continue to study and interpret, understand and model respect for cultures; we need to bring people together so that cultures can be presented and translated; and we can help people as they seek to negotiate and transform their cultural reality.

NOTES

CHAPTER ONE PROLOGUE: DOCTOR, LAWYER, INDIAN CHIEF

Most of this chapter originally appeared as "Doctor, Lawyer, Indian Chief" in *Natural History* 89, no. 11 (1980): 6–24. Reprinted with permission. Copyright the American Museum of Natural History, 1980.

1. See, for example, various fieldwork narratives: Bronislaw Malinowski, *A Diary in the Strict Sense of the Term* (New York: Harcourt, Brace, and World, 1967); Alma Gottlieb and Philip Graham, *Parallel Worlds: An Anthropologist and a Writer Encounter Africa* (New York: Crown Publishers, 1993); George D. Spindler, *Being an Anthropologist: Fieldwork in Eleven Cultures* (New York: Holt, Rinehart, and Winston, 1970).

2. Research was supported by a generous grant from the Social Science Research Council and a Fulbright-Hays Research Fellowship.

3. In northern India this system is referred to as *jajmānī*.

4. "Kərən," which sounds like "Kurin," is more usually transcribed as "Karan," "Kuran," and "Kurran," though given the short vowels in Punjabi, all can sound the same. There is no positive evidence linking the Nunari to a historical Raja Karan, although there are several famous personages identified by that name. Given the genealogy recited by Hedayat, the founding of the tribe by the four brothers appears to have occurred sometime between 440 and 640 years ago, depending on the interval assumed for each generation. On that basis, the most likely candidate for the actual or imputed Nunari progenitor is Raja Karan, ruler of Anhilvara (Gujerat), who was defeated by the Khilji Ala-ud-Din in 1297 and again in 1307. Although this is slightly earlier than suggested by the genealogical data, such genealogies are often telescoped, are missing some ancestors, and do not necessarily reflect actual ancestry.

Nevertheless, several aspects of Hedayat's account make this association doubtful. Hedayat clearly identifies Raja Karan's conquerors as Mughals, whereas the Gujerati Raja Karan was defeated by the Khiljis. Second, Hedayat places the Nunari ancestor's kingdom only twenty-seven miles from Delhi. The Gujerati Raja Karan ruled several kingdoms, none closer to Delhi than several hundred miles away.

Other circumstances, however, offer support for this identification of the Nunari ancestor. According to Hedayat, Raja Kərən's father was named Kam Deo. Although the historical figure was the son of Serung Deo, the use of *deo,* a popular title for the rajas of the Vaghela and Solonki Dynasties, does seem to place the Nunari founder in the context of medieval Gujerat. Furthermore, Hedayat clearly identifies the *pīr* (saint) said to have initiated the conversion of the Nunaris to Islam. This saint, Mukhdum-i-Jehaniyan, was a contemporary of the historical Raja Karan.

Also of interest, but as yet unexplained, is that several other groups living in Nunari settlement areas specifically claim to be descended from Raja Karan of Gujerat, who is said to have migrated northward into the Punjab after his defeat. Controverting this theory, the available evidence indicates that Raja Karan fled not toward the Punjab but southward to the Deccan, and that his patriline ended with him. It is his daughter, Deval Devi, who is remembered: she is the celebrated heroine of *Ashiqa,* a famous Urdu poem written by Amir Khusrau in 1316. She was married to Khizr Khan, the son of Karan's conqueror; I have not found any historical information about her progeny.

5. My father is Saul and his father Julius. Julius came from Lithuania via Latvia in the early 1900s. His surname, like those of other Jewish immigrants from eastern Europe and the Baltics, was likely shortened or drastically modified or even made up. I know nothing of the Kurin genealogy before Julius. Any actual genealogical connection to the Nunari seems quite far-fetched.

CHAPTER TWO   INTRODUCTION: BROKERING CULTURE

1. For an idea of how Senegal was represented, see *Festival of American Folklife Program Book* (Washington, D.C.: Smithsonian, 1991).

2. David Maybury-Lewis, *Millennium: Tribal Wisdom and the Modern World* (New York: Viking, 1992); Ivan Karp and Steven Lavine, eds., *Exhibiting Cultures: The Poetics and Politics of Museum Display* (Washington, D.C.: Smithsonian Institution Press, 1991); John MacAloon, *Rite, Drama, Festival, Spectacle: Rehearsals toward a Theory of Cultural Performances* (Philadelphia: Institute for the Study of Human Issues, 1984); Richard Handler and Jocelyn Linnekin, "Tradition: Genuine or Spurious," *Journal of American Folklore* 97, no. 385 (1984): 273–290; James Clifford, *The Predicament of Culture* (Cambridge:

Harvard University Press, 1988); Robert Cantwell, *Ethnomimesis: Folklife and the Representation of Culture* (Chapel Hill: University of North Carolina Press, 1993).

3. Marshall Sahlins, *How "Natives" Think, about Captain Cook, for Example* (Chicago: University of Chicago Press, 1995); Gananath Obeyesekere, *The Apotheosis of Captain Cook: European Mythmaking in the Pacific* (Princeton: Princeton University Press, 1992); Clifford Geertz, "Culture War," *New York Review of Books* 42, no. 19 (1995), pp. 4–6; Robert Gordon, "People of the Great White Lie," *Cultural Survival* 15, no. 1 (1991): 49–51; Geoffrey White, "Museum/Memorial/Shrine: National Narrative in National Spaces," *Museum Anthropology* 21, no. 1 (1997): 8–27; Amy Henderson and Adrienne Kaeppler, eds., *Exhibiting Dilemmas* (Washington, D.C.: Smithsonian Institution Press, 1997).

4. Nestor Garcia Canclini, *Hybrid Cultures* (Minneapolis: University of Minnesota Press, 1995); Virginia Dominguez, "The Marketing of Heritage," *American Ethnologist* 13, no. 3 (1986): 546–555; Robert Baron and Nicholas Spitzer, *Public Folklore* (Washington, D.C.: Smithsonian Institution Press, 1992); Ivan Karp, Christine Kraemer, and Steven Lavine, eds., *Museums and Their Communities* (Washington, D.C.: Smithsonian Institution Press, 1993); Curtis Hinsley, "The World as Marketplace: Commodification of the Exotic at the World's Colombian Exposition, Chicago, 1893," in Karp and Lavine, *Exhibiting Cultures,* pp. 344–365.

5. *Cultural Survival Quarterly* (Cambridge, Mass.: Cultural Survival, Inc.).

6. A. L. Kroeber and Clyde Kluckhohn, *Culture: A Critical Review of Concepts and Definitions* (Cambridge: The Museum, 1952).

7. Maybury-Lewis, *Millennium,* p. 262.

8. Alan Lomax, "Appeal for Cultural Equity," *World of Music* 14, no. 2 (1972).

9. Robert B. Reich, *The Work of Nations* (New York: Vintage Books, 1992), pp. 88, 178, and *passim.*

10. This is also expressed in terms of systems or complexes of brokering by Daniel Mato in "Complexes of Brokering and the Global-Local Connections: Considerations Based on Cases in Latin America" (paper presented at the Nineteenth International Congress of the Latin American Studies Association, September 28–30, 1995).

CHAPTER THREE   BROKERING THE SMITHSONIAN'S 150TH ANNIVERSARY

An earlier version of part of this chapter was presented at the invited session of the Society of Cultural Anthropology, Public History/National Narrative at the 94th annual meeting of the American Anthropological Association, Washington, D.C., November 15–19, 1995. Much of this chapter, excluding the treatment of the Birthday Party on the Mall, was published as "From Smithsonian's America to America's Smithsonian" in

Museum Anthropology 21, no. 1 (1997): 27–41, and appears with the coopera-
tion of the American Anthropological Association. A short review of the
traveling exhibition was published as "America's Smithsonian: What and
Where's the Story?"
The Grapevine, issue 24 (November 1996), the in-house newsletter for the
Smithsonian Forum on Material Culture.

1. Bronislaw Malinowski, *Magic, Science, and Religion* (Garden City: Doubleday,
   1954).
2. John MacAloon, *Rite, Drama, Festival, Spectacle: Rehearsals toward a Theory of
   Cultural Performances* (Philadelphia: Institute for the Study of Human Issues,
   1984); Terrence Ranger, *The Invention of Tradition* (New York: Cambridge
   University Press, 1983); Neil Harris, *Cultural Excursions: Marketing Appetites
   and Cultural Tastes* (Chicago: University of Chicago Press, 1990); Michael
   Kammen, *Mystic Chords of Memory: The Transformation of Tradition in American Culture* (New York: Alfred A. Knopf, 1991).
3. Max Gluckman, ed., *Essays on the Ritual of Social Relations* (Manchester:
   Manchester University Press, 1962); Victor Turner, *The Ritual Process*
   (Chicago: Aldine, 1969); Clifford Geertz, *Negara: The Theater State in Nine-
   teenth-Century Bali* (Princeton: Princeton University Press, 1980); McKim
   Marriott, "The Feast of Love," in Milton Singer, ed., *Krishna: Myths, Rites, and
   Attitudes* (Chicago: University of Chicago Press, 1969), pp. 200–212.
4. James Clifford, *The Predicament of Culture: Twentieth-Century Ethnography,
   Literature, and Art* (Cambridge: Harvard University Press, 1988); Cornel West,
   "The New Cultural Politics of Difference," in Simon During, ed., *The Cultural
   Studies Reader* (London: Routledge, 1993), pp. 203–220.
5. For detailed histories of the Smithsonian, see James Conaway, *The Smith-
   sonian: 150 Years of Adventure, Discovery, and Wonder* (Washington, D.C.:
   Smithsonian Institution Books and New York: Alfred A. Knopf, 1995);
   Geoffrey Hellman, *The Smithsonian: Octopus on the Mall* (Philadelphia:
   J. B. Lippincott, 1967); see also Margaret Chrisman, *1846: Portrait of the
   Nation* (Washington, D.C.: Smithsonian Institution Press, 1996).
6. *The Smithsonian. Smithsonian Year* (Washington: Smithsonian Institution,
   1985–95).
7. Mark Bello, *The Smithsonian Institution: A World of Discovery* (Washington,
   D.C.: Smithsonian Institution, 1993); Commission on the Future of the
   Smithsonian Institution, *E Pluribus Unum: This Divine Paradox.* Report of the
   Commission (Washington, D.C.: Smithsonian Institution, 1995).
8. The Smithsonian is often thought of as the place where all sorts of stuff
   ends up. Ross Perot, in the 1992 election campaign, suggested that the fancy
   alligator shoes of lobbyists should be sent to the Smithsonian, presumably
   because when he became president, they would not be necessary anymore.
   The Smithsonian collection is legendary, and thus all sorts of things are
   supposed to be there. When I was growing up in New York City in the 1950s,

the word about the Smithsonian was that it even had the penis of John Dillinger in its collection. This was thought to be a rather extraordinary organ. The *Wall Street Journal* reported on this urban legend in 1994. Anthropologists in the National Museum of Natural History have been asked about this so many times that one curator actually took a plastic model, put it in a specimen jar, and labeled it John Dillinger's penis.

9. A public opinion survey was conducted by Northern Illinois University's Public Opinion Laboratory with Leo J. Shapiro and Associates, resulting in a final report by William C. McCready and Leo J. Shapiro, "Smithsonian Institution Marketing Study: The Smithsonian in the Minds of Americans" (manuscript, 1995). Peter D. Hart Research Associates conducted focus groups among donors to major cultural institutions, resulting in "Smithsonian Institution: Focus Groups" (manuscript, 1993).

10. "The Smithsonian Institution: Connecting People, Knowledge, and the World," *Business Week,* no. 3365 (April 4, 1994).

11. Lonnie Bunch, "Exhibiting American Culture in Japan: A Curator's Odyssey," *Museum News* 73, no. 2 (March/April 1994): 32.

12. Thomas B. Allen and Norman Polmar, "Blown Away," *Washingtonian* 30 (August 1995): 58.

13. Martin Harwit, *An Exhibit Denied: Lobbying the History of "Enola Gay"* (New York: Springer-Verlag, 1996); Geoffrey White, "Memory Wars: The Politics of Remembering the Asia-Pacific War," East-West Center Issue Paper no. 21 (July 1995).

14. John Ross, "The Nation's Treasures Take to the Highways for a 12-City Tour," *Smithsonian* 27, no. 2 (May 1996): 49–59.

15. *America's Smithsonian: Celebrating 150 Years* (Washington, D.C.: Smithsonian Institution Press, 1996).

16. Study of membership at America's Smithsonian, Smithsonian Office of Institutional Research, 1996.

17. Sharon Waxman, "A Peek into the Nation's Attic," *Washington Post,* February 10, 1996, p. D1.

18. Exhibition attendance figures were as follows: Los Angeles, 300,972; Kansas City, 375,723; Providence, 271,065. New York was a disappointing 187,764.

19. Paul Goldberger, *New York Times,* February 11, 1996; Frank Rich, *New York Times,* June 22, 1996.

20. See articles on working at the Smithsonian in the *Festival of American Folklife Program Book* (Washington, D.C.: Smithsonian Institution, 1996).

21. 150th Smithsonian Birthday Party on the Mall, program guide (Washington, D.C.: Smithsonian Institution, 1996).

22. "Around the Mall," *Smithsonian* 27, no. 7 (October 1996): 24.

23. 150th Birthday Party on the Mall, Publicity Report, Office of Public Affairs, Smithsonian Institution, 1996.

24. I. Michael Heyman, "Smithsonian Perspectives," *Smithsonian* 27, no. 8 (November 1996): 18.

CHAPTER FOUR   MAKING A MUSEUM OBJECT

1. Betsy Broun in remarks at a November 12, 1987, meeting of the Smithsonian Ways of Knowing Forum on Culture Exhibited.

2. See Karl Marx on the fetishism of commodities, in *Das Capital* (New York: International Publishers, 1967), 1:71–83; Marcel Mauss, *The Gift* (New York: Routledge, 1989).

3. Arjun Appadurai, ed., *The Social Life of Things: Commodities in Cultural Perspective* (Cambridge: Cambridge University Press, 1986).

4. See Elaine Gurian, "Noodling Around," in Ivan Karp and Steven Lavine, eds., *Exhibiting Cultures: The Poetics and Politics of Museum Display* (Washington, D.C.: Smithsonian Institution Press, 1991), pp. 176–190.

5. Rajeev Sethi expressed this in an especially compelling way during the Smithsonian's "Museums in the New Millennium" conference in September 1996. Exhibits, which can so appeal to sensuality, are voluntarily forsaking their distinctive advantage when they fail to do so.

6. Warren Robbins, "The Malling of a Museum," *Washington Post,* September 29, 1996.

7. Some of my colleagues at the Conservation Analytic Laboratory, particularly Diane Van Der Reyden, have expressed the idea that all human action upon the object has a physical effect upon it and thus in some way can be measured. This to me, is a naive realism—meaning, intention, motive, and all sorts of nuances of behavior leave no distinguishing trace on material objects.

8. Richard Kurin, "The Hope Diamond: Gem, Jewel, and Icon," in Amy Henderson and Adrienne Kaeppler, eds., *Exhibiting Dilemmas* (Washington: Smithsonian Institution Press, 1997), pp. 47–69.

9. Earl Nyholm, "The Use of Birchbark by the Ojibwa Indians," in *Festival of American Folklife Program Book* (Washington, D.C.: Smithsonian Institution, 1981), pp. 6–9.

10. See Thomas Vennum, "American Indian Culture and Access to Resources," *Festival of American Folklife Program Book* (Washington, D.C.: Smithsonian Institution, 1989); Thomas Vennum, *Wild Rice and the Ojibwe People* (St. Paul: Minnesota Historical Society Press, 1988); Thomas Vennum, *American Indian Lacrosse: Little Brother of War* (Washington, D.C.: Smithsonian Institution Press, 1994).

11. A memorandum of understanding between the Heye Foundation and the Smithsonian was signed by Secretary Robert McC. Adams on May 8, 1989, in the presence of Senator Daniel Inouye and Representative Ben Nighthorse Campbell. This paved the way for the passage of P.L. 101-185, creating the new National Museum of the American Indian on November 28 of that year.

12. A copy of the letter is in the files of the Smithsonian's Center for Folklife Programs and Cultural Studies.

CHAPTER FIVE   EXHIBITING THE ENOLA GAY

This chapter is based on concluding remarks made to the symposium sponsored by the Smithsonian Institution and the University of Michigan, "Presenting History: Museums in a Democratic Society," Ann Arbor, Michigan, April 19, 1995.

1. Thomas B. Allen and Norman Polmar, "Blown Away," *Washingtonian* 30 (August 1995): 58; Lonnie Bunch, "Fighting the Good Fight: Museums in an Age of Uncertainty," *Museum News* 72, no. 2 (March 1, 1995): 32; Edward Linenthal, "Can Museums Achieve a Balance between Memory and History?" *Chronicle of Higher Education,* February 10, 1995; Richard H. Kohn, "History and the Culture Wars: The Case of the Smithsonian Institution's *Enola Gay* Exhibition," *Journal of American History* 82, no. 3 (1995): 1036–1063. Geoffrey White, "Museum/Memorial/Shrine: National Narrative in National Spaces," *Museum Anthropology* 21, no. 1 (1997): 8–27; Geoffrey White, "Memory Wars: The Politics of Remembering the Asia-Pacific War," East-West Center Issue Paper no. 21 (July 1995).

2. Martin Harwit, *An Exhibit Denied: Lobbying the History of "Enola Gay"* (New York: Springer-Verlag, 1996).

3. A written summary of the symposium is available as "Presenting History: Museums in a Democratic Society," from the Smithsonian Associates. A full audiotape of the symposium is available as Folkways Cassette Series, S00001, S00002, S00003, and S00004, from Smithsonian Folkways Mail Order, 414 Hungerford Drive, Suite 444, Rockville, Maryland 20850; phone: (301) 443-2314.

4. Ibid.

5. Harwit, *An Exhibit Denied.*

6. William C. McCready and Leo J. Shapiro, "Smithsonian Institution Marketing Study: The Smithsonian in the Minds of Americans" (manuscript, 1995).

7. Presidential press conference, April 18, 1994.

8. Comments by Barbara Clark Smith at "What About Increase? The First Science and Humanities Dialogue," held at the National Zoological Park in Washington, D.C., March 12–14, 1995.

9. This point of view was clearly and eloquently presented by Bunch at a provost's workshop on interpretation at the Smithsonian, October 29, 1996.

10. See, for example, Anthony Wallace, *Rockdale* (New York: Norton, 1980).

11. James Clifford and George Marcus, *Writing Culture: The Poetics and Politics of Ethnography* (Berkeley: University of California Press, 1986).

12. *Enola Gay,* Script 1, January 14, 1994, p. 5.

13. This is made very clear in an exchange of letters to the editor of the *Washingtonian* in September and October 1995 by Tom Crouch, Richard Hallion, and Richard Kohn.

14. Harwit, *An Exhibit Denied.*

15. White, "Museum/Memorial/Shrine."
16. John Shy, remarks at the "Presenting History" symposium.
17. Barbara Kirshenblatt-Gimblett, remarks at the "Presenting History" symposium.
18. President Clinton, press conference, April 18, 1994.
19. Herman Wolk, remarks at the "Presenting History" symposium.
20. Smithsonian Directive 603, Exhibition Planning Guidelines, was promulgated on August 25, 1995.
21. Lonnie Bunch expressed these ideas at a provost's workshop on interpretation at the Smithsonian, October 29, 1996.

CHAPTER SIX   WHAT'S WITH ANTHROPOLOGY?

This chapter is based on comments made to the Smithsonian Council during its meeting on October 22, 1994, in Washington, D.C., and included in the January 1995 *Anthropology Society of Washington Newsletter.*
1. Curtis Hinsley, *Savages and Scientists* (Washington, D.C.: Smithsonian Institution Press, 1994).
2. Personal communication.
3. The Smithsonian Council Report from 1994; see especially report of Linda Cornell.
4. Claude Lévi-Strauss, *Trieste Tropics,* trans. John Russell (New York: Criterion Books, 1961); Clifford Geertz, *Agricultural Involution* (Berkeley: University of California Press, 1966).
5. George Stocking, *Race, Culture, and Evolution: Essays in the History of Anthropology* (New York: Free Press, 1968).
6. George Stocking, ed., *The Shaping of American Anthropology, 1885–1911: A Franz Boas Reader* (New York: Basic Books, 1974).
7. Margaret Mead, in *Redbook* 145, no. 3 (1975): 38–40; Margaret Mead, *And Keep Your Powder Dry: An Anthropologist Looks at America* (New York: William Morrow, 1942); Margaret Mead, *Coming of Age in Samoa: A Psychological Study of Primitive Youth for Western Civilization* (New York: William Morrow, 1928).
8. Sherry Ornter, "Anthropologists and Multiculturalism: Why Are We Not Included in the Debate?" *Chronicle of Higher Education,* December 16, 1992.
9. Jomo Kenyatta, *Facing Mount Kenya* (New York: Vintage Books, 1965). Indian social anthropologists like Veena Das, Andre Beteille, and others have long been involved with public debate over issues such as caste and community. Mexico has a lengthy tradition of anthropological involvement in social, economic, and political issues. One of my colleagues, Princeton anthropologist Jacinto Arias, a native Chiapaneco, became director of the Native Writers Project in Chiapas and went on to become the mediator in the struggle between the Mexican government and the Zapatistas.

CHAPTER SEVEN   DEBATING RACIALLY AND CULTURALLY SPECIFIC MUSEUMS

This chapter started out as a presentation to the "Awards for Museum Leadership" seminar, July 24, 1992, organized by Rex Ellis, director of the Smithsonian's Office of Museum Programs (now Center for Museum Studies). An abridged version of my presentation was originally published in the May 1993 *Bulletin* (vol. 1, no. 1) of the Office of Museum Programs. I was assigned to argue in the negative; Claudine Brown, then deputy assistant secretary for museums and head of the African American Museum Project, was assigned to argue in the affirmative. Her remarks were published in the October 1993 *Bulletin* (vol. 1, no. 2). The argument in the affirmative below is not Claudine's but my own.

1. John Kinard's presentation to the Congress of the United States, House of Representatives, Committee on Government Operations, Subcommittee on Government Activities and Transportation, Hearing on Smithsonian Institution Minority Employment Practices, March 14, 1989. Transcript available at the Anacostia Museum, Washington, D.C.

2. *Willful Neglect: The Smithsonian Institution and U.S. Latinos* (Washington, D.C.: Smithsonian Institution, 1994).

3. Constance Bond, "If You Can't Bear to Part with It, Open a New Museum," *Smithsonian* 26, no. 1 (April 1995).

4. I take the use of "community-focused museum" from Claudine Brown's presentation.

CHAPTER EIGHT   THE FESTIVAL ON THE MALL

This chapter is a reworked, combined, and expanded version of Richard Kurin, "The Festival of American Folklife: America on the National Mall," *Trends* 32, no. 2 (1995): 4–11; and Richard Kurin, "The Festival: Making Culture Public," in *Festival of American Folklife Program Book* (Washington, D.C.: Smithsonian Institution, 1994), pp. 6–11.

1. Bruce Babbitt, "The Festival, Culturally Speaking," in *Festival of American Folklife Program Book* (Washington, D.C.: Smithsonian Institution, 1994), p. 5; and Bruce Babbitt, "Cultural Conversation on the Mall," in *Festival of American Folklife Program Book* (Washington, D.C.: Smithsonian Institution, 1993), p. 8.

2. S. Dillon Ripley, "The Festival—A Living Museum," in *Festival of American Folklife Program Book* (Washington, D.C.: Smithsonian Institution, 1973), p. 4.

3. S. Dillon Ripley, quoted in Ken Ringle, "Of Lawyers and Other Folk: Even Barristers Join the Blend at the Smithsonian's Festival of Diversity," *Washington Post*, June 25, 1986.

4. I. Michael Heyman, "Smithsonian Perspectives: The Festival of American Folklife," *Smithsonian* 26 (August 1995): 7.

5. Festival attendance is difficult to measure, given the openness of the National Mall, the volume of the crowd, free admission, and the fact that people may visit several times. Formal efforts by the Smithsonian to count the crowd have been under way since 1992. Volunteers record entries along pathways by clicking counters—the same method used at the museum entrances—and fill out forms by the hour. For a report on the method, see Richard Kurin, "Counting One Million Visitors," *Talk Story*, no. 8 (Fall 1995), the newsletter of the Smithsonian Center for Folklife Programs and Cultural Studies. The 1996 festival recorded more than 1,236,000 visits. In 1995, there were just over 1 million, and in a very hot 1994, more than 800,000. Visits are correlated to food sales and trash volume, and studies have shown similar correlations with the museums as a whole. The National Park Service generally asks the Smithsonian for its figures but sometimes makes its own estimates. National Park Service estimates are usually based upon aerial photographs of crowds—fine for a parade or a speech but not very effective for events like the festival, where people come and go over the course of days and most events are under trees and tents, and thus not accessible to photographic assessment. Estimating Mall crowds often becomes politicized when the event is a rally or a march. Crowd size becomes a measure of the popularity of a political position. Politicization reached an apex with the estimates over the Million Man March, with organizers claiming they had surpassed their goal and the National Park Service asserting that attendance was about 400,000. This led to open conflict in the media, a threat of a lawsuit against the National Park Service, and alternative studies of aerial photographs of the assembled crowd. In the federal budget for 1997, the National Park Service was relieved of responsibility for estimating crowds on the National Mall. Spitzer, in Robert Baron and Nicholas Spitzer, *Public Folklore* (Washington, D.C.: Smithsonian Institution Press, 1991), p. 101, uses an obviously wrong National Park Service figure in a similar way to make his own point about the festival.

6. *Life*, July 1994; Henry Allen, *American Culture: Going Too Far Enough* (Washington, D.C.: Smithsonian Institution Press, 1994).

7. A sample of books and articles on the festival includes: Laurie Sommers, a special issue of *Folklore in Use* 2, no. 2 (1994); Linn Shapiro, Rosie Lee Hooks, and Bernice Reagon, eds., *Black People and Their Culture: Selected Writings from the African Diaspora* (Washington, D.C.: Smithsonian Institution, 1976); Robert Cantwell, *Ethnomimesis: Folklife and the Representation of Culture* (Chapel Hill: University of North Carolina Press, 1993); Richard Conroy, *Old Ways in the New World* (New York: St. Martin's Press, 1994); Bert Feintuch, ed., *The Conservation of Culture: Folklorists and the Public Sector* (Lexington:

University of Kentucky Press, 1987); Ivan Karp and Steven Lavine, eds., *Exhibiting Cultures: The Poetics and Politics of Museum Display* (Washington, D.C.: Smithsonian Institution Press, 1991); Baron and Spitzer, *Public Folklore;* Victor Turner, *Celebrations: A World of Art and Ritual* (Washington, D.C.: Smithsonian Institution Press, 1982); Richard Bauman, Patricia Sawin, and Inta Gale Carpenter, *Reflections on the Folklife Festival: An Ethnography of Participant Experience* (Bloomington: Indiana University Folklore Institute, 1992); Richard Price and Sally Price, *Maroons on the Mall* (Bloomington: Indiana University Folklore Institute, 1995); Olivia Cadaval, "The Latino Community: Creating an Identity in the Nation's Capital," in Francine Curro Cary, ed., *Urban Odyssey: A Multicultural History of Washington, D.C.* (Washington, D.C.: Smithsonian Institution Press, 1996); Richard Kurin, "The Politics and Economics of Culture," in *Proceedings of the Fifth Annual Australian National Folklife Conference* (Canberra: Australia Folk Trust, 1993); Richard Kurin, "Culture on the 1990s Agenda," in *Festival of American Folklife Program Book* (Washington, D.C.: Smithsonian Institution, 1993), pp. 9–14; Richard Kurin, "The Festival of American Folklife: Not Just a Festival," in *Festival of American Folklife Program Book* (Washington, D.C.: Smithsonian Institution, 1992), pp. 7–14; Richard Kurin, "The Festival of American Folklife: Building on Tradition," in *Festival of American Folklife Program Book* (Washington, D.C.: Smithsonian Institution, 1991), pp. 7–20; Richard Kurin, "Folklife in Contemporary Multicultural Society," in *Festival of American Folklife Program Book* (Washington, D.C.: Smithsonian Institution, 1990), p. 8; Richard Kurin, "Why We Do the Festival," in *Festival of American Folklife Program Book* (Washington, D.C.: Smithsonian Institution, 1989), pp. 8–21; Richard Kurin and Carey Cauthern, "Promotional Value and Public Image: Press Coverage of Tennessee at the Smithsonian's Festival of American Folklife," *Tennessee's Business* 6, no. 1 (1995): 45–55; Xun Gallo, *Mis Ojos Vieron* (Chiapas: Gobierno del Estado de Chiapas, 1992); "Met Marrons door Washington: Een Opmerkelijke Wandeling," *De Ware Tijd,* September 24, 1992. Documentary films on the festival include, among others, *Celebrating Hawaii's Cultures* (Juniroa Productions, 1990); *The Festival* (Hawaii Public Television, 1990); *The U.S. Virgin Islands at the Festival* (USVI Public Television, 1991); *Our Bahamian Heritage* (ZNS Television, 1995); *The Stone Carvers* (Marjorie Hunt and Paul Wagner, 1985); *Iowa Folks and Folklife* (Iowa Public Television, 1996); *Chiapas en el Festival de Culturas Tradicionales Americas* (Chiapas Television, 1992). Documentary recordings based on or growing out of the festival include, among others, *Iowa State Fare* (SF 40083); *Heartbeat: Voices of First Nations Women* (SF 40415), *Music of Indonesia,* vols. 1–12; *Old Believers: Songs of the Nekrasov Cossacks* (SF 40462); *Musics of the Soviet Union* (SF 40002); *Crossroads, Southern Routes* (SF 40080); *Royal Court Music of Thailand* (SF 40413); *Tuva: Voices from the Center of Asia* (SF 40017); Hazel

Dickens and Alice Gerrard (SF 40065); *Borderlands* (SF 40418); *Hawaiian Drum Chants* (SF 40015); *Musics of Hawai'i* (SF 40016); *Music of New Mexico: Hispanic Traditions* (SF 40409); *Music of New Mexico: Indian Traditions* (SF 40408); *Puerto Rico en Washington* (SF 40460); *Puerto Rican Music of Hawaii* (SF 40014); *Musics of Struggle* (with Columbia Records); *The Roots of Rhythm and Blues* (with Columbia Records).

8. William Seale, *The President's House* (Washington, D.C.: White House Historical Association, 1986).

9. Therese O'Malley, "A Public Museum of Trees: Mid-Nineteenth Century Plans for the Mall," in Richard Longstreth, ed., *The Mall in Washington, 1791–1991*, Studies in the History of Art no. 30 (Center for Advanced Study in the Visual Arts, Symposium Papers 14, Washington, D.C.: National Gallery of Art, 1991), pp. 61–78.

10. Cynthia Field, "The Mall: Our Front Yard," *Smithsonian Preservation Quarterly* (1995): 1–2.

11. Thomas Hines, "The Imperial Mall: The City Beautiful Movement and the Washington Plan of 1901–1902," in Longstreth, *The Mall in Washington*, pp. 79–100.

12. J. Carter Brown, "The Mall and the Commission of Fine Arts," in Longstreth, *The Mall in Washington*, pp. 279–295.

13. S. Dillon Ripley, quoted by Ringle, "Of Lawyers and Other Folk."

14. Edwards Park, "S. Dillon Ripley Retires after Twenty Years of Innovation," *Smithsonian* 15, no. 6 (September 1984): 76.

15. Gary Everhardt, "The Festival: Living History," in *Festival of American Folklife Program Book* (Washington, D.C.: Smithsonian Institution, 1975), p. 4.

16. Manuel Lujan, Jr., "The Quincentenary: Understanding America's Cultural Heritage," in *Festival of American Folklife Program Book* (Washington, D.C.: Smithsonian Institution, 1992), p. 6.

17. Everhardt, "The Festival: Living History."

18. P. J. Craul, "The Condition of the Soil and Vegetation of the National Mall" (Report to the U.S. Department of the Interior, National Park Service, National Capital Region, 1990, manuscript).

19. G. B. Runion, H. H. Rogers, C. W. Wood, S. A. Prior, and R. J. Mitchell, "Effects of Traffic on Soil Physical Characteristics and Vegetative Resources of the National Mall," *Journal of Soil and Water Conservation* 48, no. 5 (September–October 1993): 389–393.

20. G. B. Runion, H. H. Rogers, and S. A. Prior, "Preliminary Report: Evaluation of the Health of Elm Trees on the National Mall" (1993, manuscript).

21. Dean Anderson, under secretary of the Smithsonian, speaking at the opening of the 1986 Festival of American Folklife.

22. There has been a good deal of contention over the credit for the founding of the festival. Ripley, Morris, and Rinzler all contributed. From Smithsonian archival records, memos, and correspondence it is clear that Ripley wanted

to do something performative and public on the Mall. Morris, who had created the short-lived American Folk Festival in Asheville, North Carolina, came up with the idea of the festival, and it was under his supervision that it started and continued during its first ten years. Rinzler, hired by Morris as a consultant in February 1967, held the title of festival artistic director in 1967 (and director from 1968) and was responsible for the curatorial thrust of its programs. Disputes between Morris and Rinzler led to a split between them, with the festival emerging under Rinzler and the newly created Office of Folklife Programs in 1977.

23. See the program books for the Pennsylvania Folklife Festival in the early 1960s. Also see Roger Abrahams, "Ralph Rinzler (1934–1994)," obituary in *Journal of American Folklore* 108, no. 429 (1995): 325–326.

24. The *Highlander Center* newsletter and *Sing Out!* magazine provide numerous examples of how the folk song revival fit in with the Civil Rights Movement.

25. S. Dillon Ripley in internal Smithsonian memoranda. Ripley wrote in *Sacred Grove* (Washington, D.C.: Smithsonian Institution Press, 1969): "I would hope that eventually a new kind of museum could be created . . . to study the persistence of older cultures, folk life and folkways in the face of the pressures of increasing homogenization of life today" (pp. 90–91).

26. The conference, held during the first festival, produced this and other recommendations, some of which developed into legislative proposals and eventually the law that founded the American Folklife Center at the Library of Congress. The idea of a national folk troupe was dropped by the time legislative proposals were introduced by Senator Ralph Yarborough in 1969.

27. This language emerges in the introductions and secretary's statements for the festival program books in the late 1960s and early 1970s. It also emerges in speeches by various members of Congress, for example, Mark Hatfield at the 1977 Festival of American Folklife and Fred Harris at the 1971 folk hearing on the Mall.

28. Margaret Mead, *Redbook* 145, no. 3 (July 1975): 38–40.

29. "The Smithsonian Institution: Connecting People, Knowledge, and the World," *Business Week*, no. 3365 (April 4, 1994), special advertising section.

30. Conroy, *Old Ways in the New World*, p. vii.

31. James Boon, "Why Museums Make Me Sad," in Karp and Lavine, *Exhibiting Cultures*, pp. 259–260.

32. The extent to which this occurs is often debated, with examples and counterexamples constantly being offered. See Barbara Kirshenblatt-Gimblett, "Objects of Ethnography" in ibid., pp. 386–443.

33. Peter Seitel, personal communication.

34. Cantwell, *Ethnomimesis*.

35. This survey of participants was conducted in 1995. Feedback from participants in the festival in the form of notes, letters, and conversations, both before and since, seems quite consistent with these findings.

36. 1995 survey of participants.
37. Price and Price, *Maroons on the Mall*.
38. Various proposals and oral presentation by program curators, Ken Bilby and Diana N'Diaye.
39. Price and Price, *Maroons on the Mall*.
40. Unsolicited letters and verbal communications from Maroons involved in the program, particularly the Jamaican leaders, directly contradicted the Prices' reports.
41. Price and Price, *Maroons on the Mall*.
42. Bilby and N'Diaye presented their written response to the Prices. N'Diaye noted to me that she believed the Prices wrote her off as a Smithsonian propagandist. Bilby's comments, which I have never seen, apparently consist of very detailed material that counters at least some of the Prices' perceptions and analyses. I have encouraged Bilby to publish his commentary.
43. Kathy Neustadt, *Clambake: A History and Celebration of an American Tradition* (Amherst: University of Massachusetts Press, 1992), pp. 8–9.
44. See reviews by Frank Korom, in *Museum Anthropology* 19, no. 2 (Fall 1995): 99–103; Rebecca Joseph, "Practicing What We Preach at the Festival," *Folklore in Use* 2, no. 2 (1994): 275–279; Pat Sawin, *American Ethnologist* 23, no. 3 (1996); Richard Handler, *Museum Anthropology* 19, no. 2 (1995): 98–99.
45. Richard Kurin and Diana Parker, "A Short History of the Festival of American Folklife and Michigan's Contribution to Smithsonian Practice," *Folklore in Use* 2, no. 2 (1994): 159–180.
46. Sommers, "Michigan on the Mall," in Bauman, Sawin, and Carpenter, *Reflections on the Folklife Festival*.

CHAPTER NINE   THE FESTIVAL OF INDIA

An earlier version of this chapter appeared as "Cultural Conservation through Representation: Festival of India Folklife Exhibitions at the Smithsonian Institution," in Ivan Karp and Steven Lavine, eds., *Exhibiting Cultures: The Poetics and Politics of Museum Display* (Washington, D.C.: Smithsonian Institution Press, 1991), pp. 315–343. Information on post-1991 developments has been added. For background on the exhibitions, see Pria Devi and Richard Kurin, "Aditi—A Celebration of Life," in *Aditi: The Living Arts of India* (Washington, D.C.: Smithsonian Institution Press, 1985), pp. 31–183; Richard Kurin, "Mela! An Indian Fair," in *Festival of American Folklife Program Book* (Washington, D.C.: Smithsonian Institution, 1985), pp. 66–71; Richard Kurin, "Making Exhibitions Indian," in Michael Meister, ed., *Making Things in South Asia* (Philadelphia: University of Pennsylvania South Asia Regional Studies, 1989), pp. 196–210.

1. Lory Frankel, ed., *Festival of India in the United States, 1985–1986* (New York: Harry N. Abrams, 1985).
2. This approach mirrored many others of a "civilizational" type. It was motivated mainly by Rajeev Sethi, who brought a design perspective, rather than a historical or geographic perspective, to representing India.
3. Sethi's use of traditional Indic categories as organizing principles in modeling cultural traditions and their representations resonated well with an ethnosociological approach to India promulgated at the time by McKim Marriott, Ralph Nicholas, Ron Inden, and others. See McKim Marriott, "Constructing an Indian Enthnosociology," *Contributions to Indian Sociology*, Special Issue: Toward an Ethnosociology of India, n.s. 23, no. 1 (1989): 1–40.
4. "Animation," as in making the exhibit animated—alive—might not be such a bad term, recalling as it does ideas of "soul" or life presence by physicians and movement by cartoon illustrators. Recall that before the festival, Dillon Ripley thought of the Mall as a cemetery. There was a tremendous difference between the *"Mela!"* just before it opened for the first time and the moment afterward. The Mall was animated, the presentation sparked to life. Festival staff often speak of the festival as metaphorically birthed. Museums can sometimes be spoken of as having the life squeezed out of them; cf. Warren Robbins on the African Art Museum, in "The Malling of a Museum," *Washington Post*, September 29, 1996.
5. Venu Sandal, "India's Traditional Folk Artists Fight for a Place in the Future," *Smithsonian* 16, no. 3 (1985): 44–53; Carla M. Borden, ed., *Contemporary Indian Tradition* (Washington, D.C.: Smithsonian Institution Press, 1989). Kate Rinzler and Manjula Kumar developed educational materials on Indian cultural traditions; these continue to be circulated.
6. Salman Rushdie, *Midnight's Children* (New York: Avon Books, 1980).
7. This has a long and complex history, documented in only a limited way by the literature developed under the various cooperatives and self-help schemes Bhule Bisre Kalakar, Nehru Kala Kunj, and Saarthi.
8. Cf. the catalog for the "Aditi" exhibition in London at the Barbicon Centre: Rajeev Sethi, *Aditi* (New Delhi, 1982).
9. Maura Moynihan, coordinator for *"Mela!"* and the daughter of Senator and Liz Moynihan, secured the promise of Rajiv Gandhi during a visit with him accompanied by artists from Shadipur.
10. Dr. Mei Zegers has produced reports over the years documenting the classes, a clinic, and other community development initiatives in Shadipur.
11. The Dehli Development Authority issued a letter confirming an allocation of funds to develop the site. A model and blueprints for the site have been made.
12. The level of sales and the volume of sales activity—items for sale, cash registers, salespeople— at *"Mela!"* was higher than for any other Smithsonian festival. It was as close to a bazaar as we could get.

13. Banku Patua, "The Ballad of Washington, D.C.," as printed, with photographs of each of his panels, in Richard Kurin, *Cultural Conservation through Representation: Festival of India Folklife Exhibitions at the Smithsonian Institution* (Washington, D.C.: Smithsonian Institution, 1991), pp. 25–26.

14. Barbara Kirshenblatt-Gimblett, "Objects of Ethnography," in Karp and Lavine, *Exhibiting Cultures*, pp. 386–443.

15. Milton Singer, *When a Great Tradition Modernizes* (New York: Praeger, 1972).

CHAPTER TEN   BROKERING POST-COLD WAR FOLKLORE

An earlier version of this chapter originally appeared as "Presenting Folklife in a Soviet-American Cultural Exchange: Public Practice during Perestroika," in Robert Baron and Nicholas Spitzer, *Public Folklore* (Washington, D.C.: Smithsonian Institution Press, 1992). New information on post-1992 developments has been added.

 1. Ormond Loomis, *Cultural Conservation: The Protection of Heritage in the United States* (Washington, D.C.: Library of Congress, 1983); Barbara Kirshenblatt-Gimblett, "Mistaken Dichotomies," *Journal of American Folklore* 101, no. 400 (1988): 140–155; Robert McCarl, "Occupational Folklife in the Public Sector: A Case Study," in Bert Feintuch, ed., *The Conservation of Culture: Folklorists and the Public Sector* (Lexington: University of Kentucky Press, 1988), pp. 132–153. See also the following three articles, all in Feintuch, *Conservation of Culture:* Shalom Staub, "Folklore and Authenticity: A Myopic Marriage in Public Sector Programs," pp. 118–131; Jack Santino, "The Tendency to Ritualize: The Living Celebrations Series as a Model for Cultural Presentation and Validation"; and David Whisnant, "Public Sector Folklore as Intervention: Lessons from the Past, Prospects for the Future," pp. 233–247. Also see David Whisnant, *All That Is Native and Fine* (Chapel Hill: University of North Carolina Press, 1983).

 2. Theodore Levin, "Soviet Asia: A Multi-Ethnic Non-Melting Pot," in *Festival of American Folklife Program Book* (Washington, D.C.: Smithsonian Institution, 1988), pp. 30–33; Margarita Mazo, "Song in Rural Russia," in ibid., pp. 26–29; *Musics of the Soviet Union,* Smithsonian Folkways Recordings (SF 40002); *Tuva: Voices from the Center of Asia,* Smithsonian Folkways Recordings (SF 40017); *Shashmaqam: Music of the Bukharan Jewish Ensemble,* Smithsonian Folkways Recordings (SF 40054); *Bukhara: Musical Crossroads of Asia,* Smithsonian Folkways Recordings (SF 40050); *Old Believers: Songs of the Nekrasov Cossacks,* Smithsonian Folkways Recordings (SF 40462).

 3. Richard Kurin to Kennedy Schmertz, memorandum, November 5, 1986.

 4. Peter Seitel to Vasily Zakharov, cable, April 29, 1987.

 5. Ralph Rinzler to Aleksander Potemkin, May 1987.

6. See "Guidelines for Research and Development of Programs at the Festival of American Folklife" (Smithsonian Institution, Center for Folklife Programs and Cultural Studies, manuscript), various revised versions 1988–96.

7. Thomas Vennum, Jr., and Nicholas Spitzer, "Musical Performance at the Festival: Developing Criteria," in *Festival of American Folklife Program Book* (Washington, D.C.: Smithsonian Institution, 1986), pp. 101–104.

8. Zakharov to Adams, June 1987.

9. Alan Dundes, "Nationalistic Inferiority Complexes and the Fabrication of Fakelore: A Reconsideration of Ossian, the Kinder- und Hausmarchen, the Kalevala, and Paul Bunyan," *Journal of Folklore Research* 22, no. 1 (1985): 5–18.

10. Kurin to Demchenko, October 22, 1987.

11. Ibid.

12. Levin, "Soviet Asia"; Mazo, "Song in Rural Russia"; *Musics of the Soviet Union,* Smithsonian Folkways Recordings (SF 40002).

13. Nick Spitzer, "Back in the U.S.S.R.," Washington, D.C., Radio Smithsonian, 1988.

14. John MacAllon, *Rite, Drama, Festival, Spectacle: Rehearsals toward a Theory of Cultural Performances* (Philadelphia: Institute for the Study of Human Issues, 1984).

15. Michael Herzfeld, *Ours Once More: Folklore, Ideology, and the Making of Modern Greece* (Austin: University of Texas Press, 1982); Felix Oinas, "The Political Uses and Themes of Folklore in the Soviet Union," *Journal of the Folklore Institute* 12 (1975): 157–175.

16. Cf. Smithsonian Folkways productions, n. 2 above.

17. Joe Wilson and Richard Kurin to Anatoli Kargin, July 15, 1989.

18. Ministry of Culture, draft project manuscript. Emphasis added.

19. Secretary Adams conveyed this in spoken remarks, personal communication.

20. Richard Kennedy, "A Russian-American Cultural Exchange," and Margarita Mazo, "Molokans and Old Believers in Two Worlds," in *Festival of American Folklife Program Book* (Washington, D.C.: Smithsonian Institution, 1995), pp. 83–89.

21. Samarin to the Smithsonian, August 9, 1995.

CHAPTER ELEVEN   AMERICA'S REUNION ON THE MALL:
A PRESIDENTIAL INAUGURAL

The initial form of this chapter was presented at "Anthropologists Negotiating Policy: Challenges to the Field," an invited session of the National Association for the Practice of Anthropology at the annual meeting of the American Anthropological Association, November 20, 1993, in Washington, D.C.; it was subsequently published in revised form as "Public Display as Cultural Policy," *Journal of Popular Culture* 29, no. 1 (Summer 1996): 3–14.

1. Edwards Park, "S. Dillon Ripley Retires after Twenty Years of Innovation," *Smithsonian* 15, no. 6 (September 1984): 76.
2. James Boon, "Why Museums Make Me Sad," in Ivan Karp and Steven Lavine, eds., *Exhibiting Cultures: The Poetics and Politics of Museum Display* (Washington, D.C.: Smithsonian Institution Press, 1991), p. 260.
3. Cf. the inaugural program, "America's Reunion on the Mall, Jan. 17–18, 1993," Presidential Inaugural Committee, Washington, D.C.
4. This statement was drafted by Richard Kurin. "America's Reunion on the Mall," in ibid.
5. *Miami Valley Sunday News,* January 24, 1993.

CHAPTER TWELVE   O JERUSALEM!

The basis of this chapter was verbally presented at "Anthropologists Negotiating Policy: Challenges to the Field," an invited session of the National Association for the Practice of Anthropology at the annual meeting of the American Anthropological Association, November 20, 1993, in Washington, D.C.; it was subsequently published in revised form as part of "Public Display as Cultural Policy," *Journal of Popular Culture* 29, no. 1 (Summer 1996): 3–14.

1. Amy Horowitz, "The Jerusalem Project," in *Festival of American Folklife Program Book* (Washington, D.C.: Smithsonian Institution, 1993), pp. 90–96.
2. Cf. interview with Suad Amiry in *Middle East Report* 23, no. 3 (May–June 1993): 21–22.
3. Horowitz, "The Jerusalem Project."
4. *Jerusalem: Gates to the City* (Washington, D.C.: Smithsonian Institution, 1997). The forthcoming book on the Jerusalem Festival project, edited by Amy Horowitz, Suad Amiry, and Galit Hasan Rohem, is tentatively titled *Living Jerusalem.*

CHAPTER THIRTEEN   WORKERS' CULTURE IN THE WHITE HOUSE

This chapter is based on work with Marjorie Hunt. Some of these findings are published in Richard Kurin and Marjorie Hunt, "White House Culture: Serving the Presidency," *American Visions,* Special Black History Month Issue: Blacks in the White House (1995): 48–51; "In the Service of the Presidency: Workers' Culture at the White House," *Prologue* 28, no. 4 (1996): 271–277. See also Marjorie Hunt, "Serving Those Who Serve: White House Workers," in Wendell Garrett, ed., *Our Changing White House* (Boston: Northeastern University Press, 1995), pp. 201–222; *Workers at the White House,* exhibition booklet (Washington, D.C.: Smithsonian Institution, 1993).

1. Marjorie Hunt, "Making the White House Work," in *Festival of American Folklife Program Book* (Washington, D.C.: Smithsonian Institution, 1992), pp. 98–102.

2. Books by key African American workers describe life in the White House in this century and present the culture of the institution from their own perspective. Alonzo Fields, *My 21 Years in the White House* (New York: Coward McCann, 1960); Lillian Rogers Parks, *My Thirty Years Backstairs at the White House* (New York: Fleet Publishing, 1961); Preston Bruce, *From the Door of the White House* (New York: Lothrop, Lee, and Shepard, 1984). Each offers a behind-the-scenes view of the institution through the eyes of a long-term worker.

3. *Workers at the White House* (Washington, D.C.: Center for Folklife Programs and Cultural Studies, in cooperation with the White House Historical Association, 1994), a thirty-two-minute video, directed by Marjorie Hunt and broadcast on PBS.

4. "Workers at the White House," an exhibition curated by Marjorie Hunt, produced by the Center for Folklife Programs and Cultural Studies in cooperation with the White House Historical Association and the National Archives, 1994–96.

5. A program honoring White House workers, attended by Hillary Rodham Clinton, was held for D.C. public school students at the Alice and Ernestine Shaed Elementary School on February 13, 1995.

6. The developments cited in this and following sections are culled from the definitive work of William Seale, *The President's House* (Washington, D.C.: White House Historical Association, 1986).

7. Ibid., p. 228.

8. Paul Jennings, *A Colored Man's Reminiscences of James Madison* [1865], in G. Franklin Edwards and Michael R. Winston, *White House History,* vol. 1 (Washington, 1983).

9. Interview with Lillian Rogers Parks, in Smithsonian Institution, Center for Folklife Programs and Cultural Studies Archives. Research for the White House Workers Program, Festival of American Folklife, 1992. All subsequent quotes from White House workers come from interviews and narrative sessions at the 1992 festival.

CHAPTER FOURTEEN   WHAT IS IT? THE AMERICAN SOUTH AT THE OLYMPICS

1. *Southern Crossroads* (Washington, D.C.: Smithsonian Institution, 1996).

2. Allen R. Myerson, "Marathon Man of the Atlanta Games," *New York Times,* February 25, 1996, Money and Business section.

3. Ibid.

4. Ibid.

5. John Shelton Reed to Leslie Gordon, ACOG.

6. *Time,* October 9, 1995.

7. Cynthia Tucker, "Revive Olympics Artsfest," *Atlanta Journal-Constitution,* February 2, 1994.

8. Howard Pousner, "Smithsonian Folklife Festival Is a Model for '96 Olympiad," *Atlanta Journal-Constitution,* July 17, 1994, Living section.

9. *Time,* July 15, 1996; *Atlanta Journal-Constitution,* July 14, 1996.

10. I believe it was George Holt who first suggested this twist of terminology.

11. In a July 15, 1996, article, Lucy Soto, a reporter for the *Atlanta Journal-Constitution,* graded these corporate exhibits as follows: AT&T, Global Village—D; Swatch Pavilion—C; General Motors—F; Budworld—B.

12. Steve Dollar, "Sights and Sounds of the South," *Atlanta Journal-Constitution,* July 18, 1996, Atlanta Games: The Park section.

13. Steve Dollar, "Crossroads Talent Loses to Flash," *Atlanta Journal-Constitution,* City Olympic section, p. 49.

14. See *Southern Crossroads* (Washington, D.C.: Smithsonian Institution, 1996).

15. Steve Dollar, "Crossroads Finds a Niche," *Atlanta Journal-Constitution,* August 2, 1996. This was similarly true for the overall Olympic Arts Festival, which had a low public profile throughout the Games. See Dan Hulbert, "Invisible Triumph," *Atlanta Journal-Constitution,* August 3, 1996, Atlanta Games: The Arts Legacy section.

16. "Atlanta's Other Olympics: The Arts, with Heart and Soul," *New York Times,* August 3, 1996, Arts section.

17. *Southern Crossroads.*

18. Steve Dollar, "Prices May Stun, But Folk Art's a Delight," *Atlanta Journal-Constitution,* July 18, 1996, Atlanta Games: The Park.

19. *Crossroads: Southern Routes,* Smithsonian Folkways Recordings (SF 40080).

20. See www.si.edu/folkways. Check out the Microsoft pages for teachers at the bottom of the Crossroads page.

CHAPTER FIFTEEN   CONCLUSION: THE NEW STUDY AND CURATION OF CULTURE

1. Ben Barber, *Jihad vs. McWorld* (New York: Ballantine Books, 1995).

2. Arjun Appadurai, "Global Ethnoscapes: Notes and Queries for a Transnational Anthropology," in *Recapturing Anthropology* (Santa Fe: School of American Research Press, 1991), pp. 191–210.

3. "Disneyland Opens in France with Mixed Views," report on National Public Radio, April 15, 1992, paraphrase.

4. Charles D. Kleymeyer, *Cultural Expression and Grassroots Development: Cases from Latin America and the Caribbean* (Boulder: Lynne Rienner Publishers, 1994).

5. Ivan Karp, Christine Kraemer, and Steven Lavine, eds., *Museums and Their Communities* (Washington, D.C.: Smithsonian Institution Press, 1993).

6. George E. Marcus and Michael Fischer, *Anthropology and Cultural Critique: An Experimental Moment in the Human Sciences* (Chicago: University of Chicago Press, 1986); Richard Handler, ed., *Schneider on Schneider: The Conversion of the Jews and Other Anthropological Stories* (Durham: Duke University Press, 1995); Simon During, ed., *The Cultural Studies Reader* (London and New York: Routledge, 1993); Raymond Williams, "Advertising: The Magic System," in ibid., pp. 320–337.

7. Anthony Seeger, "Academic and Public Sector Ethnomusicology: A False Dichotomy?" *Society for Ethnomusicology, Middle Atlantic Chapter Newsletter* 14, no. 3 (1995): 1.

INDEX